FROM TAOISM TO EINSTEIN

The symbol Yin-Yang above, which dates back to late classical times (ca. Han era) represents the ancient Chinese perception of how the world works. The outer circle symbolizes 'all things', while the black and white shapes within it represent the interaction and interrelationship of two energies, called 'yin' (the black shape) and 'yang' (the white shape), which cause everything to happen. Their significance lies in the fact that the forms are not completely black or white, just as it is in real life, and are entirely dependent on each other

From Taoism to Einstein

Ki and *Ri* in Chinese
and Japanese Thought

A SURVEY

Olof Lidin
University of Copenhagen

GLOBAL
ORIENTAL

FROM TAOISM TO EINSTEIN
KI AND *RI* IN CHINESE AND JAPANESE THOUGHT

By Olof G. Lidin

First published in 2006 by

GLOBAL ORIENTAL LTD
PO Box 219
Folkestone
Kent CT20 2WP

www.globaloriental.co.uk

British Library Cataloguing in Publication Data
A CIP catalogue entry for this book is available
From the British Library

ISBN 1-901903-78-8
    978-1-901903-78-2

Set in Gill Sans Light 11½ on 13 point by Bookman, Langley, Berkshire
Printed and bound in England by Antony Rowe Ltd., Chippenham, Wilts

To Arild, Bjørk, Elvira and Zelda

CONTENTS

Part I. Survey of the Neo-Confucian Ri-Ki Orthodoxy

Part II. Survey of Confucian Intellectuals in Tokugawa Japan

Part III Conclusions

Acknowledgements and Thanks

W hen one works on a subject for decades rather than years one has received assistance from many quarters other than books and libraries. I have received inspiration from dozens of scholars and colleagues on at least three continents. I will therefore not attempt to mention names but rather institutions and locations which have extended support during my work. After I left Stockholm University and B. Karlgren it was first the University of California, Berkeley, where D. Shively opened the doors for me; next it was the University of Copenhagen, where S. Egerod invited me to begin a Japanese programme. After retirement from there it has been the University of Tübingen and Humboldt Universität zu Berlin and K. Kracht that have provided offices and libraries. This all came to be crystallized in the present work. In addition, in Japan I have been received by the University of Tokyo, Tokai University in Tokyo, and Nichibunken in Kyoto among others. My special gratitude goes to the PS Company and T. Hirayama in Tokyo who have always offered office facilities during my stays in Japan. Special thanks go also to my assistants, N. Futami in Tokyo and K. Yonezawa in Berlin and others; and finally, heartfelt thanks go to my wife who has followed my progress with unstinting patience.

Prologue

K i came first and it is the thread that runs through the millennia of Chinese philosophy. Ri was added later in Sung times and, together, ki and ri became the mainstay and core of Chinese beliefs during the Sung (960-1279), Ming (1279-1644) and Ch'ing (1644-1911) dynasties.

The ki thought can profitably be compared with European philosophy. In China it begins with an original 'primal ki' (*genki*) which is the source of all things and affairs. The search is for the whole. In Greece and later in Europe the thinking goes in the opposite direction: it searches for the exact truth in the independent units of the cosmos – the atoms. The truth is found in the part. Thus, both Eastern and Western traditions embrace an early 'ism', '*genki*-ism' in the East and 'atom-ism' in the West.

The approach to these 'isms' has differed. The overall philosophical categories are different. The ism in the East can be called 'organism' and the ism in the West 'materialism'.[1] Since categories are the axioms of philosophy, this explains the underlying difference in East-West philosophy through millennia. They may also explain the different modernizing processes, West and East: in the East it has been the development of a philosophy of organism versus the progression towards materialism in the West, the stress being on the complete whole versus the single part. The Eastern philosophers emphasized the cosmic All, while the Western thinkers looked deeper and deeper into the Part, ending up in the infinitesimal particles of today's research. While the Chinese demonstrated scant tendency towards atomistic ideas, gradually, the Europeans lost interest in the wider perspective of Heaven and Earth.

The *I Ching* (Jpn. *Ekikyō*), *The Book of Changes*, often simply called the *Changes*, is the first Chinese classic from about 1000 BC. This is where the ki philosophy was originally presented, and the work that philosophers have turned to in all ages.[2] The ki thought of change in the *I Ching* runs parallel with the Taoist philosophy in the *Tao Te Ching* (Jpn. *Dōtokukyō*), *The Book of the Way and the Virtue*, the early Taoist work.[3] The *I Ching* is unsystematic and fragmentary while the *Tao Te Ching* presents a rather orderly ki philosophy. It is therefore natural that Buddhism, too, played an important role in the establishment of the Neo-Confucian thinking in spite of its being a foreign importation. Ki is the original stuff and comprises all reality. It has its roots in nature religion and in ancestor and spirit worship.[4]

There is a ki tone resounding throughout the long Confucian continuity from its *I Ching* and *Tao Te Ching* beginnings. Nationalism required, proudly, consciously or unconsciously, that the beginning was in ancient China. The proponents of Neo-Confucianism had, however, not only a native but also, most notably, a Buddhist background and all of them, Chu Hsi (1130-1200), the foremost amongst them, had been in Buddhist and Taoist studies and practices before becoming the creators and synthesizers of the Neo-Confucian gospel.

Buddhism remained its own tradition as one of the 'three teachings' (*san-chiao*, Jpn. *sankyō*) alongside Confucianism[5] and Taoism. Taoist vocabulary was used when Buddhist scriptures were translated into Chinese. It became in most respects a Chinese religion.

The Chinese cosmology was finally formulated during the Han era (206 BC-AD 220). Its *axis mundi* was a continuing evolution, under the name of the ten thousand changes, and the ki, the 'energy-matter', was the source of the cosmic macrocosm and the natural microcosm, forming a complex of order and harmony. This ki was both material, living and spiritual, the animated mass of life, which in endless transformations gave form to things in the process of going and coming. It was a naturally self-generating hylozoism with no mention of a creator.

If there is another concept running through Chinese philosophy, it is the Way,[6] the *tao* (Jpn. *dō*). It is not only the key term of Taoism but also of all Confucianism and later Legalist and other Chinese philosophies. It is only in present-day thought, imported from Europe, that the tao is mostly forgotten. There has, in other words, been a 'Way' piloting all ki cosmic formations from the beginning, mentioned in all scriptures through the centuries. These formations took shape in the virtues, first of all rites and ritual (*li*, Jpn. *rei*), which came to be regarded as a kind of 'natural law', reflecting the tao of Heaven.

The ri in Sung cosmology expressed the tao in each thing and therefore the two terms were often expressed together as *tao-li* (Jpn. *dōri*), 'the Way-Principle'. Above them both was always Heaven (*t'ien*, Jpn. *ten*), the origin of tao and ri. One could therefore speak about a ten-dō-ri metaphysics, competing with the Buddhist Heavens in being conducive to wisdom and sagehood.

The ki and ri concepts are repeated in every age, always within the same paradigm until in modern times when they connect with Western philosophy. The aim of this study is to present these two important concepts and their central role and continuity throughout the long and rich Confucian tradition.

Simplicity has been the key-word and the goal has been to make the work easy to read, primarily directed to the non-specialist. The long tradition of three millennia can indeed be 'threaded on one string' that runs from age to age and be made translucent and succinct.

This study has three separate but interrelated parts. Part I delineates the ki and ri philosophy as it developed in China; Part II presents Confucian study and learning in Tokugawa Japan (1600-1868); and Part III finishes with conclusions about things East and West and the situation in today's world.

The presentation is repetitious because the entire tradition is repetitious. This is natural since the thinkers moved within the same tradition ascribed to sacrosanct sages. The rich and varied dialectic witnessed through the epochs of Western philosophy did not exist in Chinese thought – a fact that makes the study less absorbing but somewhat easier. You deal with a tradition that rarely strays into unknown territories. You find adaptation but within definite limits. There are the Taoists to the left, the Confucians in the centre and the Legalists to the right. Philosophers moved within this spectrum and combined Taoism in personal life, Confucianism in social life and Legalism in political life. They could be legalistic in service, ethical in society and Taoist in poetry in the course of a single day. It was all within one spectrum. While the parameters changed again and again in the West from original Greek atomism to modern materialism, the paradigm remained the same in the East, even today when Western materialism has been accepted among intellectuals.

It is the author's conviction that even if the reasoning at times is convoluted, the presentation need not be equally convoluted. Simple things can be expressed simply and what is not simple can be made simple.

The Confucian scholars constituted the educated moral élite in both China and Japan. The salient difference was that while the Confucian scholars after examinations commonly became the political and ruling mandarins in China, they remained an erudite minority in Japan who rarely came into official service above working in lower positions in the respective domains – the han. The Confucians were therefore a more relevant class in China than in Japan where they acquired a higher social status than the masses of population by just being literate and little more – enough, however, to allow them to be contemptuous of ordinary people. They came mostly from the lower samurai strata, were often the sons of *rōnin* and doctors, and remained on the inferior *koku*-stipend level. They were described as the idle class of the realm.[7]

The sources are unmanageably vast as regards a story that stretches over three thousand years. Chinese and Japanese works are available in abundance and Western sources are numerous.

After Confucius we have an unbroken line of great thinkers who wrote copiously about Chinese philosophy, first of all in China and then also in Korea and Japan. It is impossible to cover them all. The Western literature about Chinese thought has also been extensive in recent centuries. A selection must be made, and the bibliography must be correspondingly selective. Only relevant works have been consulted and at times translated in part. Secondary sources have been greatly relied upon and the narrative is much indebted to the many fine specialists on China and Japan. It has indeed been rewarding to read numerous enlightening works by the best minds in the field.

Eras and Dynasties in China and Japan

China

Legendary Period:
The three Sovereigns and the Five Emperors

Ancient China:
Hsia Dynasty (mythical era)
Shang Dynasty (ca. 1766-1123 BC)
Chou Dynasty (1122-256 BC)

Imperial China:
Ch'in Dynasty (221-207 BC)
Han Dynasty (206 BC-AD 220)
The Three Kingdoms (220-280)
The Six Dynasties (country separated, ca. 280-581)
Sui Dynasty (581-617)
T'ang Dynasty (618-907)
Five Dynasties (907-960)
Sung Dynasty (960-1279)
Yüan Dynasty (1279-1367)
Ming Dynasty (1368-1644)
Ch'ing Dynasty (1644-1911)

Republic (1912-1949)
People's Republic (1949-)

Japan

Jōmon Period (ca. 10000-300BC)
Yayoi Period (ca. 300 BC-AD 300)
Tomb Period (ca. 300 BC-AD 552)
Asuka Period (552-710)
Nara Period (710-784)
Heian Period (784-1185)
Kamakura Period (1185-1333)
Muromachi Period (1336-1573)
Tokugawa Period (1603-1667)
Modern Japan (Meiji, Taishō, Shōwa, Heiwa) (1868-)

Part I

SURVEY OF THE
NEO-CONFUCIAN RI-KI ORTHODOXY

Introduction

It is not entirely clear when the Neo-Confucian mode of thought was introduced into Japan, but this was certainly not long after Chu Hsi (Chu Tzu, 1130-1200) died.[8] Zen monks visiting China did not only learn about *zazen* (Ch. *tso-ch'an*) 'sitting meditation' but also about *seiza* (Ch. *ching-tso*), 'quiet sitting',[9] practised by Confucian intellectuals.[10] They took an interest in the latest outpourings of Confucian thinking and they became assiduous students of Confucian metaphysics in between their meditation sessions, to the extent that a Zen abbot once complained that that there was too much philosophy and too little *zazen* in the Rinzai (Gozan) temples. However, throughout the Kamakura and Muromachi periods (ca.1200-ca.1600), the Neo-Confucian studies remained an intellectual sideline and seem never to have become the main occupation of the monks, who were Zen monks both in words and deeds.

For four hundred years[11] it was thus the Zen religion and culture that was the main interest during the Kamakura and Muromachi eras. Gradually, an interest in Neo-Confucianism arose among the Gozan monks, who blended the creeds into a *jubutsu itchi*, a Confucian-Buddhist syncretism, and even a *shinjubutsu-itchi*, a Shinto-Confucian-Buddhist eclectic syncretism. In either case the new Confucianism did not hold an independent position.

Interest was taken in (Neo-)Confucianism in Kamakura and Muromachi times. Kitabatake Chikafusa (1293-1354) was inspired by Chu Hsi when he wrote the *Jinnō shōtōki*, which was completed in 1339, and the Confucian truths were in the centre when Takeda Shingen compiled his ninety-nine admonitions in 1558. The Chu Hsi interpretations are affirmed in the Satsunan Zen school in Satsuma under Nanpo Bunshi (1556-1620), who had studied Neo-Confucianism at the Gozan temples in Kyoto. The Tosa school (the so-called Southern school) of Confucianism originated under the Zen priest Keian (1429-1508), who had come to Tosa around 1548 or 1549, and published Chu Hsi's *Tahsüeh chang-chü* in 1481. The Muromachi age was further known for its eclectic tendency. No sharp line was drawn between Confucian and Buddhist studies. Shimazu Tadayoshi (1492-1568), for example, was known for his *nichigaku*, a Three-Creeds-in-One school. It should be added that also the Kiyowara scholars in their official service in Kyoto from early times took an interest in Neo-Confucian studies.[12]

At the beginning of the Tokugawa era we find the first monks who left Rinzai and established themselves as Confucian scholars. They broke out of the Buddhist Zen eclectic syncretism, even often denied Buddhism, and started to preach the Confucian doctrine, leaning more towards the native *kami* creed than towards Buddhism, thereby giving it a distinct Japanese identity. Buddha was replaced by Confucius. Confucianism, or rather its updated Neo-Confucian form, acquired an independent stature and began an extraordinary revision of the terms of intellectual discourse.[13] It is significant that this happened in 1600, the same year that the new era, Tokugawa, commenced.

Traditionally, Fujiwara Seika (1561-1618) and Hayashi Razan (1583-1657) are mentioned as the precursors of this new Confucian age.[14] Whether they left the Buddhist orthodoxy out of conviction or convenience is difficult to say. Fujiwara Seika seems to have been the noble personality who did it out of religious earnestness; Hayashi Razan, on the other hand, might well have done it out of opportunism, hoping to rise in the new world that was being built by the first Tokugawa shogun, Ieyasu (1542-1616, r.1603-1616). Fujiwara Seika never accepted a position in official service, but Hayashi Razan happily entered shogunal service in 1607, establishing a link with the Tokugawa shogunate that would last for twelve generations, that is, throughout the Tokugawa era. The Hayashis became the carriers of the Shushigaku orthodoxy, and whatever new thinking appeared, they were in the centre.[15] Their ri thinking was so closely associated with shintoism, that the Confucian ri and the national *kami* came to exist symbiotically in a Confucian-Shinto syncretism (juka-shintō). This syncretism started with Fujiwara Seika and Hayashi Razan and continued with other Confucian scholars such as Nakae Tōju, Yamazaki Ansai and Yamaga Sokō.

1. The Neo-Confucian Ri Doctrine

How can the Neo-Confucian ri doctrine be set forth in a simple way? Ri can be visualized as the totality of the 'wiring' of the universe, as ordained by Heaven. One finds the expression *tenri*, 'Inscape of Heaven', in which one can feel the close relation between Heaven and the world,[16] synonymous with the term *tendō*, 'Way of Heaven'. Ri alone is, however, not sufficient. The 'wiring' is devoid of meaning if it were not for the ki, the 'electricity', which makes the whole net come alive.[17] The whole is an electrical grid through which the ki, that is, the life-giving energy pulsates, an enormous grid-iron upon which the cosmic wonder is enacted.

Miura Baien (1723-89) has explained the ri, using the metaphors of the branches of a tree and the ditches in the fields. The ri are the life veins of a tree and the water channels of a field:

> What is the purpose of these inscapes? Its purpose is to convey the ki, that is, the energy which in turn manifests the physical form (*katachi*), thus giving shape to the tree. If we apply this to the water needed to irrigate rice fields, then ditches have to be dug. These ditches are the routes

(ri) of the water (ki) and where they branch out, they divide themselves into thousands of branch routes. However, as long as the routes are maintained, even though the rice fields are numberless, the water following them smoothly yet irrigates them all and the countless rice plants are vitalized up to the leaf-tips. Similarly, too, the weather travels East and West, the sun and the moon revolve along their course, rivers and streams flow, kites fly and fish leap: all because of the energy (ki) of things following their respective ri texture.[18]

Another translation of the same passage:

Channels must be made to convey water through the fields. These channels are the ri of the water. The ri divides into branches. A thousand branches may become ten thousand branches, but because of the ri, even if the fields were endless, water would reach the millions of leaves of rice, to the tips of the grains, by flowing along the ri.[19]

A present-day simile would be the roads and highways which criss-cross the world. They are the ri of the world and the ever-flowing traffic is the ki.

The ri was perhaps never better explained during the long Neo-Confucian tradition. Miura Baien was one of the great exponents of Neo-Confucian thought in eighteenth-century Japan. These metaphors reflect a vision of the universe in which all things are unified in a single normative system which binds together an undivided field of organic ki.[20]

For other similes, the ki is the blood that flows through the ri arteries until reaching the farthest and minutest capillaries,[21] and the ri are the stable genes giving form to the changeable ki energy-matter. Ri has been regarded as the warp and ki the woof of the cosmic weave.[22]

To these holistic metaphors of the universe one can add Chu Hsi's view of the world as a purposive process of transformation. The world is not only a unified rational field. It is a grand, supra-historical, logical and ethical structure of all creation, an organic totality in constant and ceaseless generation and regeneration.

'*Alles hängt an allem*'. The metaphor of a growing organism is mentioned repeatedly in the Neo-Confucian cosmology. 'Ri is like a tree one hundred feet high, which constitutes one continuous whole from its roots to its branches and leaves', says Ch'eng I. Chu Hsi speaks of 'the thousand branches and myriad leaves'. There is also the analogy with the family that expands from generation to generation. The family is also a good metaphor because it presents a network like the channels in the field: parents and children form a line and one generation breeds the next. These analogies are much the same as in the Western tradition. The growing tree is found in the Bible and the family simile in both Greek literature and the works of Shakespeare.[23]

2. Investigation of and Knowledge of Ri

Ri-ism can be regarded as an empirical interpretation, built upon man's aptness to reason about things.[24] Man discerns regularities in things, lines and streaks which individuate. He sees order in the cosmos.[25] The indestructible lines and regularities are noted as the ri in things, and all these ri are, in turn, germane to the Heavenly Principle, the father of all individuated ri and the ultimate source of creation. It is the core concept in the Chu Hsi philosophy. It presents the universal measure for all things and confers the purpose and meaning of the cosmos as a living, natural order. It is the ri above things as well as in things. It is one, universal and good. The ri can be registered as the same in, for example, each horse and each man not only in physical appearance but also in mental and psychic apparatus.[26] Horses share the same ri, the ri of being horses, and men share the same ri, the ri of being men.[27]

The world is, thus, an infinity of ri archetypes within ki mutable matter. Each and every thing has its uniqueness, its ri quality and ki constitution, which make it belong to a certain class or category (lei, Jpn. rui) and function according to its potential.

As Fung Yu-lan expresses it: 'The word ri was originally a verb referring to the process of cutting, trimming and polishing jade, and came later to be used in a wider sense meaning "to put in good order" generally.' As used by Chu Hsi and other Neo-Confucianists, it means form or principle, or, in the translation of J. P. Bruce, 'law'.[28] According to W. E. Hocking, ri originally referred to 'streaks', 'veins' and fine lines of cleavage in jade and only later to virtues, goodness uppermost among them.[29] Thus, it came, allegorically, to stand for Heaven's immanence in man's world; then, beginning in the Ming era it returned to its original meaning, referring to the patterns of the material world, however, without losing its heavenly reference; last, in modern times, it has come to refer to the inscapes of material things with no reference to Heaven.[30]

Ri runs through all things in the universe. As a consequence, the universe is orderly. It is a single organism in which things go and return in complementary yin and yang ki revolutions of condensation and dispersion. The ten-dō in old Confucianism and ten-dō-ri in the Chu Hsi orthodoxy radiate in the same manner.[31] The ten-dō-ri organizes substance and gives purpose, form and appearance to the ki configurations and natural order.[32] No line can be drawn between what is seen (ki) and what is unseen (ri). Whether seen or unseen, however, it is a ri reality in a ki cosmos in which the yin force stands for stillness and the yang force stands for activity.

As Y. Abe puts it:

> According to Chu Hsi, ri, although it cannot be grasped by the senses because it is immaterial and formless, is something ultimate and so important that unless one presupposes its actual existence, the physical world will not exist. . . . All things in the universe have their laws or

principles, which cause them to be what they are. . . .
However, such [laws and] principles do not exist separately
but as a single whole of the Great Ultimate (*taikyoku*, Ch.
t'ai-chi), which is equally embodied in all the myriad things
(*wan wu*, Jpn. *banbutsu*)[33] within the universe.[34]

The Great Ultimate became the pinnacle of the ri philosophy,
'the norm of norms '. . . It took the place of a godhead in a
pantheistic reality, 'self-evident and self-sufficient, extending
everywhere and governing all things. . . . The mind, truth,
universal order, universal law and the universal principle of
creation.'[35]

Thus the basis of individual ri is the great universal ri. All ri in
the universe unite in the Great Ultimate, defined as the 'Centre
rope of creation' and as '. . . the moral order of human beings'.[36]

Like the ideal forms in Plato's world, the ri are characterized by
permanence. 'They are static, fixed and changeless.'[37] The static
image of the supersensory reality above would have an immense
impact upon the conception of the phenomena of the world. Since
the things reflect immutable heavenly ri (noumena), this world
(phenomena) is also ideally static and innovations abnormal.[38]

As A. C. Graham and J. H. Berthrong put it:

> Probing the ri-principle to the point of complete
> comprehension was the crucial step in Chu Hsi's
> programme of moral self-cultivation; for since the ri-
> principle in things and the ri-principle in man were the
> same, and since the ri-principle in man was identical with his
> nature, apprehending ri either in things out there or in
> himself was nothing but self-realization. . .[39]

And:

> Everything in the world has [its endowment of] principle
> (ri). A pattern or a structure makes a thing what it is. It
> determines how it comes to be, how it manifests itself and
> how it is to act: 'If we exhaust the principles in the things of
> the world, it will be found that a thing must have a reason
> why it is and a rule to which it should conform, which is
> what is meant by principle.'

> The individual principles finally amount to one all-embracing universal principle for which 'heaven', 'decree' and 'Way' are merely different names. It is a natural order transformed into a rational order.

Or as Chu Hsi puts it: 'A thing must have "a cause by which it is as it is" and "a standard to which it should conform".' (Ch. *so tang jan chih ku*, Jpn. *shotōzen no ko* and Ch. *so i jan chih tse*, Jpn. *shoizen no soku*.)[40]

Accordingly, thanks to ri, things are what they ought to be, that is, they have their 'oughtness'.[41] Ri is inherent in and provides the proper standard for all things in the universe, living or inert. In modern terms one could add: down to the last cell and subatomic particle. All partake of the Great Ultimate! Consider the following question to and answer by Chu Hsi:

> (Question) 'Ri is what is received from Heaven by both beings and things. Do things free from feelings also possess ri?' (Answer) 'Of course they have principle. For example, a ship can go on water while a cart can go on land.'

This has been referred to as the Chu Hsi empiricism and universalism. Chu Hsi says in the *Chu Hsi yü lei* (Jpn. *Shushi gorui*), *Chu Tzu's Conversations*: 'Each thing, even a grass or a tree or an insect, is endowed with ri.'[42] This ri empiricism was joined to a transcendent perspective which, with its demand on investigation of each thing, even a blade of grass, could lead to enlightenment (*wu*, Jpn. *satori*).

The necessary basis for the investigation was found in the *Ta Hsüeh* (Jpn. *Daigaku*, the *Great Learning*), which Chu Hsi found both coherent and easy to understand. It says (1: 1 and 4, in Legge's translation):

> Wishing to order well their states, they first regulated their families (*ch'i-chia*, Jpn. *seika*). Wishing to regulate their families, they first cultivated their persons (*hsiu-hsin*, Jpn. *shūshin*). Wishing to cultivate their persons, they first rectified their hearts (*cheng-hsin*, Jpn. *seishin*). Wishing to rectify their hearts, they first sought to be sincere in their

hearts (ch'eng-i, Jpn. seii). Wishing to be sincere in their hearts, they first extended to the utmost their knowledge (chih-chih, Jpn. chichi). Such extension of knowledge lies in things being investigated (ko-wu, Jpn. kakubutsu).

The investigation of matter was expressed with terms such kakubutsu-kyūri, 'the study and pursuit of ri in things', short as kyūri (Ch. ch'iung-li), 'the pursuit or inquiry of ri', and kakubutsu-chichi (Ch. ko-wu–chih-chih), 'to investigate things and attain wisdom'.

It was Ch'eng I who introduced the ri thought and the notion that there was a supreme ri, the Great Ultimate, in the universe. He said: 'All things under Heaven can be understood through ri (li). If there is a thing there must be a rule. Each thing necessarily has its distinct manifestation of ri.' He says further: 'Kaku (ko) means chi (chih), "arrive at", "to reach". Wu means butsu, "things", "affairs". In all things and affairs there is ri; to arrive at ri is kakubutsu (ko-wu).'

Chu Hsi, who accepted Ch'eng I's ri-ism, explains how he understands kyūri and kakubutsu in his commentary to the Ta Hsüeh. Convinced that an original kakubutsu chapter of the Ta Hsüeh had been lost, he supplied his own explication, which circulated as part of the Classic itself. It reads:

> What is meant by 'the extension of knowledge' lies in fully apprehending the ri in things, that if we wish to extend our knowledge to the utmost, we must probe thoroughly the ri in those things that we encounter. It would seem that every man's intellect possesses the potent capacity for knowing that everything is possessed of ri. But, to the extent that ri is not yet thoroughly probed, man's knowledge is not yet fully realized. Hence, the first step of instruction in greater learning is to teach the student, whenever he encounters anything at all in the world, to build upon what is already known to him of ri and to probe still further, so that he seeks to reach the limit. After exerting himself in this way for a long time, he will one day become illumined and understand all matters under heaven, the manifest and the hidden. The subtle and the obvious qualities of all things will all be known, and the

mind, in its whole substance and vast operations, will be completely illuminated. This is called 'fully apprehending the ri (li) in things'.[43]

In another context he says:

From one's own body ... to grass and plants, and insects and animals, one should investigate the ri embodied in them. One should extend further to the books of the sages and worthies, the classics and the political affairs of the various dynasties, all of which are things to be investigated.[44]

Wing-tsit Chan says as regards *kyūri*:

For Chu Hsi to investigate ri means none other than to investigate things. Thus investigation of ri has as its subject things in the empirical world; the more one is involved with inquiry of ri, the less one would deal with the transcendent world and the world of spirits and deities. No matter whether it was the study of classics or moral practice, Chu Hsi always wanted to keep his feet on the solid ground, which is none other than the human world.[45]

This external investigation should, however, always correlate with internal self-realization. 'You will understand that the truth within and the truth without unite heaven, earth and man.'[46]

No *kyūri*, therefore, should be a soulless measuring of distances or observing the stars. 'The evil comes from measuring heaven and not knowing its heart.'[47] Any study should be in the full awareness of the overshadowing Heaven. Measurement and examination should lead to an understanding of the wholeness of life, to the personal experience of enlightenment and that there is ri in everything. This did not just mean knowledge. The real aim of the *kakubutsu* 'was to reach the One Ri – the heavenly ri – via the individual ri'.[48] It was important to study the individual ri, but the goal was to attain the heavenly ri. This final apprehension was interpreted as 'sudden' and 'thorough penetration'. When, therefore, the West came with its cold scientific rationalism which measured only for the sake of measurement and observed only for the sake of cognition, it was not readily accepted in the East, where people were deeply steeped in perceiving all endeavours in a moral light and with a heavenly *raison d'être*.

How did Chu Hsi link ri with the Way (*tao*)? We should note this passage in the Chu Hsi yü lei:

> Someone asked how the tao and ri are to be distinguished. Chu said: The tao is the path. Ri is the pattern. Like the grain of a wood? the questioner asked. Yes, Chu replied. In that case, the questioner said, they seem to be alike. Chu said: The word tao is all-embracing. Ri refers to the many veins within the tao. . . The word tao refers to the whole, ri to the details.

Thus, Chu Hsi regarded ri as the normative dimension of things: no matter without form and no form without matter! The tao is not replaced, only rationalized by ri. On the metaphysical totem pole the line would go, in a descending order, from Heaven, the prime mover, via ming, its decree, to tao, its logos, and to ri, endowing the myriad things with nature and direction. This *ten(mei)-dō-ri* is accordingly the metaphysics ending up in immanently transcendent forms. The ancient Confucianism is not changed on the worldly side; the change is on the supernatural side where a simple *ten-(mei-)dō* is elongated to a *ten-(mei-)dō-ri*.

Chu Hsi, thus, equated ri with ten and dō and created the ten-dō-ri trinity, three concepts in one, above terrestrial things.[49] Ten is the will, the dō its 'way', and the ri its law pervading all cosmos into every atom and cell through innumerable 'veins'. This trinity could thereupon expand with the *jin* (goodness), and *sei* (nature), ending up as a *ten(mei)-dō-ri-jin-sei* metaphysics. Heaven is the Pole Star (ri) 'piloting' the 'plenum' (ki).[50]

How do we know of the existence of ri? We can have doubts, but by studying, rather seeing, cosmic manifestations and forms, we can deduce the existence of ri, because any manifestation presupposes form, order and purpose.[51] As Chu Hsi said: 'When the mind is bright, it can spontaneously see that this thing or event has this or that ri'; but 'when the mind is not settled, one cannot see the ri'.[52]

Order is the common denominator that links the ri of early use with that of later application. Ri is thus the ordering principle of the creative process. 'There being order, there is ri.' As it earlier denotes 'order' in a material sense 'as veins on a piece of jade', it denotes 'order' of a metaphysical dignity later, 'as order in thought, order in heaven, order on earth and in all things' – law, meaning, purpose and harmony (ho, Jpn. wa) – ORDER!

Alfred North Whitehead (1861-1947) and Chu Hsi would have understood each other. As the world requires God in Whitehead's philosophy of organism, it requires ri in Chu Hsi's. If the 'order of nature' is simply exchanged for 'ri' in the following passage, it could have been written by Chu Hsi:

> It is not the case that there is an actual world, which accidentally happens to exhibit and order nature. There is an actual world because there is an order in nature. If there were no order, there would be no world. Also since there is a world, we know that there is an order. The ordering and refining entity is a necessary element in the supernatural situation presented by the actual world.[53]

We have, at last, the question of the possible existence of a personal God in the Chu Hsi Confucian outlook. He makes himself clear on this point in the following statement:

> Heaven revolves and spreads in all directions. It is now sometimes said that there is up there a person who judges all evil actions; this assuredly is wrong. But to say that there is no ordering [principle] would be equally wrong.[54]

It was not an anthropomorphic God in a monotheistic sense but a ten-dō-ri anthropopathic moral order. He could not come closer to Whitehead.

3. The Origin and the Development of the Ri Thought

Thus, the term ri does not exist with heavenly connotations in early texts. It refers only to 'veins in jade' or markings in stones and other materials.[55] It was later that the term appeared in Taoist usage and in Buddhist scriptures with connotations that pointed in a non-physical direction. For example, we find the term *shizen no ri*, 'the ri of nature', in Taoist parlance, and the ri and *ji* (things) put side by side in Kegon scriptures, representing what is above and what is below. It is posited that the concept was 'stolen' from Taoism and Buddhism and added to Sung cosmology and that it did not just develop naturally as part of new reasoning. One thing is clear: ri was only 'veins in jade' in early classics. As a Confucian paranormal concept, it was introduced in Sung thought.

Originally, in the *I Ching*, the term representing the supernatural world was *tao*, (Jpn. *dō*), 'Way', and the term representing the physical world was *ch'i*, (Jpn. *ki*) 'instrument' or 'vessel'. Ri and ki came in their stead in the Chu Hsi system.[56]

It was thus in a later age that the ri concept changed in meaning and moved from immanence to transcendence and became a unitary principle in a conscious attempt to understand things.[57] The few times we encounter the concept in the early classics, it refers to the inner dimension of mono and koto, 'things' and 'acts', corresponding to the later *jōri*, 'order of/in things'. In the *I Ching*, for example, the ri seems to be the *jōri* patterns of matter, as ordained by Heaven, in a ki cosmos.[58] When the word occasionally appears in other classics, it also connotes pattern and order as a noun and to put things in order as a verb. In the *Mo Tzu* (468-376 BC?, Jpn. *Bokushi*) it is found seven times, connoting material order in four cases and moral

order in three cases.[59] In the *Huai-nan Tzu* of early Han the term
t'ien-li (Jpn. *tenri*) is found connoting the heavenly natural order in
the world. This is an early example of ri as the heavenly principle
of the cosmic order

The heavenly connotation was, then, not clearly established
until in the 'new Confucianism' of the Sung era, when ri came
to represent the eternal, and immutable divine tao above things.
A human precept can be altered and modified as often as
circumstances dictate it. A heavenly law embodies absolute
truth and no occurrence is allowed to interfere with it. The ri
perception became an ideological strait-jacket that enveloped
thinking, first in China and then in Korea and Japan. The Five
Relationships and Five Constant Virtues were a central part of
this jacket. Thereupon followed the rules of propriety. These
precepts had the stamp of Heaven and could lead to moral
rigour and social stagnation. As a result, change was looked
upon askance. When it took place, it was mostly accepted with
disdain. In Japan, for example, the situation in 1600 was to
remain the same forever. A 100-*koku* samurai should remain a
100-*koku* samurai from generation to generation, and a
mizunomi ('water-drinking', poor) peasant should not attempt
to rise to the status of an ordinary peasant. When economics
and foreign pressure interfered with the eternal system,
attempts were made to contain the change.

If we compare ri with other concepts in early Confucian
scriptures, we find a connection with the *rei* (Ch. *li*), 'rites', 'ritual'
or 'propriety' in Confucian ethical doctrine.[60] If ri stands for
Heaven's Way in Sung Confucianism, the same can be said for *rei*
in early Confucianism. For example, Hsün Tzu exalted *rei* and
made it into an all-pervading natural law, saying that '*rei* is the tao
of Heaven and Earth'.[61]

In the *Chung Yung* (Jpn. *Chūyō*), *The Doctrine of the Mean*, *sei*
'(inner) sincerity', was identified with the tao of Heaven. Kei
'(outer) sincerity' and ri in the Sung era (960-1279), were
expounded as 'germinating in the minutest invisible particles'.[62]
Heaven fuses sincerity (whether as *kei* or *sei*), rites and ri into a

spiritual oneness – all under the Mandate of Heaven (*t'ien-ming*, Jpn. *tenmei*).

In the *Meng Tzu* (Jpn. *Mōshi*; Mencius) ri 'describes the harmonious cooperation of an orchestra'. In the *Hsün Tzu* (Jpn. *Junshi*) and the *Han Fei Tzu* (Jpn. *Kanpishi*) 'the ri of any particular thing is its configuration, its specific form, and all the data about it which permit one to handle it successfully; all these individual ri being subsumed in the great tao which itelf had no "fixed specificity" (*ting ti*, Jpn. *teitai*).' In the Han era, ri was also a term that signified 'streaks and veins' and the order of things. During the following centuries when Buddhism was dominant, ri became *myōri*, the 'wondrous ri', to be apprehended in intuitive and mystical experience. It became a supernatural absolute. While the early Chinese conception was patterns IN the terrestrial world, the Buddhists put it BEYOND the illusory world. Ri was 'denaturalized' and identified with *buddhatā*, 'buddhahood' and the dharma-world of emptiness.[63]

As such a *nexus rerum* ri represented the unity of the cosmos also for Neo-Taoists like Liu Shao (ca. 196-250)[64] and Wang Pi (226-249). Liu Shao is generally consistent with Confucian ontology: the cosmos operates under a heavenly tao by way of yin and yang and the Five Elements. Liu Shao and Wang-pi however, can be considered precursors of the ri thought, as advanced later by the Ch'eng brothers and Chu Hsi. Earlier ri had been 'order, system and streaks' in the world; the ri that came later was a 'transcendent absolute' above the world. 'It united all things', and was 'what ought to be', in line with Heaven and Tao.

The *taikyoku* corresponded with the *t'ai-i* (Jpn. *taiitsu*), 'the Great One' in the *I Ching* and Taoism. The difference is that the *t'ai-i* represented *wu*, 'nothingness', on the numinous side while the *taikyoku* represented *yu*, 'existence' on the cosmic side. Wang Pi said: 'The *T'ai-i* is void and without form.' It became the *wu-chi* (Jpn. *mukyoku*, the 'Unlimited' or 'Limitless') in the Chu Hsi synthesis. Wang Pi said further: 'All things (*yu*) begin in nothingness (*wu*).'[65]

The non-cosmic nothingness was replaced by the Great

Ultimate. Chu Hsi likened it to 'the moon in the sky that radiates in every wave of the ocean'. He said further: 'There is only one Great Ultimate. When all ri of Heaven and Earth (including man) and the myriad things are put together, you have the Great Ultimate.'[66] It was an Indra's net of oneness and universality in which every jewel shined and reflected in every other jewel while joining in one central jewel! There was only one source, the ri reservoir in Chu Hsi's thought and the genki infinity in Chang Tsai's thought; only one continuing and ongoing evolution that subsisted of itself, equalling the Buddha nature.[67]

All individual ri were, then, manifestations of the one ri. Chu Hsi quoted Ch'eng I: 'Ri is one and its manifestations are many' (li-i fen-shu, Jpn. riichi bunshu), 'all things have their ri but as a whole they are simply the one ri', 'originally there is only one Great Ultimate',[68] 'each of the myriad things partakes of it, and yet each holds the Great Ultimate in entirety' and 'the myriad things all have their ri but all ri come from the one source and are one and the same'.[69]

Chu Hsi 'laid down that everything in the universe possessed ri, an ideal form or essence, which prescribed the norm and nature'. If it were not so, 'oxen would give birth to horses or peach trees would produce plum blossoms'.[70]

The virtues, 'goodness', jen (Jpn. jin) first among them, became the ri and Heaven in man. In the Ta Hsüeh, Great Learning, it is said that 'the Way of Great Learning lies in making clear the clear virtue; it lies in loving the people, it lies in resting in ultimate goodness'. Ri was equal to this clear virtue in man's moral life, it was Heaven and Heaven's Way in man, as in all other things. It was the raison d'être running through all things, linked to the Unlimited (wu-chi). It was above all things and yet present in all things. From the Great Ultimate emanated the yin and yang, and out of their complementary duality and the interaction of the Five Elements (gogyō) (wood-fire-earth-metal-water (moku-ka-do-kin-sui)[71], all things were produced. This was a coherent system, both close to and independent of religion, yet an objective reality, 'outside the mind which sought to apprehend it'.[72]

With Chu Hsi, the meaning of this philosophical ri is completed: it is the principle that makes all things what they are, with their being and goodness, as well as the principle that makes the universe what it is, with its being and goodness.[73]

Neo-Confucianism had accordingly, its (ethical-)religious dimension, more so than the early Confucian teaching which was rather (religious-)ethical. It was sacred in its own right, striving for the spiritual life which is the goal of all religions. Wei-ming Tu says that 'being religious in the Neo-Confucian sense can be understood as being engaged in ultimate self-transformation as a communal act'.[74] It involved achieving the inner illumination that led to good conduct in political as well as in personal life.

4. The Original Ki Thought

'**K**i is a core concept of Chinese thought shared by Confucians, Taoists and other scholars (*chu-tzu pai-chi*, Jpn. *shoshi hyakka*, "The Hundred Schools") throughout history.'[75] The term can be traced back to classical texts, even oracle bones. It has roots both in folk religion and in ancestor worship. In the course of time it appears with the approximate meaning of life, breath and matter. The graph ki cannot be clearly explained.[76] From the late Chou era the word enters prominently into speech, both Confucian and Taoist, and from the Han era it has an important place in all Confucian, Taoist and even Buddhist discourse.

'The concept has a broad as well as a narrow meaning. In its broad sense ki is a primal and undifferentiated force that permeates the entire cosmos – everything.'[77] 'It fills up all between heaven and earth.'[78] It is the 'building block of the universe'.[79] It is both substance of all things and the divine flow of energy, the cosmic stuff and its pneuma. Thus, it is a psychophysical term, wider than the Western notions of energy and matter, combining both. All is one and the whole is divine. The entire world of time and space is constituted by it. In all its forms, whether perceptible and tangible or imperceptible and intangible, it is elusive and difficult to name. Therefore, it remains mostly untranslated and rendered in Japanese: ki (occasionally in original Chinese: ch'i). When a translation is attempted, it is with the double term: 'energy-matter'. It is energy, invisibly, and matter, visibly.[80]

In Taoism, ki is the universal 'stuff' of space and time. From it emanates the orderly formations of the cosmos. 'It is the "breath" of nature which congeals and coagulates to form the experiential world.'[81] It is not a creation by a god but rather a natural, self-generating and of itself – ex nihilo – life-force. From the pre-existing undifferentiated chaos (konton, Ch. hun-tun) the unitary, primal ki divides and becomes yin and yang and as heaven's Way the process continues by itself in the orderly concourse of time and change. Like Confucius' ch'ün tzu (Jpn. kunshi), 'the superior man', it does not 'contend'; it only comes into being, follows and responds.[82] The human body is a ki microcosm that displays the 'free travel of the divine ki inwards and outwards'.

It is 'the vital force that condenses and dissolves in perpetual change, alternating between the yin and the yang in endless relationship, interplay and harmony, a ceaseless flow of energy passing between them in the cosmos'.[83] Ki is, in fine, the source of life, the energy that permeates the universe on the macrocosmic side and links with the human world on microcosmic side. Reality is the aggregation of ki and destruction and death the dispersion of ki.[84] Ki interweaves with the Five Elements and all cosmic things are created.

However, 'when the ki becomes differentiated and individuated to form the things in the universe, it varies in purity'.[85] We have 'the great ki' (taiki), which stands for the whole cosmic order, the air that envelops us, and is the beginning of life and 'the empty ki', the air that we breathe in and out. A third term, *funiki*, also refers to the atmosphere around us, it is the 'air' that affects us socially; it is the ambience, the *genius loci*, as a dictionary expresses it. We have *iki*, respiration, which relates to *ikiru*, 'to live', meaning 'living ki or 'ki of life'. Further, we have *kōkiatsu* and *teikiatsu*, 'high air pressure' and 'low air pressure', and *jōki* and *suijōki*, 'steam', 'vapour'. Then we have the five atmospheric ki forces (*goki*), rain which is under the influence of wood, weather which is under the influence of metal, heat which is under the influence of fire, cold which is under the influence of water, and wind which is under the influence of earth. One notices how close the ki is to the Five Elements. It links with *genki*, the primal ki, 'the protoplasm of Chinese theories of evolution' (Mathews). It is the cosmic process that inter-connects and is all-encompassing.

Ki broadens to:

> ... embrace properties which we would call psychic, emotional, spiritual, numinous and even 'mystical'.... In much of its colloquial use in both Chinese and Japanese, ki refers to ... states of emotion, dispositions of sentiment, and attitudes.... It applies to moods, tastes and exists even in the void, in the blanks and in the energy of light. If there is any commonality in all these modes, it is that they refer to the all-pervasiveness of ki rather than to entities as such. If anger is a state of ki within a human person, the weather may equally be said to be a certain state of the heavenly ki (*tenki*, Ch. *t'ien ch'i*).[86]
>
> Man's mental abilities are referred to as his power of ki and his moral qualities as his ki endowment.[87]

In the end all organs and bodies are 'spheres of ki'.

In the *I Ching* cosmogony ki originated in the Great Undifferentiatedness (*konton*).[88] This was the primal ki, defined as 'the mass of seeds (*tuan*, Jpn. *tan*)'.[89] The grosser ki, being heavy, settled down to become the earth, while the refined ki, being light, rose to become the sky. Man, being half-way between the two, became a 'harmonious blending of the two'.[90] The impetus was the complementary ki, that is, the yin and yang, which function together in an eternal and spontaneous dialectic as the forces in nature and society. The four seasons of the year are the best example of this interplay. The ki force waxes during spring and summer and wanes during autumn and winter. It engenders man both physically and mentally and keeps him alive, soul, spirit and mind. Man's ki waxes as he grows up and it wanes as he grows old. His physical and mental ki forces work mysteriously together psychosomatically. The *genki* permeates the entire cosmos and is 'all in one and one in all' – in both Taoist and Confucian philosophy.[91] It is a 'vital energy field' that pervades all things. 'It is both energy and matter, both structural and functional, a unification of material and temporal forms that loses all coherence when reduced to one or the other "aspect".'[92] To translate the *Gogyō* as the 'Five Elements' is, therefore, not correct since it has to do with a cyclical ongoing transformation of the primordial stuff that is both moving and alive.

The ki concept is linked to millennia of Chinese thinking. The *I Ching* belongs to the general Chinese philosophical tradition, serving as a source for both inner and outer thought. It presents a monistic cosmology, codifying the patterns of design of a universal harmony. It states that 'Heaven feeds man with five kinds of ki, which enter his body from the nostrils and are stored in his heart. These five kinds of ki are pure and subtle and therefore go to form man's spirit, senses, voice and so on.' On the other hand, 'earth feeds man with five tastes which enter his body from the mouth and are stored in the stomach. These five tastes are impure and therefore go to form man's body, bones and flesh, blood and veins, as well as six emotions.'[93] As a result, man has two kinds of soul, a *hun* (Jpn. *kon*) soul at the macrocosmic level which is made up of the refined, heavenly ki and a *p'o* (Jpn. *haku*) soul at the microcosmic level which is made up of the grosser, earthly ki. The former soul was referred to as the *hun ch'i*, (Jpn. *konki*), the 'spiritual soul', while the latter soul, *p'o ch'i*, (Jpn. *hakki*), 'the sentient soul' or *hsing-p'o*, (Jpn. *keihaku*), as the 'form soul'.[94] The two souls pull the human beings upwards and downwards, and when they tear apart – the *hun* soul ascending to Heaven and the *po* soul descending to Earth, it means death. Eventually they return to the ki totality.[95]

The thought presented by the *Lao Tzu* in the sixth century BC, by the *Chuang Tzu* in the fourth century BC, the *Lieh Tzu* in the third century BC and the *Huai-nan Tzu* in the second century BC, is similarly ki-oriented: all is understood as an unceasing rhythm of natural ki alteration.[96] Y.-s. Yü apprises in a footnote that this was the universe of cosmic interaction that, in one way or another, dominated into the Han era via Mencius and others.[97] The question is whether the Chinese ever left this faith. By and large, through the whole Chinese history the underlying perception of reality has been a dialectics of a yin ki and yang ki process of formation and transformation. With yin and yang in order the seasons follow in the right order, agriculture is flourishing and the crops are rich. With yin and yang out of order, on the other hand, all kinds of disasters arise, floods, drought, epidemics and other disasters take place. There have been variations depending on time, place and circumstance but the dialectic tone and force have remained the same.[98]

The Taoist ki cosmology is expressed in the *Tao Te Ching*, Ch. 42:

> Tao produced the One.
> The One produced the two.
> The two produced the three.
> And the three produced the ten thousand things.
> The ten thousand things carry the yin and embrace the yang, and through the blending of ch'i (ki) of the void they achieve harmony.[99]

That the ki thinking was deeply rooted in the Confucian humanistic tradition is proven by the cases of Mencius (Meng Tzu, ca. 372-289 BC) and Hsün Tzu (ca. 298-238 BC). Mencius interpreted the world as a 'flood-like ki' reality (*hao-jan chih ch'i* (Jpn. *kōzen no ki*) and Hsün Tzu described a ki world, amazingly close to Aristotle's psyche universe.[100] That the ki concept was decidedly alive in the following centuries is registered by Needham who lists both scholars and titles of works that discuss the 'vital force' of ki in nature.

The ki of the *Kuan-tzu*, a pre-Han work,[101] runs parallel with Mencius' 'flood-like ki'. It is considered 'the universal fluid, active as yang and passive as yin, out of which all things condense and into which they dissolve. . . At its purest and most vital level it is *ching* (Jpn. *sei*), the "quintessential".'[102]

> . . . In all things the quintessential transforming becomes the living. Below it generates the Five Grains, above it becomes the constellation of stars. Flowing between heaven and earth, call it the divine (*shen*, Jpn., *shin*, *kami*) and the spiritual (*kuei*, Jpn. *ki*, *oni*).[103]

The ki has personal as well as cosmic dimensions. On the personal level it is the vitalizing energies of the body and the breath that is inhaled and exhaled. The mystical ki-oneness is realized in the personal luminous awareness of the activity of Heaven and Earth. 'Concentrate on the ki . . . and all the myriad things will be present at your disposal.'[104]

Also in the following religious Taoism all nature is a process of ki transformation, cyclic and unending. Ko Hung (Jpn. Kakkō) (283-343) imagined a Primal Origin, *Hsüan* (Jpn. *Gen*), the Mystery or the Chaos, giving rise to ki, from which in turn Heaven and Earth and the myriad things are born. All is endowed with motion and quiescence, sharing the sublimity of the Way of Heaven. 'The universe is always coming into being and passing away.' Man is beset by the same law and must be at pains not to waste his endowed ki. To preserve and nourish the vital ki force, various Taoist breathing and sitting techniques were employed.

From Han to Tang times when Buddhism and Taoism dominated we can follow a line of thinkers who favoured spontaneity and a universe that proceeds smoothly according to its own harmonies. They connected with the early Sung thinkers, first Chang Tsai (1020-77) who, closely reflecting the *I Ching*, depicted a monistic ki cosmos, both transcendent and immanent, and a 'so-of-itself' reality.[105] As the primal ki revolved, the impure ki gathered at the centre and earth was formed. The pure ki became the sky and heaven. The influence of the *Huai-nan Tzu* and other pre-Han sources is apparent. Also the cosmogony that followed in the Sung era saw a unitary ki, encompassing all reality. Chang Tsai was followed by Chou Tun-i, in turn followed by Ch'eng I and Chu Hsi who all made ki the basis and the beginning of heaven and earth. 'That all things develop without doing harm to one another and all ri realize themselves without contradicting one another, this is what makes Heaven and Earth great.'[106]

The early world outlook was amazingly like Greek philosophy in the same centuries. The Five Element theory goes back to the fourth century BC and became the basis of traditional speculation about the world. Together with the yin-yang thought, which dates even earlier, Chinese naturalism was given form, interpreting reality in ways only modified but never replaced until in a recent century. Above them was a Heaven that dictated change and motion, observed in nature. Those were manifested in human life, thus also in history. This Chinese proclivity to seeing the Five Elements on the material level and the yin-and-yang balance on the supra-material level can be followed through Chou times and into Han times. It is a culturalism dealing with relations and processes, but not with matter and substances. One can speak about natural law but not about *Wissenschaft*; about sentiments but not about inquiry; about ki but not about ri. It was therefore strikingly different from the Greeks whose elements were substances, not processes or qualities, that is, until Aristotle.

In Han times this naturalism took a long step towards a pre-modern science[107] when the Five-Element correspondences were correlated to become a metaphysical reality both within and beyond things.

Tung Chung-shu (179?-104?) wrote about 135 BC:

> ... Wood has its place in the East and has authority over the ki of spring. Fire has its place in the south and has

authority over the ki of summer. Metal has its place in the West and has authority over the ki of the autumn. Water has its place in the north, and has authority over the ki of the winter. This being so, Wood takes charge of life-giving, and Metal of death-dealing; Fire of heat, Water of cold. Men have no choice but to go by this succession; officials have no choice but to operate according to these powers. For such are the calculations of Heaven.[108]

It was in its Han synthesis that the yin-yang – Five Element theory was handed down to later ages, even to the present age. There were many fanciful and imaginary elaborations and interpretations over the centuries, for example, divination, astrology and geomancy, but they remained within the confines of the original naturalism, rarely deviating towards the mechanical cause and effect that characterized Greek and European naturalism. The thinking was frozen within established boundaries which stifled innovative ideas. When the Confucian philosophers in the late T'ang era began to develop new thought that would coalesce into Neo-Confucianism during the Sung era, they therefore built on a continuous tradition. It was not a Renaissance of ancient times but a development over centuries, ending in the Chu Hsi synthesis by 1200.

In Japan the ki thought was accepted early and the word ki is today still a popular word that is heard daily and found in hundreds of terms. For example, the word genki, the 'primal ki', is used in routine contacts, whenever one asks about a person's health. Its original meaning of 'primal ki' and its Chinese provenance is never thought of. In a saying like 'ki wa kokoro' kokoro is equalized with ki. Ki ni iru, 'to like' and 'ki ni ireru, 'to be liked', are two other 'ki expressions' often used in everyday conversation. Almost all the terms and phrases have, with time, obtained new meanings and are used in contexts which do not correspond to original Chinese usage.

5. How Do Ri and Ki Relate to Each Other?

W hich comes first and which comes second? Ri or ki? Which takes precedence over the other? If ki comprises Heaven and Earth and all things, it should logically come first because ri must anticipate ki. Only in ki does ri find meaning. If ki does not exist, there is no place for ri. From this point of view, ki is basic. Ri is, however, the activating agent that must come into and reside in ki. As Chu Hsi says: 'In the universe there has never been any ki without ri or ri without ki.'[109]

Then he says:

> What are called ri and ki are certainly two entities. But considered from the standpoint of things, the two entities are merged one with the other and cannot be separated with each in a different place. However, this does not destroy the fact that the two entities are each an entity in itself.

And:

> The ri is incorporeal, one, eternal and unchanging, uniform, constituting the essence of things, indestructible, the reason for creation and always good. On the other hand, the ki material force is necessary to explain physical individuality and the organic process. It is transitory and changeable, unequal in things, constituting the physical substance, destructible, the vehicle and material for creation, and involving both good and evil.[110]

Thus, everything is a union of ki and ri, forming the inextricable two sides of the coin: one does not go without the other; neither exists without the other. Or as Chu Hsi expresses it, 'Ri is never separate from ki; however, ri is *keijijō* while ki is *keijika*'.... 'When ki congeals, ri is in it.'[111] The heavenly ri intermingles with the earthly ki and things are formed. This inseparability of ri and ki is at the heart of the Chu Hsi orthodoxy. The conclusion is that the *keijijō* and the *keijika* constitute closely united though separate entities. They are two components, independent but complementary: 'Ri dwells within ki ... and never parts from ki.'[112] But 'ri comes first and ki follows', which suggests *keijijō* dominance.[113]

In Chu Hsi thought, ri has therefore the priority and is more essential than ki. It represents Heaven it is tenri, 'Heaven's ri', in nature. This demonstrates how closely nature is connected with Heaven. Ki represents Earth and comes second. Heaven and its ri come first. In the human moral world, ri is the timeless, essential and immutable part conjoining the ki emotional and mutable part. It compares with a supernatural principle in deistic assumptions. Ri is innate and the same in all things, while ki is allotted in differing quantity and quality. Ri and ki are in opposition in the nature of man, which is volatile and indeterminate, but in nature otherwise it seems that ki and ri go hand in hand, one functioning due to the other, one existing because of the other.

Chu Hsi was ambivalent when answering questions about which comes first, ki or ri. He says on the one hand: 'First there is the ri of Heaven, then there is the ki. The ki agglomerates to form matter (*chih*, Jpn. *shitsu*). It is the preparatory raw material for the "nature".' Then, however, he says: 'One cannot really say which comes before and which comes after, ri or ki.'[114]

Again he says: 'Ri is never separated from ki. But ri is above form while ki is below form. If one has to speak of above and below in this way, there can hardly be a before and after.'

And: 'One cannot really speak of any priority or posteriority of time as between ri and ki; it is only if one insists on considering their origins that one has to say that ri comes first. Ri is not something separate, it has to inhere in ki.'

And, finally: 'Fundamentally one cannot say that there is any difference between them (ri and ki) in time, but if one goes back to the beginning of all things, one cannot help imagining that ri was first and ki came after.'[115]

C. Shirokauer expresses it thus: 'For Chu Hsi they are both (ri and ki) irreducible, with ri holding logical and ontological but not temporal priority over ki.'[116] J.P. Bruce says: 'It is a ri-ki dualism, the pure ri world "above forms" (keijijō, Ch. hsing-erh-shang) versus the impure ki world "below forms" (keijika, Ch. hsing-erh-hsia), which resolves itself into monism.'[117] Then, ri has the logical precedence over ki. It is the 'rider on the horse'.[118]

The conclusion is that Chu Hsi assigns higher value to ri. Ri is the root and purpose of all things while ki is the raw material of all things. Things must have ki for its nature and ri for its form. Ki is the fundamental 'stuff' of the universe, formed by the inherent ri.[119] 'When ki condenses, it is governed by the ri of condensing, and when ki disperses, it is governed by the ri of dispersing; whether ki disperses or condenses, it is governed by ri.'[120] Ri and ki are not to be confused, neither are they to be separated; they are two entities in one.

In Taoist thought no rider on the horse is mentioned: Only the horse is of interest. The ri, the Creator, the Prime Mover, or a godhead above things are not asked for. Matter with its entelechial force becomes in and of itself all things. There is only a natural regeneration within ki matter. Metaphysical purpose is exchanged for a spontaneous dialectic which continues endlessly – on and on and on.[121]

A comparison can be made with both Plato and Aristotle. Chu Hsi comes close to Plato, who visualizes ideal forms which correspond to ri. He comes likewise close to Aristotle who noted form and matter, both, *mutatis mutandis*, compatible with ri and ki.[122] The difference seems to be that while Chu Hsi's ki is alive, Aristotle's matter is dead.

In his commentary on the Chung Yung Chu Hsi clarifies the ri-ki-ism.[123] He says:

> Human nature (hsing, Jpn. sei), is li (ri), principle. Heaven produces the ten thousand things with the ki of yin and yang and of the Five Elements; this ki becomes the body, with ri endowed therein . . . It is as though it had been commanded. At birth every human being receives endowed ri, and thereby is constituted of the invariable Five Constant Virtues

(i.e. benevolence, righteousness, propriety, wisdom and trustworthiness). . . . When human beings and other creatures each follow what is natural to their natures, there is not one who does not take the proper path in day-to-day affairs. This is then the so-called tao. . . . While the nature and the tao are the same for all, the allotments of ki differ, and consequently there cannot but be errors of excess and deficiency. Sages follow the path that people ought to take and regulate it so that it becomes the model for all under heaven; this is called instruction. Such are the rites, music, penal law and government. It seems that people know that they themselves possess human nature but do not know that it comes from Heaven; they know that there is a tao to affairs but do not know that it follows their human disposition; they know that the sages offer instruction but do not know that it accords with what we possess originally and regulate it.

The ki is thus the clay shaped by the ri. Heaven is the rationale, providing the direction and the script, and the tao imparts the ri. For example, in the billions of cells of the human body the ri directs in accordance with the tao, all forming one organic whole, with Heaven present in every cell. It is a holism where all lives in all. Man, being no exception, is endowed with Heaven's nature (ten no sei, Ch. t'ien chih hsing),[124] and is an integral part of one gigantic cosmic whole.

The scriptural authority was found in the Four Books, the Lun Yü, the Meng Tzu, the Ta Hsüeh and the Chung Yung. The latter two works were chapters from the Li Chi (Jpn. Raiki), The Book of Rites, one of the early Five (Six) Classics. These Four Books (ssu-tzu, Jpn. shisho), also referred to as the 'Four Confucian Books', displaced the Five (Six) Classics as the central texts to become the core of Confucian truth until modern times. Chu Hsi put the Ta Hsüeh first among the four, followed by the Lun Yü, the Meng Tzu and the Chung Yung. The Chung Yung should be read only after the other three books. The Ta Hsüeh introduces the ri, ko-wu, chih-chih and other concepts which crown the Chu Hsi philosophy.[125] These Four Books became the Confucian New

Testament, while the earlier Five (Six) Classics sank back to be the Confucian Old Testament.[126]

5.1 Yi-T'oe-gye and the Four versus the Seven

The Korean Neo-Confucian philosopher Yi T'oe-gye (1501-70)[127] elucidated the ri and ki in the Neo-Confucianism with his consideration of the 'Four' versus the 'Seven'. The 'Four' are the 'Four Beginnings [of Virtue] (shitan, Ch. ssu tuan)', representing the ri heavenly nature. They are commiseration, shame, propriety and wisdom. As Mencius says:

> The feeling of commiseration is the principle of goodness (or benevolence) (jen, Jpn. jin); the feeling of shame is the principle of righteousness (i, Jpn. gi); the feeling of modesty is the feeling of propriety (li, Jpn. rei); and the feeling of appoving and disapproving is the principle of wisdom (chih, Jpn. chi).'[128]

Mencius also says:

> What belongs by his nature to the superior man are goodness (or benevolence), righteousness, propriety and knowledge. These are rooted in his heart and their growth and manifestation are a mild harmony appearing in the countenance . . .[129]

The 'Four' correspond to the 'Five Constant Virtues' (gojō): goodness (or benevolence), righteousness, propriety, wisdom and trustworthiness (jen, Jpn. jin), (i, Jpn. gi), (li, Jpn. rei), (chih, Jpn. chi) and hsin (Jpn. shin). The fifth virtue, trustworthiness, is added, perhaps to reach the sacrosanct number of five in the Chinese tradition.[130] Not least the propriety rules represent the moral obligations on humans. They connect Heaven and man directly and indicate the original goodness of human nature.[131]

The 'Seven' are the seven emotions (shichijō, Ch. ch'i-ch'ing), pleasure, ki (yorokobi), anger, nu (ikari), sorrow, ai (awaremi), fear, ku, love, ai, hatred, aku (nikumi) and desire, yoku. They belong to the earthly ki nature in man and are mentioned and discussed in the Li Chi.[132]

Hand in hand with the Five Constant Virtues go the Five Relationships (*gorin*): the relationship between (1) Father and Son, (2) Lord and Servant (Ruler and Minister), (3) Husband and Wife, (4) Elder and Younger Brother and (5) Friend and Friend. The first four relationships are hierarchic and depict the vertical society. Only the fifth relationship – between friend and friend – is on the horizontal level, but even here seniority requires awe and respect. Among them the relationship between Father and Son, referred to as Filial Piety (*kō*), and the relationship between Lord and Servant, referred to as Loyalty (*chū*), were the most important and where Chinese and the Japanese differed. While the Chinese usually put Filial Piety first, the Japanese tended to put Loyalty first. These two relationships were often combined with the Husband and Wife (*fūfu*) relationship, together referred to as the Three Bonds (*san-kang*, Jpn. *sankō*).

6. Confucius and Mencius

Confucius (Kung Fu-tze, 551-479 BC, Jpn. Kōshi), the foremost icon and cultural hero of China – even a byname for China itself – is looming so high and great in the Chinese humanistic learning that only Chu Hsi some 1600 years later can measure up by his side.[133] The second great name in the Confucian world is Mencius (Meng-tzu, ca. 371-289 BC, Jpn. Mōshi) who is considered the second great name and follower of Confucius. If Confucius was the great moralist, Mencius was the great ki-ist. Together they championed the ancient tradition and formed the first Confucian synthesis.

On the background of Heaven and its tao Confucius

established a social ethics that emphasized the right forms of behaviour in accordance with rites and rituals, the *rei* (Ch. *li*), found in the Five (Six) Classics, which, according to tradition, he edited. *The Analects* (*Lun yü*, Jpn. *Rongo*) presents in twenty chapters precepts for correct ethical life in the light of goodness (or compassion) and righteousness, the indissoluble pair of virtues which relate to all other virtues, offering rules for man's conduct and human society. The land should be ruled by sacred law and not by means of punishments and force. Transcendental matters are on the other hand avoided. They are mentioned but not discussed.[134] It is man's moral life, and his social relations that are in the centre. Their cultivation is of utmost importance not only for the person himself but for the whole human society. Rites are internalized and expressed in external behaviour.

The primary objective of Confucius' gospel was the attainment of the golden mean, a middle way between excess on the one side and shortcoming on the other. Virtue must come first: 'it is the root'. 'Possessing virtue gives the ruler the people; possessing the people gives him the territory; possessing the territory gives him the wealth.'[135] He is the superior and noble man (*chün-tzu*, Jpn. *kunshi*) who 'stands erect in the middle, without inclining to either side' and 'follows his heart without transgressing'.[136] It is a call for ethical excellence for all people and all ages.[137] The ultimate concern was that family and political morality should form a coherent whole.

It was not until in Han times (202 BC-AD 220), some 350 years after his death, that Confucius came to be recognized as 'China's greatest sage' and a cult arose around him. Temples were erected in his honour and attempts were made to make Confucianism a state religion. As a patron saint of the teachers and scholar-officials he has been reverenced until the present day. If we define religion in broad terms, he was deeply religious. He believed in a Heavenly order and stated that at fifty he knew the biddings of Heaven.[138]

Paradoxically, Confucius probably considered himself a failure, but he has dominated Chinese civilization for two millennia;

practising neither unrestrained hedonism, nor rigorous moralism, he teaches the way of the Mean.[139]

Mencius was in most respects the respectful follower of Confucius. In the *Meng Tzu*, divided into seven chapters, he is the amplifier of Confucius. If Confucius is laconic and short, Mencius is lengthy and argumentative. He believed in the fundamental goodness of human nature and the essential harmony among men (*jen-ho*, Jpn. *jinwa*) and emphasized that sagehood was accessible to everyone. He admonishes: 'Seek and you will find it; neglect it and you will lose it.' And further: 'He who exerts his mind to the utmost knows his nature. He who knows his nature knows Heaven.' And: 'The great man is one who does not lose his child's heart.' Like Confucius he affirmed sociability and moral values and extended the humanistic doctrine to the realm of state matters. His idealism was often close to Taoism when he embraced universal love and advocated equalization of land distribution. As for the Mencian famous theory of the four beginnings, see above.

In his emphasis on the 'flood-like ki' spiritual force in human affairs, Mencius had an affinity to Taoism. Chang Tsai was, in turn, close to him in Confucian thinking. Seeing a cosmic purpose as regards Heaven and Earth and all things, it gave his views a distinct religious overtone and made him a forefather of both the ki and ri idealism.

Confucius and Mencius lived in the feudal Chou age, and the ethics and norms they propagated reflected the era. The graded social hierarchy was espoused and the family as the centre of moral life and the society as the family writ large. Their thinking was most influential in ages to come and connects with and forms the foundation of the Chu Hsi philosophy.

7. The Development of Neo-Confucian Thought in China

The early Confucianism, as represented by Confucius, Mencius and others was mainly socially oriented. It was, as a German scholar puts it: 'Die Reglementierung alles Daseins in einer hohen Ethik und Soziallehre.'[140] All the concepts were there in philosophical discourse, but remained unsystematic and never treated as a comprehensive system of philosophy.

After almost a millennium of Buddhist dominance, a Confucian Renaissance arose in late T'ang times (618-906) and a new Confucian epistemology was fully developed in Sung times. The new Confucian thinking was called Chu Hsi Confucianism with reference to the final organizer, Chu Hsi, the Ch'eng-Chu Confucianism with reference to the Ch'eng brothers and Chu Hsi, the Learning of the Way (dōgaku) with reference to Heaven's Way and the Sung Confucianism following the name of the era. In the West it has been called Neo-Confucianism – also in this work – in contrast to earlier Confucianism.

Plenty was borrowed from Taoism and Buddhism, perhaps mostly from Buddhism, which had a long spiritual lore which the founders were steeped in through years of study. From Zen Buddhism came, probably, the meditation techniques used in seiza – quiet sitting. All the primary conceptions, however, originated from the I Ching, even the ri, which is discussed in this oeuvre. The ontology, which assimilated metaphysics, nature, social relationships and government, was first presented by Chou Tun-i in graphic form, describing with typical Chinese brevity all being and becoming.

Considerable controversy has originated from the lack of a creator in the Neo-Confucian thought. The thought of a spontaneous cosmos has been difficult to accept. It need not, however, be far-fetched. Chinese philosophy has its own spirituality, only with other dimensions than we are used to in monotheism. For the Confucian, creation is the automatic yin-yang pulsating of the divine providence which emanates from the universal essence. It is eternal, orderly and harmonious. It performs a sacred drama under a Heaven that is the only stable part of the All. Surely there is no personal god to turn to, but in a syncretic multi-religious reality there are deities aplenty – in case spiritual succour be needed besides the inner peace achieved by introspective *seiza*. Heaven itself is no insignificant godhead. It has interested this writer how often Heaven is referred to synonymously with God in the Christian world. The difference between East and West – as in the world generally – is probably not great in times of distress.[141]

Neo-Confucian thought went through its own rich development during more than 600 years of intellectual dominance in China, Korea and Japan. From the Chu Hsi moralism it passed through 'several phases with changing emphases'. From its balanced ri-ki dualism in Sung it turned to inner ki monism during Ming and, perhaps as a reaction, to outer ki monism in Ch'ing, however, always within the same Confucian boundaries.[142]

7.1 The 'Five Great Masters'

The Neo-Confucian thought developed from the late T'ang era, when Confucians felt the lack of a cosmology and metaphysics to compete with the Taoists and the Buddhists. The resurgence began with numerous and successive thinkers. It was, above all, Han Yü (768-824), Liu Tsung-yüan (773-819) and Li Ao (ca. 800), great T'ang intellectuals, who reasserted the superiority of the Confucian Way over Buddhism and Taoism. In the Southern Sung era (960-1011) Confucianism moved to the forefront of Chinese intellectual life. This continued into Northern Sung (960-1127) when thinkers like Shao Yung (1011-77), Chou Tun-yi (1017-73), Chang Tsai (1020-77) and the Ch'eng Brothers (Ch'eng Hao (1032-85) and Ch'eng I (1033-1107) – the Five Great Masters –

gave it the Gestalt which was systematized in Southern Sung (1127-1279) by Chu Hsi (1130-1200).

Both Chou Tun-i and Chang Tsai were at first as much Taoists as Confucianists and the Ch'eng brothers, both Ch'eng Hao and Ch'eng I, had been in Buddhist training for years before they turned Confucian. Chu Hsi, too, had both a Buddhist and Taoist past.

The 'Five Great Masters' were related or acquainted with each other and it is therefore natural that their thinking was alike and overlapped. They operated within the same Confucian parameters and worked mainly with the same concepts. They differed however sufficiently to be worth individual consideration. Chu Hsi is mostly considered the fifth and last among the Masters while Shao Yung is omitted. Here Shao Yung is presented as the first among the five and Chu Hsi afterwards as crowning them all.

7.2 Shao Yung (1001-77)

Shao Yung regarded change, based on the *I Ching*, as the metaphysical origin of all things. It took the place of a creative godhead, in a yin and yang evolutionary dialectic. The Five Elements are thereupon the basis of the correspondences of the multiplicity of things which come and go in eternal circulation. Ki is the 'stuff' of both Heaven and Earth. The difference between the two realms is that whereas the ki of Earth has forms, the ki of Heaven is just pure ki – devoid of form. This thinking was accepted by Chou Tun-i and by Chu Hsi. All notions had the origin in the *I Ching* but came also from Taoist thinking. The same dialectical cosmology was repeated by every Neo-Confucian scholar in the following seven centuries with only variations in vocabulary and interpretation.[143]

Shao Yung was a contemporary of Chou Tun-i but is less known. The reason might be that his thinking ended up in elaborate diagrams, in which cosmological and ethical ideas and numerology intermingled and was not easily understood. Another reason might be that Chu Hsi criticized him for his excessive interest in metaphysics and hardly mentioned him in his commentaries.[144] He was, however, in line with the new trend that stressed the Confucian order in the universe. All changes were manifestations that ended in the Great Ultimate. He tended to an idealized stance and was close to Ch'eng Hao when he expressed the view that 'the myriad things are all in myself';[145] likewise, when he said that 'The human *kokoro* (*hsin/kokoro*) contains Heaven and Earth and the *tao* of the myriad mysteries is complete in every person's spirit.'[146]

7.3 Chang Tsai

For Chang Tsai all cosmos was a meta-reality, a 'great harmony' (*t'ai ho*, Jpn. *taiwa*) of ki, from which everything derived and to which everything returned. It was a ki monism of vital energy-matter, a *t'ien-tao-ch'i* (Jpn. *ten-dō-ki*) metaphysical world, operating according to a heavenly design. There is a single ki reality that integrates and disintegrates, and the appearance and disappearance of things are a matter of tao.

Chang Tsai drew his inspiration from the *I Ching*, and, further, from the *Huai-nan Tzu*. Reflecting the cosmology of these works he wrote:

> In its original state of the Great Vacuity (*taikyo*, Ch. *t'ai hsü*) ki is absolutely tranquil and formless. Acted upon, it engenders the ki of yin and yang and through their integration gives rise to forms. As there are forms, there are opposites. Heaven and Earth were in the beginning nothing but the ki of yin and yang. This single ki was in motion, turning around, and after the turning had become very rapid, there was separated out a great quantity of sediment. There being no way by which it could escape from within, it coagulated and formed an earth in the centre. The purest ki became the sky, the sun, the moon and the stars.

And:

> Ki fills the cosmos, ascending and descending, never stopping. This ki is the beginning of things, of movement

(tung, Jpn. dō) and stillness (ching, Jpn. sei) and of hard and soft. What is going up is the clear yang ki and what is going down is the unclear yin ki. The yin and yang function together, condensing and dispersing, become wind and rain and frost and snow. That all things take on forms, that mountains soar up, that rivers flow down and that there are also sediments is explained by this.[147]

And:

The Great Vacuity of necessity consists of ki. Ki of necessity integrates to become the myriad things. Things of necessity disintegrate and return to the Great Vacuity. Appearance and disappearance following this cycle are all a matter of necessity. . . . He who apprehends integration and disintegration, appearance and disappearance, form and absence of form, and can trace them to their source, penetrates the secret of change.[148]

They are equally real, the undiffentiated ki of Heaven which is above form and unmanifest and the lower differentiated ki of Earth, which is within form and manifest; one could not do without the other, they are the two sides of the same reality. What is above and what is below is however 'threaded on one string', that is, the ki that now condenses and now disperses. Things come and go but the underlying ki is not destroyed. Chang Tsai likens it to ice congealing and melting, with the water always remaining the same. It is the ki of the 'Great Vacuity' that is the origin of all things in the world. Consequently, although there are numerous things, they are all one, the unity in diversity and the diversity in unity – the one ki in the many and the many in the one ki. All ki formations are temporary 'guests' (k'o, Jpn. kyaku) in the world. The process of attraction and repulsion of ki is for everyone to see; there is nothing illusory about physical matters as the Buddhists wish to have it. There is a principle of motion operating in circles: day becomes night and night becomes day; summer replaces winter and winter replaces summer in endless alternation, as in the picture below, illustrating the cyclic nature of the the yin and yang order driving the universe.

It should be noticed that the yang contains a fleck of yin and the yin a fleck of yang. 'The essence of yin and yang conceals [within itself] the dwelling place of the other ... They possess each other and overcome each other.... This is why the ki contracts and expands without limit, revolves and moves without rest.'[149] The same complementarity concerns human psychic life: 'When you have grasped the easy and simple, then you are able to know the difficult and complex. After you have grasped the principle of the easy and simple, then you can string the world on one thread.'[150]

This was the ri of Heaven, but it differed from the ri of the Ch'eng brothers and Chu Hsi. The ri was secondary and related to the natural forces and tao within the ki. There was only one thread running through the realms of Heaven, Earth and man. The difference between the orthodox Chu Hsi Neo-Confucianism and Chang Tsai was that Chang Tsai did not emphasize the concept of ri. 'For him, ri, in the sense of orderliness, was a property of ki, and therefore it did not occupy the central position in his philosophy that it did in Ch'eng-Chu metaphysics.'[151] It was a ki Heaven condensing and dispersing in yang and yin configurations – beyond the reach of our understanding.

Chu Hsi also 'strung it all on one thread' – only that, for him, the 'colour or tone' differed on the keijijō and keijika sides. He preferred Chou Tun-i's 'Great Ultimate' to Chang Tsai's Great Vacuity. Otherwise, Chang Tsai and Chu Hsi were two variations on the same melody. For both it was an orderly universe. In fact, Chang Tsai's Grand Vacuity and Chu Hsi's Great Ultimate were much the same, both uniting all things and representing Heaven's tao on Earth. Jen, 'goodness', was the great radiating virtue for both of them.

The difference was that Chang Tsai regards all change taking place within a ki ocean – the one mass of ki that comprises all creation while Chu Hsi regards change as taking place in accord with natural law within the same ocean of ki. Chang Tsai's ki monism was only expanded with the purposeful ri, and the ri and ki became the two entities which make the Chu Hsi synthesis dualistic. It might seem that for Chang Tsai the cosmos was an automatic self-governing ki clock while for Chu Hsi the clock had its independent ri order. There were, however, patterns and standards also in Chang Tsai's cosmos of ki which brought it close to ri thought. He mentions even a heavenly principle (*tenri*) in the swirl of events. Chang Tsai, affirming the sacrosanct heavenly harmony, was also an exponent of Confucian religiosity. His ideas were accepted by Chu Hsi and so was the belief that the kokoro unites *tao* (ri) and ki and controls human nature and emotions. To sum up, even if Chu Hsi perhaps differed with Chang Tsai occasionally, they were in general agreement – even as regards ki.[152]

7.4 Chou Tun-i

Chang Tsai and Chou Tun-i (1017-73) have been depicted as the pillars of the new Confucianism. If Chang Tsai presented the ki colour to the canvas, Chou Tun-i added the ri pictorial background. They were contemporaries and lived in Northern Sung about 100 years before Chu Hsi. Both of them instructed the Ch'eng brothers who in turn inspired Chu Hsi.

Chou Tun-i's graphic diagram, the *T'ai-chi-tu* (Jpn. *Taikyoku-zu*), 'the Diagram of the Great Ultimate', is a graphic abstraction of the creation, presented in symbolic discourse.[153] It is simple, as can be seen. The accompanying succinct explanation provided the Neo-Confucian creed with the cosmological foundation and became the basis of the Neo-Confucian creed. Its principal source of inspiration was the *I Ching* in which work the Great Ultimate is first presented. It says:

> The Unlimited and the Great Ultimate! When the Great Ultimate moves, it produces the yang. When the motion reaches its limit, it comes to a standstill. In standstill, it produces the yin. Subsequent to the standstill, motion returns. But motion is followed by another period of standstill; these alternatively constitute the primordial factor. When either the yin or the yang is diffused, the one or the

other constitutes a function – one of the two functions. By the cyclical transformation of yin and yang, fire, water, earth, wood and metal are produced. These Five Elements are diffused causing the rotation of the four seasons. The Five Elements are no other than the yin and the yang, the yin and the yang are no other than the Great Ultimate and the Great Ultimate is rooted in the Unlimited.

When the Five Elements are produced, each has its own nature. The truth of the Unlimited and the essence of the two functions and the Five Elements are integrated in a wonderful union. The *tao* of the *Ch'ien* (first diagram of the *I Ching*, meaning Heaven) brings out the male; the *tao* of *K'un* (second diagram of the *I Ching*, meaning Earth) brings out the female. Out of the mutual affection of these two vital forces grows the manifoldness of things. By the process of production and reproduction a variety of things spring up infinitely.

Man is, however, endowed with the best and is the most spiritual of beings. Man is born with the shape of a man, and is endowed with knowledge by the gift of spirit. He lives through the mutual workings of the Five Elements, As a result, good and evil, and thousands of kinds of action diversify themselves. The sages decided the fundamental principles of *chung* (Mean), *cheng* (Fairness), *jen* (Goodness) and *I* (Righteousness) and set up the criteria for human dignity. They co-operated with Heaven and Earth with regard to moral excellence, just as the sun and moon co-operate with regard to light. As there is order in the four seasons, so there is peace in human society. A man of noble character pursues these virtues, and incurs good fortune. A small man disobeys the laws of the universe and so incurs misfortune.

The tao of Heaven is yin and yang. The tao of Earth is softness and hardness. The tao of man is goodness and righteousness. When one is familiar with what is the beginning and what is the end, one understands all about life and death. Great is the *I Ching*! It presents the ultimate truth.[154]

The explication has been subject of controversy ever since it was written because of its terse simplicity that allows various interpretations.[155] The opening phrase is one of the enigmatic sentences in Chinese philosophy. It presents the infinite Unlimited as the yonder side of the hither Great Ultimate with the absolute quality of a godhead in Western or Indian religions. The two concepts are the two sides of the same coin as expressed by Chou Tun-i: 'The Unlimited and the Great Ultimate' (*wu-chi erh t'ai-chi*, in Jpn. *mukyoku ni shite taikyoku*).

The Unlimited might be interpreted as pre-Big-Bang, pre-cosmic and reminiscent of the Buddhist emptiness and Taoist nothingness.[156] Confucian scholars generally kept to what was within comprehension, but Sung thinkers – Chou Tun-i perhaps first among them – raised the thought from the floor to the ceiling, from the mundane to the divine. Chu Hsi also assumed this other side when he said: 'The Great Ultimate, rooted (*moto*) in the Unlimited.'[157] The *wu-chi*, the Unlimited, was an equally fundamental part as *t'ai-chi*, the Great Ultimate; they formed the inseparable two halves of reality. The balance of the All demanded it. This was as clear to Chu Hsi as it was to Chou Tun-i.[158]

The explication togther with the diagram became the manifesto of Sung thought and Chou Tun-yi has been commemorated as the father of the Neo-Confucian cosmology. It proves that a message has to be short to convince. Beginning with Chu Hsi, it was copied and discussed in Neo-Confucian works, not only in China but also in Korea and Japan. It was a vision close to the Eastern soul and has remained so until this day. Chou Tun-yi laid the foundation for the discourse of the Ch'eng brothers and Chu Hsi.

Chou Tun-i was thus one of the founders of the ri-ki philosophy. The Ch'eng brothers and Chu Hsi followed in his footsteps. His veneration of quietude was also the same as for all following Sung thinkers.

7.5. Ch'eng Hao and Ch'eng I

The two brothers, Ch'eng Hao (1032-85) and Ch'eng I (1033-1107), 'canonized the metaphysics of ri as the key to the philosophical puzzle of the cosmic order'. Ri became the most important notion of the Neo-Confucian philosophy and as concretized initially by them and then by Chu Hsi, it became the basis of Chinese, Korean and Japanese Confucianism in the following centuries.

Both brothers aimed at personal self-transcendence, but while the elder asserted the cultivation of one's inner life, the younger focused more on the investigation of outer nature. Both emphasized the ri as the definite feature of everything that exists. Ch'eng Hao was more traditional. He counselled that one must concentrate on and extend one's own consciousness – the store-room of ri. Looking into one's own nature, one attains the equilibrium when 'the universe and I are one body'.[159] Thereupon one can further humanity as a whole. 'One's duty is to understand ri and preserve jen, "goodness", (inner) sincerity (ch'eng, Jpn. sei) and (outer) sincerity (ching, Jpn. kei), that is all.'[160] The reinterpretation of the tradition came with Ch'eng I as regards the ri concept. 'Greatly disturbed by the allure of Buddhism', he responded with the ri metaphysics which was accepted by Chu Hsi in the final Neo-Confucian synthesis. For him any object, even a blade of grass, could reveal the ri and lead to the experience of illumination. The brothers worked with the same concepts, but their views on nature and ri differed. They foreshadowed the two mainstreams the ri thought was going to take, the 'inner' idealistic and monistic (Lu Hsiang-shan) and the 'outer' rational and dualistic (Chu Hsi), the first known as hsin-hsüeh, study of the mind (the Lu-Wang school), and the second as li-hsüeh, 'study of ri' (the Ch'eng-Chu school).

Ch'eng Hao simplified the way to enlightenment, when he eliminated the strait-jacket of the many steps of learning and declared that the immediate capacity for sagehood was inherent within the mind. His brand of Neo-Confucianism is therefore called the hsin-hsüeh (Jpn. shingaku), 'learning of the mind'. He embraced a sudden 'penetration' rather than a gradual process. One should always 'be doing something without expectation. . . . Let there be no artificial effort to help it to grow! . . . Not to exert the slightest effort: that is the way to preserve the goodness (*jen*) [of the mind].'[161] The mind itself is 'the seat of the unfolding of ri' and the practice of self-cultivation becomes 'an internal process of correcting that which is already there'.

Then, what about the ki in Ch'eng I's vision? The primal ki (*genki*) was as real for him as for any other Sung thinker. It is the ocean in which all 'fish swim'. Everything emanates from there and it is where everything returns. The ocean is the ki and the ri are the fish. 'Man lives in the ki of Heaven and Earth exactly as fish live in the ocean.' The ki envelops him, it is what he breathes in and what he breathes out. The mysterious interaction of yin and yang leads to the myriad things of our world.

One wonders what Ch'eng I and then Chu Hsi would have said if they had heard that a man consists of one hundred thousand billion regenerating and co-ordinated cells – and that they differ among six billion people, each having a 300 gram big muscle that pumps nourishment to the very last cell? It would have proven their point, would it not?

8. Chu Hsi

N ext to Confucius, Chu Hsi ranks as China's great philosopher, the epitome and apex of Neo-Confucianism. He can also compete with Confucius in terms of impact on Eastern history. 'Without question he is one of the greatest men in the whole development of Chinese thought.'[162] He has also been characterized as 'one of the greatest synthesizers in world history'.[163] He integrated the various tenets of the whole Chinese tradition, shifting, amplifying and forming the consummation that was transmitted to later generations. Like Confucius, further, his great reputation came after his death. In his life he was not generally accepted. Before his death he was in disgrace, denounced as a 'heretic' whose spirituality was suspiciously close to Buddhism.[164]

Han scholars, Tung Chung-shu among them, had created the first systematic Confucian cosmology.[165] What had been mostly natural concepts in the *I Ching* and moral precepts in Confucius' *Lun Yü* and other classical works were appraised by them and built into a coherent whole to become a state-espoused orthodoxy and an elaborate state cult. The 'Five Great Masters' of the early Sung era inherited this orthodoxy. The final systematization came with Chu Hsi. He combined Chang Tsai and Chou Tun-i with the Ch'eng brothers and adding his own views, the result was the Neo-Confucian philosophy, the *rigaku* (alternatively called *rikigaku*), the Ri (Riki) Study. 'His genius and diligence enabled him to bring together the various strands of texts, practices and ideas that had accumulated in Confucian thought and weave them into a powerful and coherent system.'[166] Lastly, he drew heavily on both Buddhism and Taoism, which he had studied for years.

Chu Hsi interpreted Chou Tun-i's Great Ultimate to be the ultimate principle and the highest good within the ki cosmos. It was the same beyond things and within things. The ri of one thing was the ri of all things. It became the basis that naturally and logically resolved all existence. The Chang Tsai's ki thought and Ch'eng I's ri thought joined in a single vitalistic dimension. 'The world could be explained as the ceaseless unification of principle (ri) with energy-matter (ki). . . . In humans it is the role of the mind-and-heart (*kokoro*) to unify its nature *qua* ethical principles and virtues with the dynamic power of energy-matter (ki) as passion or emotion.'[167]

Chu Hsi recommended a strict approach to study and learning. It should be for self-cultivation and one's moral enlightenment. It should not just be for the civil service examinations and worldly success. It had to be systematic and in proper order. With this aim in mind he set up a graded curriculum for the disciple. He should begin with the *Ta Hsüeh*, which is logical and coherent, and thereupon turn to the *Lun yü*, and the *Meng Tzu* and finish with the more difficult work, the *Chung Yung*. Chu Hsi singled them out as the primary works for teaching the Confucian truth. The *Lun yü* was the central prescriptive teaching, which should be read meticulously, and the *Meng Tzu* should be the elucidation of the *Lun yü*. To make this study truly thorough, Chu Hsi wrote commentaries which soon became as important as the original texts. The Confucian Four Books with the Chu Hsi commentaries became the axial programme of education for all students in the Yüan, Ming and Ching China. The previously authoritative Five (or Six) Classics[168] became the second round of study, undertaken only after the study of Confucian classics had been covered and were not considered as important as the Four Books, which were learned by heart, recited aloud and memorized. They formed a unit, in which one book had little or no meaning without the other three.[169] The day the commentaries on the Four Books were completed in 1190, the Chu Hsi era commenced. For six centuries, under the Yüan, Ming and Ch'ing dynasties (1313 – 1911), they were the standard texts for the official examinations.[170]

Chu Hsi was further responsible for the establishment of the orthodox transmission of the Way (the *tao-t'ung*, Jpn. *dōtō*) in the Confucian tradition. It begins with the ancient sages, continues with Confucius and Mencius and, leaving the Han and T'ang eras out, continues with Chou-Tun-i and ends with Ch'eng I. Chu Hsi meant that the line was broken following Mencius and only revived after a thousand years with the Ch'eng brothers. He was later himself added to the list.[171]

With his coherent and elaborate approach Chu Hsi presented an intellectual alternative that fitted the Chinese mind and pride. His ri synthesis could successfully counteract the Buddhist and Taoist faiths that had dominated for a millennium. It offered an alternative for the intellectual elite that preferred the exoteric, abstract and practical to the esoteric, mythologized and occult.

The magic and superstitions of the Buddhist creed were condemned and a down-to-earth empiricism aiming at the Great Ultimate took its place. With the addition of meditation, perhaps a loan from Buddhist practice, the serenity was achieved which spelled the peace of mind on the one hand and positive social activity on the other.

Chu Hsi was the pivot on the axis of the Neo-Confucian thought. He matched inner self-cultivation with outer study of things and social concerns, emphasizing both observation and intuition. Others espoused either side of the axis. His contemporary and friend Lu Hsiang-shan (Lu Chiu-yüan) (1139-92) emphasized reflection and the cultivation of the mind. Another contemporary, Ch'en Liang (1143-94), endorsed the outer aspect of the Confucian life and was concerned with practical, also political, matters.[172] This division of Sung philosophy into central, inner and outer reflected the same cleavage in classical times.[173]

Among Chu Hsi's numerous works, the *Chin-ssu lu* (Jpn. *Kinshiroku*), *The Essentials of Learning*, which he compiled in 1175-76 with the help of a friend, Lü Tsu-ch'ien (1137-81), is a compact work which is the best summation of his thinking. It is an anthology of the principal doctrines, intended to serve as an introduction of the Confucian Books and the ri thinking. It is considered one of the most influential works of philosophy produced in all East Asia during later dynasties.[174]

Chu Hsi nourished a religious attitude of reverence towards Heaven throughout his life, cultivated by *kyūri* and *seiza*.[175] W. -t. Chan concludes that 'he was an intensely religious person'.[176] His *kyūri* 'aimed at a thorough comprehension of the multitude of things by realizing that all principles constitute one ultimate principle – a step from mere intellectualism or empiricism towards a religious perspective. Therefore, the Chu Hsi position may safely be said to be congenial to a religious state of mind, and, in fact, Chu Hsi sought such spiritual transcendence.'[177]

9. Wang Yang-ming (1472-1529)

Chu Hsi's antipode in the Confucian world was Wang Yang-ming (Ō Yōmei) who lived around the middle of the Ming Dynasty (1368-1528). If the former was the foremost representative of Sung Neo-Confucian scholarship, the latter headed Ming Confucianism. His thinking was in line with Lu Hsiang-shan and together they are usually referred to as the 'Lu-Wang' school. In his studies it dawned upon him that the mind and ri could never be separated and that truth was to be found in the 'sincere intention' (ch'eng-i, Jpn. seii), not in external objects and affairs (shih-wu, Jpn. shibutsu).[178] External kakubutsu was discarded, and internal kakubutsu became the way to sagehood.[179] 'The universe is my mind and my mind the universe'; thus he reduced the ri and ki to a mind-only unity.[180] 'Mind itself is the world of truth, and intuition the key to it.'[181] All people have 'the truth within themselves' and it cannot be lost. It can only be obscured by the clouds of selfishness as when 'clouds obscure the sun, but how could the sun ever be lost?'[182] His approach was thus introspective and referred to as 'learning of the mind' like Ch'eng Hao's thinking earlier. His meditation was close to Zen and he was accused of being a 'Zenist in disguise'.[183] Intellectual speculation was concerned with the mind, its cultivation and preservation. One can sense an affinity with George Berkeley (1685-1753) in the conclusion that what exists are minds and their sensory experiences.

Wang Yang-ming's lifelong concentration was therefore on the human mind, which he equated with ri. 'The kokoro is ri' (hsin chi li, Jpn. shin-soku-ri). All ri is inside the kokoro, not outside of it, requiring exhaustive investigation of things external to the mind.[184] 'There is no ri outside human nature; there is no thing (mono) either outside human nature.'[185] Human nature is fully formed and perfect at birth, and if it is kept free from the obscurantism of the ki endowment, it joins hands with Heaven and Earth and all people. There is therefore no special need for the classics or the investigation of things. Only one's innate good knowledge (*liang chih*, Jpn. *ryōchi*) is to be one's teacher. It is immmanent in the heart of man and is both physical and nonphysical. Also for Wang Yang-ming goodness (*jen*) is the root of all other virtues and made manifest in the pursuit of daily life.[186] Filiality was emphasized as the central virtue in later Japanese Wang Yang-ming thinking. (See Nakae Tōju in Part II.)

Self-cultivation should aim at enlightenment, attained within one's own nature and experienced in a sudden flash of illumination rather than through step-by-step transformation.[187] The 'inner light' should lead to the unity of knowledge and action (*chih-hsing ho-i*, Jpn. *chikō gōitsu*) and to the highest good (*chih-shan*, Jpn. *shizen*).[188] Knowing what is good, one acts accordingly. 'Knowledge is the beginning of action; action is the completion of knowledge.'[189] Wang Yang-ming lived up to this ideal by serving as a civil servant and a general.

Wang Yang-ming made a distinction between 'real knowledge' (*chen chih*, Jpn. *shinchi*) and 'ordinary knowledge' (*chang chih*, Jpn. *jōchi*). Real knowledge is the true knowledge when 'the perfected person is as clear as a mirror: accurately and concisely "reflecting" the situation at hand'.[190] Ordinary knowledge is a superficial knowledge of just knowing about a matter. With real experience a person knows of the matter, reacts directly in ways that a person with ordinary knowledge does not. 'You can not really know what love is until you have been in love, and you can not really understand what compassion is until you have acted compassionately.'[191] The 'real' person reacts and acts without hesitation while the ordinary person takes all things at the outset into consideration. The majority of politicians would fit under the second category, people freshly in love under the first.

In the centre of the quest for mental illumination lies (inner) sincerity. Self-cultivation must make a person extend sincerity to the utmost and guard against wayward impulses, whether resting or moving. This conscious effort does not disregard the study of the classics and meditation, but knowledge or quietism *per se* should not be the goal. This would be like heating a pot – cooking nothing.

Wang Yang-ming's emphasis on introspective examination and intuitive perception had overtones of religion when he referred to the innate moral faculty as the 'good knowledge' and stated that 'The thousand sages are all passing shadows; the good knowledge alone is my teacher.'[192] What had been part of Mencius' philosophy became the centre of Wang Yang-ming's philosophy, metaphysics as well as ethics. In spite of divergent views, Wang Yang-ming was close to Chu Hsi and in time included among the Neo-Confucian philosophers. His idealism exerted a wide influence on the Ming era and its popularity gave rise to schools which were also active in early Ch'ing.

10. Heaven (*t'ien*, Jpn. *ten*), and the Way (*tao*, Jpn. *dō*)

In all Confucian thought, Heaven is the bottom as well as the top line. When it distances itself from and forgets Heaven, as has happened in modern times, it is no longer true Confucianism.[193]

Heaven has been a concept in Chinese philosophy from earliest times. It is found already in the *I Ching*, alternately with the concept of *ti* (Jpn. *tei*) and *Shang Ti* (Jpn. *jōtei*), Lord-on-High, with the connotation of a divine ruler or God. Afterwards the concept is found in other classics and later works with overtones of deism. If, as it seems, it had a godly connotation in pre-

Confucian times, the question is how it should be considered in ages beginning with Confucius. That Heaven was experienced as a Celestial Lord (*t'ien ti*, Jpn. *tentei*) before Confucius is quite clear. It is also quite clear that Confucius never doubted the existence of Heaven.[194]

From the time of Confucius, Heaven seems to have become anthropopathic, transcendent as well as immanent, with a will and power over cosmos, nature and man. It functions so automatically that people do not even notice its being there. Whether anthropomorphic or anthropopathic, however, the Chinese were conscious of the Mandate of Heaven that governs nature, man (the Emperor, 'Son of Heaven' (*t'ien-tzu*, Jpn. *tenshi* first of all)) and the myriad things. As such Heaven was also seen by the Neo-Confucian thinkers, not least by Chu Hsi. No Neo-Confucian philosopher forgot to refer to Heaven and Heaven's Will in his writings.

The *I Ching* and especially Lao Tzu present Heaven and Earth as an unending ki evolution and as a 'great transformation' (*ta-hua*, Jpn. *taika*): 'All modalities of being, from a rock to heaven, are integral parts of a continuum'[195] in an all-embracing cosmic pattern.[196] No mention is made of a higher lawgiver or creator; all comes naturally in an evolutionary process of generation and change. All is bound up with forces working from within, not from without. Instead of an anthropomorphic being or anthropopathic essence, the Way is expounded as a 'being so of itself' (*tzu-jan*, Jpn. *shizen*) and a spontaneous, self-generating natural order. 'Tao belongs to Nonbeing (*wu-wei*, Jpn. *mui*). Things belong to Being but tao controls all actions', says the Taoist work *Kuan-tzu*. 'When has Heaven ever stopped working?'[197] Chu Hsi asks rhetorically. Hsün Tzu was close to the same view, when he said: 'The fixed stars make their round; the sun and the moon alternately shine; the seasons succeed each other. . . . These changes are known to us, but we do not know the invisible source: this is what is called Heaven.' Hsün Tzu obviates the question of a creative deity, but ends with a caveat, asking about 'the invisible source': Heaven, which exists above and shines into one's life.[198]

In following centuries Confucian thinkers often rejected supernatural matters. Wang Ch'ung (AD 27-100?), the greatest sceptic among them all, questioned whether the dead would survive as spiritual beings or ghosts and whether Heaven could interfere in human matters. He says: 'All things are spontaneously produced, when the ki of Heaven and Earth come together, husband and wife unite and children are naturally born.'[199] Wang Pi (226-49) was opposed to the thought that the virtue of Heaven takes action with regard to the myriad things. Neither, however, denied the existence of Heaven.

The belief in an anthropomorphic or anthropopathic Heaven did not vanish and in the Chu Hsi synthesis of the Confucian philosophy it is, in one way or another, the superstructure of the keijijō, expressing direction, law and principle as tao (dō) and ri (li). It is the 'encompassing' which transcends the world and man and is the source of everything finite.[200] The great innovation was the elevation of the ri to a position where it equalled Heaven's way in importance. Rigaku and tengaku became synonymous. Chu Hsi also juxtaposed Heaven with a 'Lord-on-High' when he said that 'we can serve Heaven and offer sacrifices to the Lord-on-High'.[201]

Closely linked with Heaven is the Way (tao), so closely, in fact, that the two terms are usually written together, as tendō. When Heaven is expressed, the Way is often included, and when the Way is expressed, Heaven is always included. Together they form the upper, supernatural essence. For the Chinese, generally, tao has become such an accepted term, connoting both religion and philosophy, that it is untranslatable. For both the Taoist and the Confucian it was synonymous with Heaven, the natural order and the very structure of things. It has become an axiomatic term without need for explication or translation. For this reason also in this work it is used interchangeably with the term 'Way'. Thus it has priority over the temporal world and even the sages who 'functioned as the discoverers of the way'. In Japan Ogyū Sorai 'reversed the sequence of the sage and the Way', indicating that the sages had invented the Way of Man.[202]

The Taoists have called tao 'the mother of the universe' and given, it seems, priority over Heaven.

Among the two, Heaven (ten) and Way (tao, dō), Heaven comes first in Confucian scriptures – it is always written tendō, never dōten. The metaphysical lord is thus Heaven and the Way is the handmaiden of Heaven.[203] Together they refer to the ultimate reality of things. If Heaven is the master, the origin of life and the unmoved mover, the Way syncretizes heaven and subsumes the flux and flow of cosmic life, embracing all change. It is the omnispatial, omnipresent, omnipotent and omniscient essence. 'It is eternal and unceasing, transcending time, space, substance and motion. It is characterized by the universal harmony found in nature as well as in man.'[204] In the cosmic sense it belongs to the Taoist order while in the ethical sense it belongs to the Confucian order. In the Chu Hsi synthesis the cosmic tao and the human tao link together in unity.

Tao, joining Heaven, thus, overlaps the entire Chinese philosophical tradition. It is the origin of everything and ends in simple ethical maxims which pervade world and society. It is incumbent on man to apprehend its distinct manifestations, and thereupon to live and follow the great way of Yao and Shun.

Chu Hsi's accomplishment was to add the concept of ri to the ten and the dō and create the triad of the ten-dō-ri. A broad Confucian metaphysics was established with Heaven's Way being the spirituality beyond and in things.[205]

The Absolute had, in the end, many names and aspects which came together under Heaven, the ABSOLUTE above all other Absolutes. Tao (dō) was one, li (ri) was another, t'ai-chi (taikyoku) was a third, jen (jin) was a fourth, hsin (shin, kokoro) was a fifth, ch'eng (sei, makoto, sincerity) was a sixth and chiao (kō), (filial piety) was a seventh. There were other terms and internal virtues that encompassed the 'all-in-all' totality. Transcendence had as many names in Neo-Confucian times as in the I Ching and

Confucius and Mencius. They just express different aspects of the same cosmic purpose.

11. Goodness or Benevolence (jen)[206]

The virtues both begin and end with goodness, benevolence or humaneness (jen, Jpn. jin).[207] 'It is indeed the one principle that penetrates through Confucian teachings.'[208] Since this is a pervasive term, difficult to render, it is often left untranslated as jen, also in this work. The preferred translation here is 'goodness'. It is the prime virtue of man. All other virtues are comprised by it. Man is originally good and all evil can be blamed on natural aberration. The good person (jinsha) unites with Heaven and Earth and all things. This optimism of early Chinese thinking remains unaltered in Neo-Confucianism. Chu Hsi says that 'jen is the Way of the mind, sincerity its firmness'. The dualism of good and evil can be traced from early Heaven and Earth thought via yin-yang polarity to Neo-Confucian ri-ki-ism. The jen is the most central theme of the Lun Yü, occurring over one hundred times, and around it the whole Confucian edifice is constructed. In the Neo-Confucian traditionalism it is the axis leading from Heaven and tao to man. 'Jen was given a metaphysical dimension during the Chinese Middle Ages, Sung and Ming dynasties, and became identified with the cosmic life force itself.'[209]

For Confucius and Mencius, goodness (jen) was the universal and ultimate virtue, the Great Good, that correlated with righteousness. Both of them emphasized the natural equality of all men at birth, an equality that exists in spite of social inequality later. Confucius said that 'within the four seas all men are brothers' and Mencius said that 'every human being can become a *Yao* and a *Shun*'. Confucius said also succinctly that *jen* is to 'love people' (*ai-jen*). It cannot be said shorter and better.[210]

Jen is thus the chief topic in Confucius' conversations as in most Confucian literature. It reaches its most beautiful expression in sayings like 'Repay hatred with uprightness and repay virtue with virtue',[211] the greatness and nobility of which equals – even excels – the Christian love demand.

The Christian golden rule is also found in Confucian garb, but put in a more sophisticated negative form, 'What you do not wish others to do to you, do not do to them.'[212] The rule has been found from classical times in the discussions of human interrelatedness and interdependency. This rhetoric has been concerned with graded versus universal love. The Chinese have soberly tended to accept love with distinctions in social relationships. Universal and equal love was preached, but it was graded love that was socially actualized.

Han Yü (768-824) advocated universal love (*hakuai*, Ch. *po-ai*). Sung scholars followed in his footsteps and treasured it as highly. Because of its all-embracing usage, goodness tended to be identified with both human nature, ri, and Heaven and Earth. According to Ch'eng Hao, for example, the man of *jen* forms 'one body' with all things, and righteousness, propriety, wisdom and truthfulness are all expressions of *jen*.[213] The purport of goodness, signifying the total democracy and unity of all human beings, was well expressed by Chang Tsai (1021-77) in his *Western Inscription* (*Hsi ming*, Jpn. *Seimei*):

> Heaven is my father and Earth is my mother, and even such a small creature as I finds an intimate place in their midst. Therefore that which extends throughout the universe I consider as my body and that which directs the universe I consider as my nature. All people are my brothers and sisters, and all things are my companions. . . . Even those who are tired and infirm, crippled or sick, those who have no brothers or children, wives or husbands, are all my brothers who are in distress and have no one to turn

to. . . . If in life I follow and serve (the Way), in death I will be at peace.[214]

Chu Hsi expresses the meaning of goodness as well in his Treatise on *jen*:

> The mind of Heaven and Earth is to produce things. In the production of man and things, they receive the mind of Heaven and Earth as their mind. Therefore, with reference to the character of the mind, although it embraces and penetrates all and leaves nothing to be desired, nevertheless, one word will cover all of it, namely, *jen*.[215]

Jen implies that everything, the cosmos, living things, everyday affairs, are one in goodness. 'In the Confucian learning *jen* comes first, righteousness matches it, propriety follows as also loyalty and uprightness on the worldly side.'[216] In the end, it includes all virtues. The truly *jen* man is a living sage, forming a trinity with Heaven and Earth. Chu Hsi subscribed to this moral thought and developed it to its highest excellence. He emphasized its creative vitality, which denotes unceasing generation and regeneration (*seisei*, Ch. *sheng-sheng*) of things, and constitutes the *raison d'être* of creation. Taoist inspiration is evident. It is a pity that goodness was more spoken about than lived up to, either in China, Korea and Japan – or in the world otherwise.

Among the later Confucian philosophers who attempted to define *jen*, no one did it better than Ogyū Sorai. He says in the *Bendō*, Ch. VII:

> In the Way of the ruler only *jen* constitutes the great virtue . . . mutually to be affectionate, mutually to love, mutually to grow, mutually to attain perfection, mutually to assist, mutually to nourish, mutually to protect, mutually to relieve, is the way man's nature is constituted.[217]

12. Human nature (*hsing*, Jpn. *sei*, or *tensei*) and Kokoro (*hsin*, Jpn. *kokoro, shin*)

H uman nature has been at the centre of Chinese philosophy and is part of '*das feste Repertoire des konfuzianischen Diskurses*'.[218] So it was in classical times and so it was in the Neo-Confucian centuries. The fundamental question has been whether the human mind is good or evil, or something else. The Chinese were moralists and their perennial question seems to have been, 'What ought I to do that is right?'

Tradition usually mentions Mencius first, who optimistically declared that the human nature was good, immediately adding Hsün Tzu, who affirmed that human nature was evil. For some fourteen centuries every Chinese thinker worth his salt expressed his opinion on the matter until the doctrine of the goodness of human nature was declared Confucian orthodoxy in Sung times.[219] Chang Tsai, the Ch'eng brothers and Chu Hsi were all inclined to agree with Mencius that human nature is good. It is endowed with and identical with Heaven and Earth and all things, whether as ki (Chang Tsai) or as ri (the Ch'eng brothers and Chu Hsi). Chu Hsi adds that it is good at birth and that evil enters afterwards. The evil part is derivative of the ki endowment from the day we are born until the day we die. Human nature, hence, necessitates continuous and lifelong care and discipline. Chu Hsi stresses that this self-cultivation must continue during all waking hours.[220]

Man in the world is likened to a pearl in muddy water.[221] In the *Chin-ssu lu* (Jpn. *Kinshiroku*) Chu Hsi compares human nature (*sei*) with the clear water that, flowing downward, turns turbid but is still the original water whose purity can be restored. Man can likewise cultivate his nature and regain its purity. He says:

That whatever issues from the Way is true and good may

be compared with the fact that water always flows downwards. Water is always the same. Some water flows to the sea without becoming turbid. . . . Some flows only a short distance before growing turbid. Some flows a long distance before growing turbid. . . . Although water differs in being clean or turbid, it does not cease to be water. With purification, the water will be become clear, and when it is clear, it is the original water. . . . The original goodness of human nature is like the original clearness of water'.[222]

The kokoro (hsin, Jpn. shin, 'mind-and-heart')[223] 'envelops human nature and is the repository of virtues. It is the ruler of the body, without form, yet the lord of the entire man', says Chu Hsi. He says further: 'It represents Heaven in man, it is what Heaven imparts to man and it controls the functions of human nature and emotions.' And further: 'It dwells in the centre and governs the five faculties; hence it is called the heavenly lord (tenshu).'[224] Mencius said earlier: 'He who fathoms his kokoro knows his nature; if one knows his nature, he knows Heaven'.[225] The Kuan-tzu says, 'Within the kokoro there is another kokoro and this inner kokoro contains the human intellect.'[226]

'The kokoro is the apex and pivot of man's soul', according to Mencius, 'his innermost sanctuary, the meeting point of his intellect and the will'.[227] Heaven and Earth, ri and ki meet and relate there and together form one body, ri embedded in ki, ki in ri, and the kokoro embedding them both. Further:

The kokoro identifies with consciousness, to the active side of living beings, which, on account of its very dynamism, is capable of evil . . . The ri in human mind is called nature. Nature belongs to the kokoro. . . . Nature comprises all the Way's principles, which are received from Heaven and present in the mind. When manifest in cognition, perceptions, thoughts and anxieties, we have emotions.[228]

The kokoro is consequently at the 'heart' of man's struggle to become a fully moral human being.[229] It is where Heaven and Earth meet. Hence, man has both his 'heavenly nature' (*honnen no sei*), and his 'earthly nature' (*kishitsu no sei*), corresponding to 'the *kokoro* of *tao*' (*dōshin*) and 'the *kokoro* of (earthly) man' (*jinshin*). *Dōshin* is the the pure *kokoro*, the *kokoro* of Heaven, while the *jinshin* is the the impure *kokoro*, the *kokoro* of the world. Man, as a conscious being, has the ability to cleanse his *kokoro*. For Ch'eng Hao, the *seiza* was the way. For Ch'eng I and Chu Hsi, the *kyūri*, was as important. With his balanced view Chu Hsi was as close to Ch'eng Hao as to Ch'eng I, Lu Hsiang-shan and Wang Yang-ming.

When the virtues and emotions attain proper measure and degree, they appear as the Mencian goodness, righteousness, propriety and wisdom. A tranquil *kokoro* precedes active life. It is the '*kokoro no kokoro*'. When it prevails, man becomes vacuous and calm, and he is not overcome by things.[230]

Chu Hsi purported that a combination of *seiza* meditation and *kyūri* learning generated the composed *kokoro*. In this manner one avoided an 'over-reliance upon individual intuition' and the 'drift into radical subjectivism' as among the Lu Hsiang-shan scholars.[231] Through the extensive study of the classics one learnt the correct rites and rituals which corresponded to heavenly law, and through the *kakubutsu* one attained the 'sincere will' (*cheng'i'*, Jpn. *seii*). Chu Hsi said that one should 'abide in reverence and fathom principle' (*chü-ching ch'iung-li*, Jpn. *kyokei-kyū-ri*). Only when the reverent *kokoro* had achieved inner oneness with all things, 'the vessel can be filled with water', that is, we are ready to serve the world. It begins with individual enlightenment and ends with sharing one's illumination with all human society.[232]

The *kokoro*, as a result, oscillates between unmanifest stillness (*wei-fa*, Jpn. *mihatsu*), which relates to the nature of Heaven, and manifest activity (*i-fa*, Jpn. *ihatsu*), which appertains to the nature of Earth. It is incumbent on man to cultivate his *kokoro* and allow its heavenly ri to become apparent.

On the celestial level there is 'heaven's *kokoro*' (*t'ien-hsin*, Jpn.

tenshin) 'the mind of heaven', synonymous with the 'moral mind' (*tao-hsin*, Jpn., *dōshin*). It is 'a natural, spontaneously creative force present in nature as well as in Heaven'.[233] This heavenly *kokoro* is the lord (*chu-tsai*, Jpn. *shusai*), that wills all creation, and 'a positive metaphor for unity with Heaven, Earth and the myriad things'. It represents the active purpose whereas the Great Ultimate serves as the passive ministrant.

13. Taoism and Buddhism

It is easy to trace Chu Hsi's views partly to Taoism[234] and Buddhism. These creeds appealed to the Chinese mind with their refined mystic ideas. The ri thought that became the cornerstone of the Chu Hsi system may be regarded as a direct development from and a parallel to Indian dharma thought which via the Chinese *chu-tsai* (Jpn. *shusai*) ended up as ri. Ri came to be synonymous with both heaven (*ten*) and the way (*tao*) and we meet with the terms *tenri* and *dōri*. Chou Tun-i and Chang Tsai were heavily stimulated by their Taoist and *I Ching* studies and saw the total universe as a fluid ki unfolding, rarely mentioning ri except as the order – *jōri*[235] – within matter and activities. For both of them there was instead the Great Ultimate, bringing order to the ki – a Great Ultimate that is not mentioned by the Ch'eng brothers. The more speculative part of the system came from the *I Ching*, Taoism and Buddhism and the less speculative part from Confucius and Mencius. It was, then, Chu Hsi's genius that made an amalgam of what derived from disparate sources and created a Confucian rationalism.

Chu Hsi studied Buddhism for some ten years when young

and was on friendly terms with Buddhist priests throughout his life, but his practical mind made him turn away from the illusions of their world-negative religiosity. He wrote that he had indeed approached Buddhism in his search for truth, but disappointed, set it aside for the time being and devoted himself to Confucian thinking. Apparently the world-positive Confucius suited him better and he never returned to Buddha. The Chu Hsi synthesis stood, however, not far away from either Buddhism or Taoism. It balanced on the sharp edge, as it were, between professing a Buddha or a sage.

Among the things Chu Hsi criticized in Zen Buddhism was its doctrine of sudden *satori*. In his sober Confucian approach, the way to illumination was a step-by-step intellectual undertaking, a gradual process that would take years rather than a moment. It could result from an extended study of books which contrasted with the wordless Zen approach. With a dry Chinese sense of logic he also ridiculed the *kōan* riddles. The biggest fault was, however, the negation of the world; for a Confucian Chinese this was the acme of idiocy. When Buddha abandons his father and mother and gives his life to feed a hungry tigress, what kind of morality is that? In social thought the Confucian and the Buddhist were thus poles apart, the Confucian aiming at serving the world, the Buddhist at rejecting it.

Taoism was indigenous and shared the same ancient ideals, and was therefore close to Confucianism. However, its concept of nothingness was close to the Buddhist concept of emptiness. The 'inner' wing of Neo-Confucianism, Ch'eng Hao, Wang Yang-ming and others, were naturally adjacent both to Taoism and Buddhism. Chu Hsi was as attracted to Taoism as to Buddhism in his search for truth but left them both when he turned to the sages. A number of concepts are identical in the Chinese traditions, whether Taoist, Confucian or Legalist, for example tao and ten, although with different connotations. The cosmology of Chou Tun-i, accepted by Chu Hsi, stood with one leg in Taoism when it declared that whatever exists, begins in the Unlimited. Chang Tsai was close to Taoism in his pan-ki-ism which considered nature self-sufficient, neither created nor governed. It was Ch'eng I who broadened the cosmology with the ri thought which ended in the Chu Hsi ri-ki orthodoxy. Chu Hsi was close to the Neo-Taoist Wang Pi who said: 'The shapeless, nameless moment is the father of the myriad things, while the shaped and named moment is the mother who nurtures and makes it grow.'[236] Nature is infinite time and space, equating with tao, Heaven and the One.[237] Chu Hsi read widely and absorbed the Taoist creed for his synthesis of both cosmogony and the world.

Hence, we cannot deny the assmilation of transcendent elements from Taoism and Buddhism. From them, Sung Confucianism received the impetus for a wider metaphysical orientation and for a richer reverent life. It became more than a means for self-centred potential bureaucrats. Confucius had not bolstered up his thinking with undue reference to religion. He had rather declined to discuss what was beyond. Wisdom for him was to learn to be human. In Chu Hsi's doctrine, learning and contemplation became the Confucian way to achieve a good ethical life and ultimately sagehood.

14. Learning and Quiet Sitting (seiza)

S tudy and learning (hsüeh, Jpn. gaku) are necessary in order to be in accord with the moral way. They are man's foremost duty and pleasure. For the true Confucian it means, as expressed in the Kuan-tzu, 'to give wings to your ears and to make your eyes long'.[238]

To acquire knowledge and to overcome obstructions one must learn, and the way is the study of the works of the sages and worthies. They have left instructions of unchanging validity of how to return to the original infinite nature and how to become a Yao or a Shun.[239] The commitment to the ideal of the sage starts with learning and this should be a life-long undertaking. The example was granted by Confucius himself who said: 'At the age of fifteen I set my heart upon learning.' This enabled him eventually to 'know the biddings of Heaven without overstepping the boundaries of right'.[240] Chu Hsi likewise professed the importance of scholarship, 'In the pursuit of learning we must aim at the Way, and in being a man, we must aim at being a sage'.[241]

Learning for its own sake was useless. True learning should have the high goal of acquiring the truth, the tao, that is, the sages' Way. It should not be 'examination learning', directed towards becoming an official,[242] but aim at the truth as articulated by the sages of the early Three Dynasties. Learning to be a sage was the only true 'learning'; to engage in literature without this objective was to be narrow and vulgar (rō).[243]

Confucian learning had, in the end, to be for the service of man. This was the practical goal of the Confucian scholar. He was illumined to be anxious about the world's troubles. 'The superior man dares not but exert himself in service to his father, in service to his lord, in service to his elder brother, in service to his friend. This is what marks the superior man.'

The emphasis on learning was nothing new in Confucianism. Already the initial sentence in Confucius's Lun yü endorses study and 'to learn' is the first word of the work. The Ta Hsüeh has even the word learning in its title 'Great Learning'. Chu Hsi discussed 'learning' and gave it an exact ri orientation. He emphasized that one shall not seek the truth swiftly. Learning is likened to climbing a mountain: one cannot reach the summit without climbing, one step at a time, the long way upwards.[244]

Chu Hsi's teaching about learning stood, however, on two legs. He certainly said that 'knowledge comes first' but he warned against 'one-sidedness'. One should seek knowledge not only outside but also within oneself. The question is which leg should come first: the seiza internal leg or the kyūri external leg. A conclusion is that Chu Hsi considered both activities equally important and wished to see an equilibrium: one would not do without the other. The goal was, however, the same whether one stood more on the one leg than on the other: to attain the truth and become, not a Buddha, but a sage.

The way to wisdom was, for Chu Hsi, a long way that led from the Great Learning via Confucius and Mencius to ethical life and to 'being in accord with – and attuned to – the proper situation'.[245]

If study and learning were the erstwhile way to the illumination of the mind, the 'quiet sitting' (*ching tso*, Jpn. *seiza*), was the complementary way to the 'shattering experience of oneness with all things'.[246] It is not until Sung learning that we hear of *seiza* or quiet sitting.[247] It was in this era that the Confucian thinkers, through contact with Taoism and Buddhism, found that to sit silently and achieve an inner equilibrium was as important as being submerged in learning and studies. The state of reverence for Heaven, so central in the Neo-Confucian creed, demanded quietude and innerness to match outer activity. A nourished mind was necessary for a poised personality. Chu Hsi presented no precise formula for the seiza, and he stressed that it must not be a goal *per se*. This would come dangerously near Buddhist *dhyana* trance and to become a 'Confucian Buddha'. The settled mind should lead to active political and social life. Therefore, he emphasized that the observation of nature (ri) should go *pari passu* with quietism and meditation.

Chu Hsi cautioned that the practice of contemplation should fit into the total process of learning, referring to the *Chung Yung*, which says: 'Before pleasure, anger, sorrow and joy are evoked, it is called equilibrium (*chung*, Jpn. *chū*). When these feelings are evoked and each and all attain due measure and degree, it is called harmony (*ho*, Jpn. *wa*).'[248] At first, he took less interest in *seiza* meditation but eventually compromised and advocated the practice of *seiza* as supportive of the ri study, ending with the formula, 'a half-day quiet sitting and a half-day study' (*pan-jih ching-tso pan-jih tu-shu*, Jpn., *han-nichi seiza, hannichi dokusho*).[249] Thus, like Ch'eng I, he asserted the necessity of balancing extension of knowledge and moral effort. The *seiza* should come first.[250] After the mind was clarified in detached *seiza*, it was ready for the observation of things.

The purpose of *kakubutsu* and *seiza*, whether reading books or introspection, was in the inner realm of self-cultivation. It was a lifelong commitment, necessitating a strict schedule of practices until the day of death. Reverence or seriousness, *ching* (Jpn. *kei*) was paramount. As Ch'eng I states: 'Moral self-cultivation requires reverence; the pursuit of learning depends upon the extension of knowledge.'[251] 'Abiding in reverence' (*kyokei*) means spiritual cultivation, rectification and the attainment of earnestness. One must ripen steadily and one day arrive at the consummation when the inner and the outer are uniform, and one is ready to serve the world. Chu Hsi emphasized that the unity of seriousness and enlightenment should lead to extroverted life. He quoted the *I Ching*: 'Seriousness is to straighten one's inner life and rightousness is to square one's outer life.' They were the 'two wheels of a vehicle or the two wings of a bird'.[252]

15. Neo-Confucian Thought in Statecraft

The ri value system, as accommodated by the *Ta Hsüeh*, the *Chung Yung*, the *Lun Yü* and the *Meng Tzu*, came to serve as a traditional force and ideology, supporting the state and the system. The rigidity of Neo-Confucian orthodoxy was welcomed by conservative regimes that strove for the equilibrium within the limits of status quo. In China this happened already in the Yüan Dynasty when the Chu Hsi ideology was declared the state ideology (1313) and in Korea at the inception of the Yi dynasty (1392). In Japan the Tokugawa bakufu feudal order incorporated and represented the Way of Heaven, and it became incumbent on the people to espouse the bakufu seido, which was considered to correspond to and be in line with the universal ri. The feudal socio-political structure with the four classes,[253] hierarchically ordered, was a reflection and manifestation of the 'natural' order.[254] Thus Heaven remained the supreme source of legitimation for the maintenance of bushi domination and shogunal rule. It contributed to and strengthened the inherent conservatism of the systems of China, Korea and Japan.

It was the ancient times as presented in the early Five (Six) Classics that represented the basic truth for statecraft. It was therefore the duty of every forward-striving, progressive Confucian scholar to study these works, as edited by Confucius, and to apply them in official service. Thereupon came the continuous annals which should be considered in the light of the Five (Six) Classics. From the Confucian classics and other early works one learned about propriety and etiquette in personal and social life, rules which tended to increase over the centuries. First among the rules were the Five Relationships, initially the relation between lord and servant, loyalty, and the relation between father and son, filial piety. Distinction between the high and the low was considered necessary for the orderly world. Any deviation bottomed in evil ki fluctuations. When customs changed and habits turned in new directions, there was a risk that the Heavenly ri had been tampered with. Any rebel could be accused of having alienated himself from his ri and not being in control of his ki.

From the Five Relationships, the road was not long to the vertical society that was central to and characterized the Chinese and other Eastern lands through the ages. Social differences came to have heavenly sanctity. When Chang Tsai said that 'all people are my brothers and sisters and all things are my companions',[255] he evinced an egalitarian inclination with roots rather in Taoist idealism than in Confucian realism. In Sung China, as later in Yi Korea and Tokugawa Japan, the loyalty towards one's lord, the trustworthiness towards one's friends and military morality demanded strict vertical relationships. At the top of the social ladder was the literati (the samurai in Japan), and under them the common people, consisting of farmers, artisans and merchants. This hierarchy was sanctioned by ancient sages and its imposed rigidity was all-important. If these four classes, comprising the majority of the population, were kept in proper hierarchical order, other groups of people could be managed easily. This was the sages' way and its institutions could only be modified due to place, time and circumstance.[256]

Maruyama Masao does not hesitate to put the blame on Chu Hsi for this feudal state of affairs in his discussion of 'nature (*shizen*) and invention (*sakui*)'.[257] 'Nature' refers to Chu Hsi's ri thought whose eternally immovable forms had resulted in feudal stagnation where everything remained uniform from generation to generation, while 'invention' refers to the social and political customs and laws, which could alter from age to age.

16. Neo-Confucian Historical (Ki) Realism

In orthodox Chu Hsi-ism absolute standards unify the Great Ultimate and its many manifestations. History not less than international relations were considered among these manifestations. The Way of Heaven was timeless and unchanging and its application was also timeless and unchanging; any interfering with it was to belittle the sages, the golden age of utopian antiquity and Heaven. This unitary thinking was challenged already in early Confucian thought that accentuated both unwritten customs and written laws, which were relative to time, place and circumstance.[258] The Way was brought down from its heavenly plane into the world and became a relative Way. It was not just the Three Early Dynasties that had accomplished a relevant Way. Each dynasty and age required the institutions which suited it. Both the Han and the T'ang dynasties also accomplished states in which the Way differed from the Way of the early golden age. Worldly success and results were the measuring stick, not obscure supersensory notions. History began with the Five (Six) Classics and the sages. Times change, ethics changes with it – and the Way changes accordingly. Nothing is constant – not even the (institutions of the) Way. Thus the Way in later ages was naturally different from the Way of earlier dynasties. The Way changed in accord with the flow of history. It was an organic reality, the 'flood-like ki' (*hao-jan chih-ch'i*, Jpn. *kōzen no ki*), mentioned by Mencius. Chu Hsi accepted historical alteration. He said that an age can last long only when moving with circumstances. Every situation has its Mean; this is 'the ri of the world' (*tenka no ri*).[259]

The sages and the Early Three Dynasties, however, never lost their Heavenly connotations. The sages 'had acted in accord with Heaven', when they 'established institutions fitting their own times'. At the beginning of Han, T'ang and Sung, likewise, wise people had created the appropriate customs and ceremonies – however, always idealizing the Three Dynasties.[260]

The Three Dynasties were the golden age when sages ruled and all was perfect. All later ages were going downhill and could only hearken back to the perfect beginning and try to learn from the customs of early times – apparently not too successfully. The Sung realists thought revolutionized the orthodoxy with their practical approach to knowledge and put the later dynasties side by side with the Early Three Dynasties. History was equalized, as sagely wisdom could appear in any dynasty, not only among the wise early emperors. Thus, wisely, Kao-tsu of Han and T'ai-tsung of T'ang had also been held up as paragons and standards for later ages. The Way was an interweave of correct institutions for their times as those of the sages for the Early Three Dynasties.

The scholars advocating the changing Way were described as practical and utilitarian, because they embraced this world and did not emphasize the eternal ri patterns. Denying the ri as a constant in history, the way to a monistic ki view of things was short generally. This one-dimensional explanation of cosmos was decried by the orthodox Chu Hsi-ists as blasphemous and scholars like Ch'en Liang who 'saw the tao as an immanent, relative, people-centred and practical truth'[261] were denounced. For Ch'en Liang the fundamental ki reality runs through history as through life and things generally. Ki thought stayed alive, and a number of scholars in the following Ming era advocated a ki monism that increasingly asserted historical relativity, often denying the ri superstructure, however, always within the limits of the age-old world view. The perpetual Way ended up entelechially in things. Scholars in Japanese thought who tended towards a comparable relativism were, for example, Itō Jinsai (1627-1705) and Ogyū Sorai (1666-1728) (see Part II).

17. Later Chinese and Japanese Ri-Ki Thought

It is ironic that at the same time that the Japanese began to persecute the Christians in about 1600, the missionaries were welcomed in China. Jesuits like Matteo Ricci (1552-1610) and Johann Adam Schall von Bell (1591-1666) introduced the new European science, which in Chinese translation found its way to Nagasaki.[262] When Shogun Yoshimune probably heard about this literature through Nishikawa Joken, he ordered that it should be studied and used as long as Christianity was not mentioned. This study, first in China and then in Japan, testifies to the fact that both Chinese and Japanese adapted new knowledge and that they could turn to new learning and yet remain Confucian literati.[263] Similarly, a Christian in Europe could turn to new learning without leaving the Christian creed – although often looked upon askance and persecuted by the church. Scholars became 'nominalists' both in the East and West, but while this trend led to empirical and systematic study of nature in the West, it did not in China and Japan. The Chinese and Japanese remained 'nominalists' until the West brought modern science.[264]

The thinking did, however, not stay stagnant. During the Ming dynasty (1289-1644) preference was increasingly afforded ki, while interest in ri decreased. One wing of the Neo-Confucianists had already in Sung times emphasized the inner side of man. Lu Hsiang-shan had been one of them and he connected with Wang Yang-ming in the Ming era.[265] Their intuitionism was a kakubutsu limited to individual man and close to Zen Buddhism. The ri was located within the experiencing mind and a favoured saying was that 'there is nothing in the universe that is not in myself'. The human mind (kokoro) was the world of truth and illumination should emanate from this inner world, not from kyūri.

The step to Lo Ch'in-shun (1465-1547) was not long. Though affirming the Chu Hsi ki and ri orthodoxy, he asserted that 'the ri is only the ri in ki. Ri must be observed in the revolving and turning of ki ... If one gains a clear understanding of this phenomenon of revolving and turning, one will find that everything conforms to it.'[266] Thus, within the Chu Hsi ri-ki paradigm, he leaned to a ki monism and the secularization of things. It is the physical side – the horse, not the rider – that is of prime interest and emotions and desires are considered to be natural parts of man's psyche and in accord with Heaven. Thus he propounded a 'proto-science' that might have led to 'modern science'.

During the Ch'ing dynasty (1644-1911) the pendulum swung

further in an empiricist direction and the tendency was to look without and not within. A new age demanded the concrete and the practical. A Chinese philosopher who motivated Japanese thinkers in this direction was Fang I-chih (1611-71) who sought 'the extended principles of things', and advanced 'the comprehension of seminal (ki) forces'. *Kakubutsu* was broadened and directed at what is material and external to our minds. Fang I-chih was cognizant of and discussed the works of Jesuit missionaries which were published in Chinese at the end of the Ming dynasty. He was impressed by the ki dimension of these studies, which he found, however, to lack the metaphysics of the ri dimension.[267] Whether geocentric or heliocentric, the universe was under a Heaven where the ki force blended and operated in yin and yang manifestations. Wang Fu-chih (1619-92),[268] likewise, under the influence of Chang Tsai, expressed that 'within the universe there is nothing but one mass of ki', that 'ri are only visible in the arrangement and pattern of ki', and that 'ri operates within the ki', and that phenomena thereby possess life and nature. The phenomena of the world are but 'the temporary forms (*kyakkei*), that is, of ri within ki'. Wang Fu-chih goes so far as to say that 'all is one'. There is only an apparent duality in phenomena – 'one and yet two, two and yet one' – where all ki and ri are the two aspects of a universe that is a living truth (*chen*, Jpn. *shin*) in dynamic equilibrium. A contemporary of Fang I-Chih and Wang Fu-chih, Ku Yen-wu (1613-82)[269] also held that scholarship had to be rooted in the objective world, external to our minds. He became interested in useful subjects such as economics, government and military defence and accused Wang Yang-ming of causing the decline and fall of the Ming dynasty with his hsin-hsüeh.[270] Yet another seventeenth century philosopher, Huang Tsung-hsi (1610-95), wrote that 'between Heaven and Earth there is only ki, there is not ri. The names ri and ki are devised by man.'[271] Other seventeenth and eighteenth century 'realist' Confucian literati were Yen Yüan (1635-1704), Li Kung (1659-1733), Tai Chen (1724-77) and Chang Hsüeh-ch'eng (1738-1801), who were also ki monists and emphasized that there is no ri apart from ki. Yen Yüan is known for his total rejection of Neo-Confucian speculative intellectualism and Tai Chen, considered the greatest scholar of the Ch'ing era, for saying that *ch'i* (ki) is all that exists and that *li* (ri) is only the 'internal texture of things'. Chang Hsüeh-ch'eng was inspired by Tai Chen and known for his extensive historical scholarship and breadth of learning. All of them turned away from both Chu Hsi rationalism and Lu-Wang idealism 'in a move to vindicate the earthy, observable particular thing'. They widened their interest into new practical affairs, but 'felt no urge to break with Confucian tradition as a whole'. Their advances motivated Japanese Confucian thinkers in the eighteenth century, for example, Miura Baien who had read Fang I-chih's works.

Part II

SURVEY OF CONFUCIAN INTELLECTUALS IN TOKUGAWA JAPAN

Introduction

The Tokugawa period was both institutionally and intellectually the most vigorous of Japan's historical ages. It was the golden age of peace when the Confucian legacy was the dominant intellectual discourse that shaped the behaviour of the people. It professed to be the creed of ancient China but was in reality an outgrowth of the Sung system of ontology and the Chu Hsi mode of thought. If the Kamakura and Muromachi eras had been primarily Buddhist, now followed an age when the Confucian truths dominated within the triangle of Shinto, Buddhism and Confucianism. Buddhism remained vital, but did not flourish as before, and Shinto bided its time of glory at the end of the age. The tenets of Confucianism were already recognized by the first Tokugawa shogun, Ieyasu, as the suitable ethics of his state.[272] This was needed after the *sengoku* disorder when the *gekokujō*[273] had been an accepted ethic. Tokugawa Ieyasu understood well that even though he had conquered the land from horseback, he could not hold it from horseback. He apprehended that a firm ideology was needed to sustain the law and order he desired. Naked power was not enough. Both reading and listening to the Confucian truth, he perceived that he had found the ideological basis for his rule, however, not neglecting what support he could also gain from both Buddhist and Shinto learned priests. It was therefore the social ethics of the Confucian philosophy, not its new metaphysics, that Ieyasu and following shoguns valued and promoted. With official encouragement, the samurai turned from warfare to scholarship – from *bu* to *bun* – and a new intellectual era began. Confucian sentiments are thereupon found in many varieties of Japanese culture. In literature, for example, the principles of *giri* (duty) and *ninjō* (human feelings) are conspicuous.

The most important scholars in this Confucian unfolding will be introduced below and their postures *vis-à-vis* the Confucian truth will be presented. It will be demonstrated how they collectively followed and individually applied the Neo-Confucian philosophy. The diversity and strength of the Confucian teachings will be evident as they are presented one by one. Differences in mind and thinking will be discerned already from the beginning of the era. The Chu Hsi moralism went through 'several phases with changing emphases' over a span of 250 years. From an initial century with a relatively simple dialectics the age moved into its second and third century when the intellectual ferment became increasingly dynamic and complex. The nativist Shinto added to the commotion religiously and Dutch (*rangaku*) studies complicated intellectually from the 1750s. Chinese thought persisted, however, in the ideologocal centre, sacrosanct and unchallenged. It was the ethics of the ruling class and, having the stamp of age-old truth, it was not easily rattled. We do not hear of revolution, but rather of evolution within the parameters of the Chu-Lu traditions.[274] A Confucian axis runs from Fujiwara Seika and Hayashi Razan at the beginning of the age to Ōhashi Junzō at the end of the age.

The stimulus for Tokugawa Neo-Confucianism came via Korea from Ming China.[275] As spoils of the Korean War (1592-98), both Confucian scriptures and scholars were brought to Japan. The fundamental Chu Hsi philosophy came at the outset and remained the mainstay of Tokugawa Confucianism. This was the first wave, originating with Fujiwara Seika and Hayashi Razan. The second wave came later, beginning with Nakae Tōju, when Ming thought prevailed. The development can broadly be described as the ri-ki orthodoxy dominating at first, and the ki humanism growing pre-eminent later. Thus, earlier thinkers placed the emphasis on ri-ki idealism, while following philosophers placed more weight on ki realism. The final synthesis was the coalescence of ri and ki in the *jōri* pre-modern thinking of, for example, Miura Baien and Yamagata Bantō. The last adaptation came with the late realists, Honda Toshiaki and Satō Nobuhiro among them, and the modernists, whose greatest representative was Fukuzawa Yukichi. It was the extension of (Neo-)Confucian thought that gradually prepared Japanese intellectualism and culture for the modern world. The sharp dialectical turn came when the Meiji modernizers cleared the land from feudal valuations and created the present Japan.

Pure Confucian thought was rare. It was always an amalgam, not only of diverse mixtures of ri and ki but also of admixtures of Shinto and Taoism. Buddhism was, however, mostly kept at a distance.[276] Already in the second half of the seventeenth century scholars began to challenge the Chu Hsi orthodoxy. As in Ming and Ch'ing China the freedom of inquiry led in new directions, away from orthodox ri-ki dualism. The Japanese surpassed the Chinese in swaying towards empiricism – until they readily joined hands with the materialism and technology coming from the West. Confucianism was not rigidly enforced. It remained an individual matter, perhaps since no examination system existed. It was not until late in the age (1796) that the Neo-Confucian orthodoxy became the official creed.

Generally, the students learned the Confucian truth through Chu Hsi classes. An analysis of the school programmes and curricula affirm that learning began as a rule with the Confucian Classics, which were learned by heart (sodoku). Then followed Chinese history, Chinese prose, Chinese poetry and Japanese studies, ending with Chinese composition (kanbun). After this study, which could take years, the student might turn to subjects that interested him – or be one of the many who entered domain service and bureaucratic anonymity. He had his 'degree' and could be of use. This was the way from the original Hayashi generation at the beginning of the seventeenth century to the twelth generation in the nineteenth century and the Meiji restoration (1868).

Japanese Confucianism differed from Chinese Confucianism in various ways. First, virtually all scholars placed Shinto side by side with the Chu Hsi creed. Confucius and Amaterasu became brother and sister in a Japanese amalgam: the Chinese ri male juxtaposed with the Japanese ki female. This fusion took many forms, ending up in kokugaku nationalism. Rare was the scholar who reacted against this (més)alliance. The only one found in this study is Satō Naokata (1650-1719) who remained staunchly Neo-Confucian.[277] This is in itself was amazing, since he was a disciple of Yamazaki Ansai, who ended up as much a Shinto as a Confucian believer. The scholars were generally cognizant of their native religious tradition and strove to assimilate it with Confucian personalism. The understanding of Shinto, begun by Hayashi Razan and Yamazaki Ansai, and the studies of the past, undertaken by Arai Hakuseki and Mito Mitsukuni (1628-1700), exemplify this endeavour.[278]

While Confucian studies were official studies in China aiming at examinations, they remained private studies in Japan although under state control. Further, Confucian learning and its message reached most people in Japan, not least through the numerous temple (terakoya) schools; in China the studies stayed in ample measure with the ruling elite and had less impact on the common people. Again, being the private preserve of the scholars, Confucianism moved faster from the 'inner' to the 'outer' realm and more easily joined with the Western learning that invaded Japan from the beginning of the eighteenth century.

The Japanese also surpassed the Chinese in creating the rigid vertical society. Chinese thought had the taigi meibun principle, that is 'to do one's duty in accordance with one's place in society'. This principle was scrupulously followed in the Tokugawa society where social mobility came to be almost nil. A people that had been relatively free and mobile in the preceding Muromachi age was forced into a strait-jacket in which they had to suffer for some 250 years.

1. Fujiwara Seika (1561-1619)

Fujiwara Seika is considered the father of Tokugawa Confucianism. He was the original expounder of the Chu Hsi creed in its orthodox form and was followed by scholars who propounded the same message until the end of the age.

Seika began as a Zen Buddhist at the Shōkokuji Temple in Kyoto where the monks were as versed in Confucian philosophy as in Buddhism. Like many other Gozan monks, he put the two creeds side by side in an eclectic *jubutsu itchi* synthesis and thereafter switched to a Neo-Confucian stance, discarding Buddhism. This was under the influence of Neo-Confucian scriptures which reached Japan as an aftermath of the Hideyoshi invasion of Korea. More directly, it was due to a Korean scholar, Kang Hang (1567-1618), who was brought to Japan as a captive in 1597. He became Seika's assistant and friend. In 1600, Seika received an invitation from Tokugawa Ieyasu to come for a visit, and dressed in Confucian attire, he met Ieyasu.[279] From then onwards Seika was a Confucian scholar. The Four Confucian Books and the Five (Six) Classics became his gospel in place of the Buddhist sutras. He added kunten marks for the reading of these works together with Kang Hang. 1600 can accordingly be considered a date of great significance in the annals of Japanese thought.

Kana shōri, Nature and Principles, in Kana Script may be said to express Fujiwara Seika's Neo-Confucian convictions. He wrote this work in simple *kana* script for his mother. In short chapters he presents the precepts of the Confucian world view, which are as rooted in olden times as in the Sung era. Above things he finds 'the Way of Heaven' (*tendō*), and begins the treatise with the following passage:

> The Way of Heaven is the Lord (*shujin*) of Heaven and

Earth. Because it has no form, it cannot be seen. However,
all the orderly change of the seasons, the flowering of
plants, the birth of man ... are the doings of Heaven's
Way. Man's heart is also without form, yet is the lord of
the entire man. ... All things under Heaven are born from
Heaven's Way. The fish in the ocean are born from
Heaven and, likewise, man's heart is always born from
Heaven's Heart. Therefore, both good thoughts and bad
thoughts are rooted in Heaven, something the ruler must
ever remember. He must never forget to be prudent.[280]

Also in following passages, the tendō is presented in
anthropopathic, if not anthropomorphic, terms. It becomes the
prime mover and the supreme divine will above all human affairs.
One also finds the interpretation tentō for the term, indicating
perhaps a creator. Whatever meaning one ascribes to the term, it
implies a faith in a heaven, that is looked up to and revered.

Most of the Kana shōri reads like a Confucian reader. Under
the tendō (tentō), one finds all the usual Confucian categories:
(inner) sincerity (ch'eng, Jpn. makoto, sei), (outer) sincerity,
reverence (kei), the five relations (gorin), the five virtues (gojō) and
the bright (illustrious) virtue (meitoku). They are all bestowed by
Heaven and lodged in human nature (sei). Kokoro (shin) is
identified with human nature (sei) and tendō (also dōshin and
shindō) is the 'Heaven's heart' and the upper half of the nature
and the kokoro, while 'man's heart' (jinshin) emanates from the
worldly desires and appetites and represents the lower half of the
nature and the kokoro. The tendō is analogous with tenri,
showing that Seika belongs to the orthodox ten-dō-ri thought. He
says distinctly: 'The Way of Heaven is ri.' The term ki does not
appear in the text, but it is apparent that when he talks about
desires and passions it is the ki that is referred to, and negatively.
The aim is the 'union of Heaven and man' (tenjin-gōitsu) and the
objective to further the Way so that the bright virtue shines forth
and illumines a person's life. The goal is enlightenment as a sequel
of continued kyūri.

All earthly 'dust' (chiri) must be cleansed so that the soul's mirror shines brightly. He says about the *meitoku*: 'If one does not, day and night, cleanse one's mirror of illustrious virtue, it will be covered by the dust of selfish desires (*jinyoku*) and one will lose one's original *kokoro* (*honshin*). Bright virtue and human desires are enemies and wage battle: if one of them wins, the other loses.'[281]

He was disillusioned with the world and in the *Suntetsuroku, A Record of Pithy Sayings* (1606), he decries the loose customs and attitudes in the world where frauds and cheats (*kyōgen*) 'rely on their wits and talents or on their gifts for sophistry' to deceive people. In extreme cases, he writes in a letter to Hayashi Razan (1604), 'people, wanting something, pursue it uncompromisingly and do not even notice the blood from the stabs [they give each other] in the back'. He regrets that he lives in the wrong age. The question is whether any age or land would have been better![282]

Seika was open-minded in his Confucian approach. He accepted both Chu Hsi's 'rational' spirit and Lu Hsiang-shan's 'irrational' creed and is referred to as the Chu-Lu eclectic. His eclectic tendencies went farther and he is known for both his *nikyō-itchi*, 'Two creeds in One' and his *ju-butsu-dō-sankyō-itchi*, 'Three Creeds in One', syncretism. He then, first, placed Shintoism side by side with Confucianism, and, second, even Buddhism side by side with Confucianism and Shintoism (Taoism). The way of the sages in China paralleled the way of the *kami* and the way(s) of the Buddha(s). His Confucianism was thus not simply Chu Hsi thinking. He was the earliest in Tokugawa Confucianism to declare the Way of the sages in China and the way of the *kami* in the Japanese tradition to be equal. (He was not the last!) All the creeds, he seemed to think generously, have the same ultimate objective, the rectification of the human heart, the illumination through intuition; the abiding in a state of reverence (*kyokei*) on the personal side, and the selfless compassion towards all people on the social side. He preferred the *seiza*, sitting in stillness, practised in reclusion on the hillside in Kyoto between sessions with his disciples.

2. Matsunaga Sekigo (1592-1657)

S eika's school continued in Kyoto under Matsunaga Sekigo[283] and from it came Kinoshita Jun'an (1621-98) who in turn taught Arai Hakuseki and Muro Kyūsō. Utsunomiya Ton'an(1634-1710) was also his disciple.[284] Even Itō Jinsai attended his lectures briefly. Kinoshita Jun'an established his own Chu Hsi school, the Mokumon, in Kyoto. He was late in life invited by Shogun Tsunayoshi to teach in Edo. From his school came also Amenomori Hōshū (1668-1755), who was among the orthodox Chu Hsi scholars in the early eighteenth century. He defended the shogunal rule and the rigidly defined hierarchical order of society with the samurai as the ruling class because of 'their broad-minded visions, high ideals and profound wisdom'. He opposed Arai Hakuseki when the latter wished to give the shogun the title of 'King of Japan' (*Nippon kokuō*).

3. Hayashi Razan (1583-1657)

F ujiwara Seika was of noble stock, and probably disdained the upcoming military class. Therefore he preferred the old order and the life as a cultured recluse in Kyoto. When invited by Edo to enter official life, he declined and recommended his star student Hayashi Razan. The latter willingly left his teacher for power and prestige at Edo and from 1605 until his death in 1657 served four shoguns in official capacities. He was always at

Ieyasu's beck and call, as a scribe, as a lecturer, as a story-teller, as a companion on hawking occasions and visits to Nikkō and so on. In service, he had to take the Buddhist tonsure and wear the robes of a Buddhist priest. He adopted the Buddhist name of Dō-shun and was the first Confucian scholar (*jusha*) of the Tokugawa bakufu.[285]

Philosophically, Razan followed the Seika line: he presented the unadulterated Chu Hsi philosophy with the *ten-dō-ri* on the transcendental side, coupled with the rɪ-kɪ on the phenomenal side. Then followed the ceaseless process of creation with yin and yang formations and transformations via the Five Elements to the myriad forms of the world. All things were ri-ki compositions, seen both dualistically and monistically. As he said: 'Ri and ki are two in one and one in two according to the Sung Confucianists.' Then he added: 'The Wang Yang-ming scholars say, however, that the ri are just the patterns and forms (*jōri*) of the ki in operation, all ending in oneness.'[286] Razan, however, never deviated from the Chu Hsi orthodoxy. He was the true follower, also when he moved from simple ri-ki thought to a syncretic Confucian Shintoism. He was yet closer to Chu Hsi than his teacher when he focused more on the investigation of things than on the quiet sitting and the abiding in reverence (*kyokei*).

On the political side, the Chu Hsi teachings fitted the newly united Japan as a glove fits the hand. Ieyasu – always the political pragmatist – must have been happy with a philosopher who could give him a heavenly *raison d'être* for the stable state structure he was building. It presented the social and political orthodoxy to which the Tokugawa state should conform – and so it mostly did. The status quo necessitated rigid hierarchy and virtuous behaviour exemplified by loyalty and filial piety. This ideal Razan clearly expressed in the following statements:

> The Five Relationships governing ruler and subject, father and son, husband and wife, older and younger brother, and friend and friend have been in existence from olden days to the present. There has been no change in these basic relations, and they are thus called the supreme Way. . . .

Heaven is above and Earth is below. . . . In everything there is an order separating those above and those below. . . . We cannot allow disorder in the relations between ruler and subject, between those above and those below. The division into four classes of samurai, farmers, artisans and merchants is part of the ri of Heaven and is the Way which was taught by the sage (Confucius).[287]

To know the Way of Heaven is to respect Heaven and secure humble submission from Earth, for Heaven is high above and Earth is below. Likewise among the people, rulers are to be respected and subjects are to submit humbly. Only when this differentiation between those who are above and those who are below is made clear can there be law and order (reigi-hatto). . . . The more the rulers are respected, and the more the subjects submit humbly, and the more the differentiation is made clear-cut, the easier it is to govern a country.[288]

While Razan assailed Chistianity, Buddhism and other heretic creeds, he found Shinto useful for the social and civilized order of the nation. He thought there was a bond between the Shinto kami gods and the Way of Heaven. He praised the teachings of ancient Shinto and accepted the Yoshida school which incorporated the Chu Hsi metaphysics into Shinto.[289] This materialized in his juka-shintō syncretism, in which the Confucian virtues joined the kami Gods in bringing peace and security to the world. The Confucian ri became identical with the Shinto kami. If one obeyed the kami, one acted in accord with the Way of Heaven. He stated explicitly that 'our country is the land of the Gods' and that 'Shinto is equal to the Way of the ('kingly') sages' Way (ōdō)'.[290] For this reason, his writings concentrated on both Confucian and Shinto subjects. His Shunkan-shō, Summary of the Spring Mirror (1629) is a description of the Gojō, 'The Five Constant Virtues', in the light of Confucius, Mencius and Chu Hsi. His Shintō denju, Shinto Survey, on the other hand, presents numerous Shinto concepts and notions, although coloured by the Confucian creed.

The work that is of special interest is the Santoku-shō,

Summary of the Three Virtues (written about the same time as the *Shunkan-shō*). Its second chapter carries the title Riki-ben, 'Explication of ri and ki'. Its beginning in short form:

> Both before Heaven and Earth were 'opened' and afterwards ri was always the appellation of the Great Ultimate (*taikyoku*). When this Great Ultimate moves, it gives birth to yang, and when it is still, it gives birth to yin. The yin and yang together are the original One Ki, but divided become two. Further divided, they become the Five Elements. These are wood, fire, earth, metal and water. The interactions of the Five Elements produce the myriad things. The Five Elements condense and generate forms and also man is engendered. Earth forms his body, wood forms his hair, water forms the liquids of his body, metal forms his sinews and bones, and fire forms the warmth of his body. In addition, as for the five viscera (*gozō*), fire corresponds to the heart, wood corresponds to the liver, earth corresponds to the stomach, metal corresponds to the lungs and water corresponds to the kidneys. Thus, man's form is condensed and its functioning is named ki. What is naturally supplied in this ki is ri. This is the work of the Great Ultimate and is named the Way. . . .
>
> However, ki contains what is pure and what is impure, what is good and what is bad. When things are condensed, they take shape through ki and in accordance with the ki endowment, selfish desire appears. Looking for signs, you discern goodness in the eyes, in what is said and also in the movements of hands and feet. . . . All shapes emerge from ki, and all the workings of the myriad things are due to ki. The *kokoro* cannot work without ki. Therefore, if a thing is right, you do it, and if evil, you do not do it; this is because of the *kokoro*. For example, wishing to eat something you should not eat, you do not eat it; the *kokoro* controls ki. . . . Thus while both good and bad lodge in ki, it is clear that there is only good and nothing bad in the *kokoro*.
>
> Not only man is born by the yin-yang forces but also all plants, trees, birds and beasts. All this truth (*kotowari*) is named the Way. It is said, 'the One Yin-One Yang is the Way'. The yin and yang correlatively is called the One Yin

and the One Yang. When this motion of the yin and the yang is in stillness, there is neither space nor time for a single breathing in or a breathing out. This ri is endowed in man's shape, in man's *kokoro*, a product of nature and Heaven's Mandate. Nature is another name for *dōri*.

Confucius' *Chung Yung* says that 'Heaven's order is nature (sei)' and Mencius says that 'nature is good (*sei zen nari*)'.... Therefore, when it is said that 'you are bad', people become angry but when it is said that 'you are good', people become happy. Thus, even bad people know good and bad in their hearts. ... While knowing good and doing ill, one is influenced by one's ki and the bad habits of the world are not altered. If the teaching from above is good, the habits become good and bad habits certainly change into good habits. Consequently, speaking about good and bad as regards the the myriad things, one speaks about the good first and the bad later. Speaking about right and wrong, one puts what is right first and what is wrong second. If one does not understand this truth well, ki is flourishing and the *kokoro* is disregarded. Ki that stands for the bad gets strong and the *kokoro* that stands for the good gets weak. For this reason, one should use the *kokoro* more than ki.[291]

This is only a reworking of the (Neo-)Confucian creed. No new doctrine can be detected. This goes also for the following chapter which could be taken directly from Chu Hsi. The opening paragraph says in excerpt:

> Ri cannot function alone. When ri and ki function together as the *kokoro*, they function well.... When ri and ki operate in harmony, the *kokoro* becomes strong and mistakes are naturally not made. Piety towards parents comes from the ri of the *kokoro*.

And:

> The *kokoro* rules over the body. Man has both his nature (*sei*) and his body (*tai*). The nature has its origin in ri of Heaven and the body in ki of Earth. Man, Heaven and Earth form a trinity and man is one with the myriad things. All things in the universe come from ri and ki in

combination, and man is no exception. Man constitutes, however, a culmination among all things; he exceeds all other created things in excellence. . . . He can be wise or stupid in accordance with the allocation of the ki. He can become a sage or a worthy, but he can equally well become a moron or simpleton. . . . The goal of moral effort and education is to realize the interior experience of enlightenment – and, thereupon, to serve a peaceful world.[292]

It did not take a great deal of imagination to bring the Chu Hsi thought in line with Shinto thinking and, in the end, to equate an abstract Chinese Heaven with a personified Shinto Heaven. Generally, as H. Ooms says: 'No rigid lines separated Shinto from Neo-Confucianism; Shinto notions were a routine part of Tokugawa political discourse.'[293] This had aready begun with Fujiwara Seika and continued throughout the seventeenth century until it turned into nativism, nationalism and ultranationalism. Fujiwara Seika and Hayashi Razan were, in a sense, the founders of Tokugawa Confucian Shintoism. Razan wrote that 'The Way of the Kings transforms into the Way of the Gods, and the Way of the Gods transforms into the Confucian Way.'[294]

Razan was an avid reader and possessed a large library. He wrote copiously but was not an original thinker. He has been depicted as more re-productive than productive. His thinking can, however, be gleaned from his many writings on other subjects, for example, history. Thus we know that he considered Neo-Confucianism to be the true foundation for governance and man, that the Confucian Way of Heaven is the equal of the Shinto Way of Gods, that human society is inherently hierarchical, that an ordered world is an expression of indestructible, universal ri, that Shinto is an important foundation for the moral order of the nation, and that it is humankind's responsibility to hold fast to this rigid ethical order. The country was a coherent structure of unequal parts deserving unequal treatment and this stratification was sanctified by 'heavenly decree'.[295]

The Neo Confucian world view was, accordingly, the right

ideology for the new age and the Razan school became the mainstay for the Neo-Confucian teaching throughout the Tokugawa age. Following Razan, his son Hayashi Gahō (1618-80) ran the school. In 1691, under Razan's grandchild Hayashi Hōkō (1644-1732), the school was moved to Yushima at Shōheizaka near the Castle where it resided until the end of the Tokugawa period, always under the leadership of the Hayashi family.

Primarily, Razan's thought was an uncritical Chu Hsi creed with the adjunct of Shinto beliefs. Both Buddhism and Christianity were his declared enemies. A work such as *Hai-yaso, Anti-Jesus* (1620),[296] exhibits his aversion to Christianity, but also how limited his understanding was of the global world that had arrived with the Portuguese and been presented to him by Fabian Fucan(sai).

3.1 Fabian Fucan(sai)

Fabian Fucan(sai) (1565-1621) is of interest since, being initially a Zen Buddhist, he had learned about the Confucian creed. At about nineteen years of age he converted to Christianity and vilified both Buddhism and Confucianism in the name of Christ in *Myōtei mondō, The Myōtei Dialogue* (1605). Thereupon, returning to Zen Buddhism, he defended Chu Hsi in *Ha-daiusu, Deus Destroyed* (1620). He was thus twice a turncoat. The first of the above scriptures is important because it is an early description of the Chu Hsi creed as he reviles it as also Buddhism and Shinto. For example, he writes:

> The Confucians regard Heaven and Earth and Yin and Yang as the Great Ultimate and the Way of Heaven and do not speak of their creator; they claim that men, beasts, grasses and trees differ only to the point of material force (ki) and its manifest experiential matter, their nature being undifferentiated. Now these are properly termed delusions! Speaking in terms of the Three Creeds, there is considerable good in Confucianism. 'The three doctrines are one.' So they say, but two – *Shaka* and *Tao* – are too outrageous for words.[297]

This was in 1605, when his Christian faith was uppermost. A year later he reverted to Buddhism and in the *Ha-daiusu* (1620) he finds rather that God as a divine lawgiver is delusional.[298] He compares the ri with Dharmakaya or Tathata in Buddhism but does not go farther.[299] What surprises in both works, is his comprehensive knowledge about all the Three Creeds – Buddhism, Confucianism and Shintoism – and his critical mind. He must have been unusually perspicacious and had the open personality which came easily in touch with both outstanding scholars and priests, such as Hayashi Razan and the Jesuit missionaries. This would explain his familiarity with the intellectual situation. One can hardly imagine that scholars generally took such an interest in all creeds. Fabian Fucan was perhaps the only scholar to describe the complicated syncretic religio-philosophical situation at the inception of the Tokugawa regime and certainly alone in ending up rejecting them all. The probable reason for his being so little remembered by contemporary, mostly Jesuit writers, must be that, in their eyes, he turned an apostate – twice.[300] They did not understand the 'comfortable eclecticism' in which beliefs intertwined both before and after Sekigahara (1600).[301] Fabian's original Japanese name is not known.

It should be mentioned, in parenthesis, that Leibniz (1646-1716), took a keen interest in Chinese thought and was stimulated by what he learned in his monad thinking, as was Voltaire (1694-1778) in his deism. They probably recognized that their anthropopathic proclivities coincided with (Neo-)Confucian deistic thinking.

4. Nakae Tōju (1608-48)

It was under the influence of Chinese Ming thinking that Japanese put emphasis on the ki more than on the ri. We have, at the outset, Nakae Tōju(1608-48), who was attracted to Wang Yang-ming and began the Wang Yang-ming school (Yōmeigaku) in Japan. Thus he propagated the ri of the *kokoro*, more so than the ri of the bamboo. The *kokoro*, he says, is the inborn jewel (*reihō*) bestowed on man by Heaven. The virtue of this jewel is filial reverence, which comprises Heaven and Earth, what is within and what is without. It has to be polished at all times – in order to illumine the myriad things. Among men, it takes the shape of respect for Heaven and love of people (*keiten-aijin*).

Man enjoys the inner intuition or 'innate knowledge' (*liang-chih*, Jpn. *ryōchi*), which is coincidental with the workings of the heart and whereby being equates with non-being. This leads to the sense of spiritual transcendence comparable with the *satori*.[302] Tōju is close to the dictum in the Chung Yung that says: 'Human nature is the command of Heaven and to follow our nature is the Way.' One shall cultivate the 'illustrious virtue', which should lead to sincerity and correct action. The unity between inspired thought and activity was emphasized. As long as man acts in conformity with the inner light, he will flourish and everything is in order, but if he neglects it for even a moment, he cannot avoid Heaven's punishment. This doctrine is clearly imbued with deism and if not a deistic Heaven, there is, at the very least, an anthropopathic essence above things. Tōju bestowed more religiosity to Neo-Confucianism than it contained in the Chu Hsi orthodoxy. It is questioned whether there was Christian influence when he used terms like *tenshu*, 'heavenly lord'.

Confucius had understood the confusion of man when he wrote the *Kōkyō* (Ch. *Hsiao Ching*) *The Book about Filial Piety*, in which *kō*, 'Filial Piety', was presented as the sacred jewel and as the underlying moral force of the universe. Tōju's thinking moved from the inquiry of ri in things, to intuition and filial piety. As he said: 'Filial piety is the summit of virtue and the essence of the three realms of Heaven, Earth and man. What brings life to Heaven, Earth, man and to all things is filial reverence. It is the root of man. Therefore those who pursue learning need study only this.'[303] Piety had thus both personal and cosmic dimensions. Piety towards one's parents (*kō*) became a higher morality than just loving them. It became 'a personal virtue, sustaining human relations and the cosmic order itself', and a love of all creation, as man 'moved to an increasingly mystical and deistic path'.[304] The individual more so than than the totality of things came in the centre.

Like Wang Yang-ming, Tōju found that each man's *kokoro* can be his world of truth within which he attains his spiritual mind and chooses his proper course of action. He begins inwards and moves outwards. Ri was manifested 'in there' in the mind and not 'out there' in the world.[305] And if the inner sensibility is cultivated and one follows the dictates of one's *kokoro*, one is able to attain personal sagehood, first, and accomplish harmony and stability in the world, next.

In asserting the primacy of the mind (*kokoro*) as the basis or origin of Heaven and of Heavenly ri, Tōju therefore belonged to the subjective and idealistic side of Sung thought. The investigation of things was internalized. It was Lu Hsiang-shan in the Sung and Wang Yang-ming in the Ming who were his predecessors, more so than the Ch'eng Brothers and Chu Hsi.

Nakae Tōju first embraced the Neo-Confucian orthodoxy and read the Four Books and the Chu Hsi commentaries. He was then in Osu on Shikoku. It was not until in 1634 that filial piety, as tradition has it, made him return to his home village in Ōmi to care for his mother. He left the samurai service and status and returned to simple country life. Loyalty clashed with filial piety and he chose the latter – not usual among Japanese. He has never been forgotten for this spontaneous act. In Ōmi he continued his Chinese studies and opened a Confucian school. His studies led to the early Five (Six) Classics, and the Chu Hsi rationalism was exchanged for an idealism based not least on the *I Ching*. Somewhat later (1645) he acquired Wang Yang-ming's works which he read with great enthusiasm, and he became the initiator of the Yōmeigaku in Japan. He had come close to Wang Yang-ming before he read those works when he placed emphasis on intuition and action more so than on kyūri scholarship.

His Wang Yang-ming creed found expression in the *Okina Mondō*, a work in dialogue form which was compiled by his disciples. In it he expresses his profound belief in spontaneous activity in every situation at the moment of inspiration. The fundamental principles of life are the same for all regardless of class and station. His thinking was close to the democratic idealism of Chang Tsai. If man acts only according to worldly criteria, he loses his true heart. All truth is located in his heart, and intuition is the key to it. He must just accord with his heart's dictates and follow the course which is appropriate to time, place and circumstance (*toki-tokoro-kurai*), an old Confucian conviction that practice must respond to changing circumstances.

Tōju only taught for twelve years before his death in 1648, but his influence on following generations of students was amazing. His single-minded devotion to personal and social rectification has been remembered until this day. Individualistic scholars were drawn to and motivated by him and the Wang Yang-ming creed throughout the Tokugawa era. The intuitive spontaneity of the thought appealed to idealists like Ōshio Heihachirō (1793-1837), who put his conviction into direct action when he led an uprising to aid poor people which ended in failure and with his death. It is still deeply appreciated and, in our time, Mishima Yukio (1925-70) is said to have been motivated by it when he staged his pseudo-coup and thereupon committed *harakiri*.

5. Kumazawa Banzan (1619-91)

K umazawa Banzan, who was Nakae Tōju's principal disciple, shared Tōju's central metaphysical beliefs but never left the military caste. Further, he focused less on filial piety as the central concept of the work of Heaven and emphasized the mundane and political matters in daily life. He writes that the rites and rituals of the sages begin with food and drink, man and woman. This is where it should begin. Thus he took an independent stand. The Way is above forms (*keijijō*), but all the world below forms (*keijika*) – law, propriety and learning – must accord to time, place and circumstance. To chase after high-sounding ri is chasing after miracles and forgetting useful learning (*jitsugaku*). He accepted, however, both the ri of the kokoro and the ki of Heaven and Earth (*tenchi no ki*). He says: 'If man's *kokoro* is upright, the ki of Heaven and Earth is also pure in him.'

He became Nakae Tōju's disciple upon reading the *Okina Mondō*.[306] If Tōju was the idealist who believed in inner intuition and transcendent sentiment, he was the realist who maintained that to achieve the heart's composure with the practice of virtue only was like walking blindly in a fog without direction. He was as much in favour of the Chu Hsi empiricism as of Wang Yang-ming's spontaneous intuitionism. The scholars of the world had, according to Banzan, forgotten that both Chu Hsi and Wang Yang-ming had aimed at clarifying the sages' Way and had not set up schools which competed with each other.

Banzan accepted, on the one side, the *dōri* truth which is constant and the same whether in India, China or Japan. They represented the transcendental dimension of the nature of things. On the other hand, he acknowledged the laws of this world (*hō*) which alter from land to land and from age to age. As a result, laws of propriety, legal rules and ethico-political structures (*seido*) should change in consonance with land and times. It was a revolutionary thought for the rulers who deprecated social change. Man's studies should comprise rites and laws and both ancient and modern history. The rites provided equilibrium in man's emotional life and the laws afforded social order. History made one understand political vicissitudes over centuries and millennia. All of them offered the wide spectrum of truth needed in personal and societal life.

Banzan lived up to the Confucian ideals when he served the Ikeda family in the Okamoto domain and undertook a successful reform programme which included land and water utilization. He illustrated the true Confucian spirit when he remonstrated against the policies of the han. This led to his disgrace and he was forced to resign.[307]

Later in life Banzan propounded his beliefs in the *Daigaku wakumon*, *Discussion of the Great Learning*,[308] which he wrote about 1687, only four years before his death. In this work the situation in the country and the shortcomings of the Bakufu were severly criticized. It was written in the *taiwatai*, 'question and answer style', which was also used in the *Okina Mondō* and earlier works. The *Leitmotif* of the presentation was 'good government' (*jinsei*). He was thus a precursor of the literature on political economy (*keizaigaku*) that would come later with Ogyū Sorai, Dazai Shundai and others. In some thirty chapters he asked for socio-economic reforms. Long before Ogyū Sorai, he asked for the return of the samurai to the land (*dochaku*), the relaxation of the *sankin-kōtai* system of alternate residence in Edo, talented people in the offices and other reforms – to avoid a looming crisis. Ever since the samurai had become separated from the peasants and farm work, they had become weak and effeminate.[309] Ogyū Sorai wrote the same in the *Seidan* (1727).

Banzan was stimulated by and close to Tōju, but, as described, his spectrum was wider. He wrote in the *Shūgi washo*, *Collected Writings about Righteousness and Harmony* (about 1672): 'I am not attached to either Chu Hsi or Wang Yang-ming, I just make ancient sages my model. Chu and Wang are alike, their words appeared in accordance with and reflected their times. Chu Hsi developed the *kakubutsu-kyūri* and Wang Yang-ming his *ryōchi* because of the ills and evils. Chu and Wang did indeed not differ.'[310]

He further said, reflecting Sung thought: 'When the 'Great Ultimate moves, the yang ki grows, and when the Great Ultimate is still, the yin ki grows.' On the transcendent side, there is the Unlimited that corresponds with the Way. It is the above and beyond where stillness reigns. On the terrestrial side, there is the rhythm of the yin and yang as agents of life. The stillness appears to contain the potential for infinite productive motion. This is expressed in ways which make one believe that both a creation takes place and that a creator steers and controls. Man equals the *kokoro* of Heaven and Earth and is equipped with the illustrious virtue in his nature of goodness, righteousness, propriety and wisdom. He has, however, also his other nature of desires and appetites and can lose the purity of his *kokoro*. 'Man shall therefore strive for the unity between the ri from above and the ki from below and harmonize the two by polishing his soul's mirror and so attain the life of Goodness.'[311] There is a single Way of Heaven and Earth, whose expression in Japan is Shinto; revering the *kami* as the Way of Japan equals revering the Confucian Heaven. He says: 'One may say that it is the way of the *kami* (*shintō*) while at the same time it is the way of the sages (*seidō*) of China.' And he generously adds: 'It is also the way of the limitless great vacuity (*taikyo*)',[312] with reference to Taoism and Chang Tsai.

The *Shūgi washo* is generally close to Neo-Confucian thinking. The central ingredients of Chu Hsi metaphysics are presented. When he hints at both a creation and a creator, the influence of Nakae Tōju and Wang Yang-ming is apparent, and when he emphasizes that the truth is found within one's own *kokoro*, he professes the teaching of Lu Hsiang-shan and Wang Yang-ming. That he accepted the Tokugawa social order, each and every part, comes clear in this statement: 'When the status of high and low, noble and base, have been fixed, rank and quality can be distinguished and there is no conflict or rivalry. Hence there is peace in the world.'[313]

He preceded Ogyū Sorai when he distinguished between Heaven's Way and the laws. He declared that the laws 'were instituted by the sages to fit the time, place and circumstance and cannot be the same in olden and modern times'. He continued, 'If they conform to the times, they harmonize with the Way. If they do not conform to the times, they do harm to the Way.'[314] 'Hence he held that laws, that is to say, institutions were produced by sages and classified them as historical entities.'[315] He was often so close to Ogyū Sorai's thinking that one is tempted to suspect that Ogyū Sorai only expanded on him when he made the human Way social and historical. Banzan did, however, not go as far as Ogyū Sorai. For him, in the end, 'the Way was coterminous with Heaven, Earth and man'.[316]

As mentioned, Banzan widened his perspective when he turned to ethico-political subjects upon which Nakae Tōju never touched. When he was critical of the shogunate in the *Daigaku wakumon*, and maintained in the *Shūgi washo* that 'Japan is the country of the Gods', and hinted at the emperor, it led to problems with the shogunal authorities.

The best known Wang Yang-ming scholar of the following generation was Miwa Shissai (1669-1744), who shifted his convictions from the outer moralism of the Kimon school (Satō Naokata) to the inward contemplation of Nakae Tōju and Wang Yang-ming. He established his own school in Edo, but was also active in Kyoto and Osaka. He co-operated with Nakai Chūan in establishing the Kaitokudō school. There were other inner-mind groups in the Lu-Wang tradition, for example, the *shingaku* sect, introduced by Ishida Baigan (1685-1744), more noticed in the West than in Japanese annals.

6. Yamazaki Ansai

Y amazaki Ansai (1618-81) was the true ri-ki-ist, who adored Chu Hsi and sang his praises. At seventeen he became acquainted with Tani Jichū (1598-1649), the founder of Neo-Confucian studies in Tosa, and under him studied the Chu Hsi school of Neo-Confucianism. He ended up renouncing Buddhism and, returning to Kyoto, he opened a school (1655) where he extolled Chu Hsi's teachings as the highest expression of Confucianism. From 1657 he was attracted to the Shinto religion and studied it under Yoshikawa Koretaru (1615-94). Later he developed a synthesis of Shinto and Chu Hsi's Neo-Confucianism – a Mikyō itchi – his personal Suika Shinto creed, which emphasized the essential unity of the Shinto gods and the Confucian Heaven; further, it emphasized the absolute loyalty to the imperial system and the feudal order. Like other early Tokugawa Confucianists, however, from Hayashi Razan onwards, he kept the balance between 'reverence for the emperor and respect for the shogun' (sonnō-keibaku).

The strict Confucian ethics, propagated by his school, '(outer) sincerity' (kei), 'goodness' (jin), 'righteousness' (gi) and '(inner) sincerity' (sei), were what Yamazaki felt he had the right to beat into his disciples in his lectures. Kei and gi were emphasized together. Kei should be pursued 'sternly' and 'without idleness'.[317] 'With sincerity I straighten my inner and with righteousness I order my outer – devotion within, righteousness without', he repeated. Austere conduct was, generally, more esteemed than ethical judgement and studies. He tended to moral rigorism also in daily life. One of his disciples, Satō Naokata (1650-1719), said later that he felt as if he was descending into a dungeon every time he went to Ansai's school, and escaping from the den of a tiger when he left the school.[318]

Being the true believer, Yamazaki, fearless and outspoken, condemned indiscriminately, and he not only rejected Buddhism and Christianity, but also criticized the Hayashi School for not taking the Chu Hsi message seriously. He called Hayashi Razan a 'vulgar Confucian' and considered him 'intolerant and superficial'. He was also himself persecuted and despised by other Confucian schools. The Shinto religion was, however, never assailed, and, as in the case of Hayashi Razan, the national gods joined with his Confucian learning. In Yamazaki's *suika shintō* the Chu Hsi creed combined with Yoshida and Ise Shintō. His belief in a Chu Hsi ri Heaven linked with the Shinto thought of godliness in man (*jinshinron*). In a double sense man was related to an ultimate norm. His Kimon school in Kyoto had thousands of students and existed throughout the Tokugawa era. Great scholars from this school were Satō Naokata, Asami Keisai (1652-1711) and Miyake Shōsai (1662-1741), the Three Kimon Exemplars (*sanketsu*).

Yamazaki's Chu Hsi adherence may be perceived in, for example, *Hekii, Exposing the Heresies*, a work that he wrote in 1547. In this work he quotes Chu Hsi:

> There is only one ri (*ichiri*) in the universe. Heaven is Heaven through ri, Earth is Earth through ri. And, generally, all things and beings between Heaven and Earth come to exist through ri. . . . It is the Three Ropes (*sankō*, Chn. *san-kang*) [the duties of lord versus servant, father versus son and husband versus wife] and, further, it is the Five Constant Virtues. All is the work of the ri, and there is no place the ri does not reach. It appears and disappears, it comes up full and goes down empty in an endless circulation of going and coming; it is a perpetual beginning and ending and ending and beginning. It never stops for a moment. If the Confucian scholars accomplish the basic nature of their hearts (*kokoro no honshin*), they naturally do not allow the slightest interstice between the inner and outer and the fine and the coarse. And in cultivating their persons and honouring the people, they have the hearts that do not allow the slightest addition or deduction. Therefore, due to the ri in nature, when acting, you aid

> what grows and develops in cooperation with Heaven and
> Earth; there is nothing that is left undone ...'

About ki he says, 'When a man is born, ki accumulates, and
when he dies his ki disperses.' 'When ki assembles, ri dwells
there. Consequently, a man's body is a receptacle (gu) where fine
ki is present.'

The above quotations from the *Hekii* testify to the fact that by
the age of thirty Ansai had adopted Chu Hsi's ri and ki. He says at
the end of the work that he had read the Confucian Four Classics
when young, become a Buddhist in his teenage years and written
Thesis of Three Creeds in One (*Sankyō-itchi-ron*) at twenty-three
years of age. At twenty-five he had been acquainted with Chu Hsi
and found that the Buddhist way was wrong. He left Buddhism,
and subequently he was never to deviate from Chu Hsi's Neo-
Confucian truth; he only added the Shinto truth to it. The *Hekii*
presents the pure Chu Hsi's *ten-dō-ri* gospel.[319]

The suika-shinto Confucian interpretation of Shinto became an
influential rhetoric for later Japanese nationalists. The Five
Relationships became the central part of a double creed,
underpinning individual and collective life. They constituted the
fabric of the universe. Ethical performance (*giri*) was coupled with
reverence (*kei*), and together with Shinto obligations they formed
a moral strait jacket for the ardent believer. Reverence should be
extended uniformly to the gods, the emperor and to the Way of
Heaven, all equally permanent and unchanging.[320] It was
Confucianism ending up in patriotism, basically mystical, a matter
of faith and not a matter of intellectual understanding.

We do not need to look at any more of his writings. His
excessive Chu Hsi adherence becomes clear. He adored Chu Hsi
to the extent that he even loved the colour of vermilion, which is
the meaning of the Chinese character *chu*, the first character in
Chu Hsi's name. He said that he erred willingly – if he erred with
Chu Hsi. He represents Neo-Confucianism in its extreme ri
appearance, touching deep-felt depths of the Japanese soul in
union with Shinto. He did not represent any advance

intellectually. He reduced his studies to a limited number of Chinese classics and three Sung commentaries – among them the *Chin-ssu lu* (Jpn. *Kinshiroku*)[321] – and to the Japanese myth. He did not attach much emphasis on the wide learning (*hakugaku*) propagated by the Hayashi school. His Chu Hsi fundamentalism with emphasis on sincerity, discipline and loyalty, suited the following nativist era, and his Kimon School remained popular until the end of the Tokugawa age.

On the one hand, Ansai represented the Chu Hsi ri orthodoxy in its rigid form, and, on the other hand, he was one of the precursors of the forthcoming Tokugawa nationalism. He stood on two legs, one being Chu Hsi, the other Amaterasu. He was stern and demanding, but, paradoxically, this did not keep students and followers away.

6.1 Satō Naokata (1650-1719)

Satō Naokata was the oldest and perhaps the most outstanding disciple in Yamazaki Ansai's school. He came to the school in 1671 at the age of twenty-one and continued as an Ansai follower until his death – even after he was banished from the school. He was perhaps the disciple who lived up to Yamazaki Ansai's rigorism more than anyone else. *Kei*, '(outer) sincerity', became the key concept for him as it had been for Ansai. Sincerity and reverence in everyday life, he says, have to be pursued as if they were one's second nature. One must never relax for a moment, walking, standing, sitting or sleeping, even when alone. Everything should be treated as an important matter, with caution and circumspection. One's mind should always be fully alert for the slightest deviation. 'One should always hold oneself as if an important guest is about to arrive.' This ascetic life required spiritual training, which was achieved through quiet sitting. A tranquil heart leads to calm action. Yamazaki Ansai had placed emphasis upon contemplation and Satō Naokata is known for his singular emphasis upon quiet sitting as self-cultivation.[322] Quiet sitting is the method to acquire the calm of the soul in the middle of worldly affairs. 'It is equivalent to the rudder in the boat'. . . . 'Without this centring activity, one's life is reduced to baseness and one is swept away by the ways of the world.'[323]

Naokata was the the purest among pure Chu Hsi devotees in Japan. He never accepted the Suika Shinto proclivity of his master and considered the infatuation with Shinto a waste of scholarly talent. He ridiculed the efforts to make Japan a divine land because it had, in contrast to China, a creation doctrine and he criticized the attempts to discover a Japanese Way on a par with the Way of the sages in China. Thus Naokata remained an ardent Chu Hsi believer and never compared the *kami* of the Shinto religion with the ri of Neo-Confucian thought. This is quite remarkable since the tendency throughout Tokugawa Confucian scholarship was to combine a Confucian heaven with a Shinto heaven and to unite the two world views. Naokata's stance is proven by statements such as: 'The Nihongi has no teachings like those of the Three Dynasties.'[324] It might be difficult to find another well-known Confucian in the Japanese tradition who explicitly contravened the native creed.

For this reason he defended Chu Hsi against all the new thoughts which appeared in his time: Nakae Tōju's *Yōmeigaku*, Itō Jinsai's *kogaku* and Kaibara Ekken's *jitsugaku*. It goes without saying that he condemned both Buddhists and Taoists who lacked the true principle (ri). It was the unitary perspective of all reality that should come first. The diverse particularizations and their study would come second, if ever. A reverential attitude was essential: it was as basic for sagely learning as *seiza* introspection for a poised mind.

Among Tokugawa Sung scholars, Naokata was perhaps the most orthodox. He took an interest in the heavenly ri and discussed it in relation to the *taikyoku* and the Heavenly fundamental forces of yin and yang ri is unfathomable and only appears on the *keijika* side in the interactions of yin and yang. Thus he was in line with the true Chu Hsi scholars in Korea and China.

6.2 Asami Keisai, Miyake Shōsai and Wakabayashi Kyōkai

Asami Keisai came to Ansai's Kimon School in 1679 at the age of twenty-seven and Miyake Shōsai joined the school in the same year at 17 years of age. Yet another student, Wakabayashi Kyōkai (1679-1752), became Asami Keisai's disciple in 1702 and later his successor. Asami Keisai, Miyake Shōsai and Wakabayashi Kyōkai turned to the Shinto side of Ansai's creed without therefore leaving the Kimon thought of reverence. Thus, they differed from Satō Naokata. Other Kimon scholars were Atobe Yoshiaki (1652-1729) and Ōtsuka Taiya (1677-1750).

Splintering developed easily in the dogmatic Kimon atmosphere. We hear about disagreements among the disciples. They stopped speaking to one another and they broke off relations. Satō Naokata and Asami Keisai were even expelled from the school and did not attend the obsequies of Ansai. However, whether as Suika Shinto or as Kimon, Yamazaki Ansai's school retained its vitality and was to stimulate the intellectual world for generations to come, and even 'propelled commoners as well as warrior reformists beyond reverence into emergent forms of rebellious action'.[325] Whether inclined to Chu Hsi or Shinto, the disciples and followers were known as the Kimon School.

Asami Keisai established his own school and like Ansai is said to have numbered his pupils in the thousands. He combined Chinese studies with Shinto devotion and emphasized patriotism and loyalty to one's country. The great duty (*taigi*) was directed to the ruler(s) of Japan, the emperor or his deputy, the shogun. To avoid criticism, Keisai wrote about China, but implicitly meant Japan in works like *Seiken igen*.[326]

6.3 Tamaki Isai (Masahide) (1670-1736) and Takeuchi Shikibu (1712-67).

Tamaki Isai expounded Ansai's suika philsophy and compiled the *Gyokusenshū, Collection of Lucky Jewels*, Yamazaki Ansai's collected Shinto suika teachings.[327] He went further than his teacher. Discussing Amaterasu, he pronounced that she was the progenitor of the imperial family and emphasized that each emperor was her successor, whose every decree was an order from heaven. About the Three Sacred Regalia he wrote that they were 'The essential foundation of the Land of the Gods, the mystical spirit of the Gods, even the ri of Heaven and Earth' and further that 'the Way of human morality arises from no other source than these Three Treasures'. This kind of thinking was widely accepted among Asami Keisai's students and eventually became characteristic of the Kimon school in general.[328]

Tamaki Isai's student Takeuchi Shikibu went even farther. He opened his own school in Kyoto and teaching, among others, court nobles, openly discussed the restoration of imperial power. The nobles in turn began to give lectures to the seventeen-year-old Emperor Momozono (r. 1747-62) in 1757. This was reported to the bakufu which took swift action. The nobles were sentenced to house arrest and Takeuchi Shikibu was banished from Kyoto to Hachijōjima.

7. The Historians

The examination of ri could turn to all fields of human endeavour. From a speculative superstructure, it moved to man and from man to the world. Thus it is natural that it also turned to history which demonstrated the pervasive heavenly ri in social relationships. No one ever forgot that truth existed in the beginning and that things were perfect during the early Three Dynasties – Hsia, Shang-yin and Chou – under the sage kings. Compilations of history had been systematic from Han times after Ssu-ma Ch'ien (Jpn. Shiba Sen, 145?-86? BC) wrote the *Shih chi*,

Records of the Historian (ca. 100 BC), which became the model of dynastic histories thereafter.

The love and respect for the past had been at the forefront of Confucian intellectualism through centuries. Already Confucius, the paragon of all Confucians, had taken an interest in history and Chu Hsi did likewise in Sung times. This enthusiasm inspired the Japanese, and history was recorded beginning with the Kojiki (712) and Nihongi (720). The historiography changed under the influence of Sung philosophy in Japan as in China. Just as the interpretation of history had shifted in the direction of Buddhist and Shinto thought in the Kamakura and Muromachi eras, Tokugawa historical studies turned to Sung historians like Ssu-ma Kuang(1019-86) and their principles of historical change.

Although there were socio-political differences, scholars, steeped in Neo-Confucian ri thought, sought to apply the Chinese Confucian principles to the Japanese past. Hayashi Razan and his son Gahō (1618-80) started the trend with *Honchō tsugan*, *Comprehensive Mirror of Our Nation* (compiled between 1644 and 1670), which reflected Ssu-man Kuang's views on evolutionary history and dynastic legitimacy. It covers the past up to the year 1611. In the next century, this interest was continued by Arai Hakuseki (1657-1725), whose greatest historical work was *Tokushi yoron*, *Essays on Political History* (1712), which traces Japanese history from the beginning of the world to the time of Hideyoshi. History was interpreted as a series of turns and successions (*hen*), five of them under military rule, on the basis of Heaven's Mandate. The *Tokushi yoron* was superior to earlier historical works in the handling of political, economic and cultural conditions in a coherent historical narrative. 'Hakuseki presented the national history in which the present was made to seem like an inevitable outflow of the past.'[329] It became the model for later works, for example, *Nihon gaishi*, *Unofficial History of Japan* (1827), by Rai San'yō (1780-1832), a great scholar and historian of late Tokugawa. Rai San'yō's work, evincing a vigorous style, became the 'single most influential interpretive history of the late Tokugawa era'.[330] It covered Japanese annals from Yoritomo

(1192) to Ieyasu (1600) in 22 chapters. Other works followed in the wake of Rai San'yō; the most well-known among them was perhaps Iida Tadahiko (1799-1861) who wrote the immense *Yashi*, in 291 chapters. A nationalist tone is increasingly apparent in the histories.

The most ambitious historical project was, however, undertaken by the Mito School (Mitogaku), begun by Tokugawa Mitsukuni (1628-1700) in 1657. It was not completed until the twentieth century (1906), and the work came to be known as *Dai-Nihon-shi, History of Great Japan*. It is a monumental work in 397 volumes. The well-known Mito scholar Asaka Tampaku (1656-1737) was one of the early contributors to the work. All these works expressed a Chinese historicism, which contrasted sharply with the Buddhist and Shinto valuations of earlier works like *Gukanshō, Jottings of a Fool* by the Tendai abbot Jien (1155-1225) and *Jinnō shōtōki, The Records of the Legitimate Succession of the Divine Sovereigns* (1339-43) by Kitabatake Chikafusa (1293-1354).

The search for the universal ri in history turned more and more from China to Japan. The Mito School was nationalist in character, and became more so in the Later Mito School, which was founded by Fujita Yūkoku (1773-1826) in the early nineteenth century. They mystisized early myhological times and generated the idea of a 'national essence' (*kokutai*), a concept that would play a pivotal role in later national rhetoric. The *kokutai* became a ri principle of truth above things. National sentiments were part of the kokutai which had come as a mandate from Heaven to the exalted line of kings from the Sun Goddess, Amaterasu. What Chinese thought had expressed with abstract terms was returned to indigenous myth and re-mythologized. This might seem, strange, but, as Donald Keene says, the Confucian sentiments were from the beginning diluted in distinctly Japanese adaptations.[331]

Fujita Yūkoku, his disciple Aizawa Seishisai (1782-1863) and his son Tōko (1806-55) took an 'anti-barbarian' stand against the West, while they wished for the rebirth of absolute traditional values and the restoration of imperial rule. 'The historical perspective that governed the compilation of the Dai-Nihon-shi changed therefore considerably between the initial stage of writing in the seventeenth century and the second stage which began at the end of the eighteenth century.'[332]

Another great historical undertaking was the compilation of the *Tokugawa jikki, The Chronicle of the Tokugawa*, between 1809 and 1843. It was commissioned by the Bakufu, and some twenty scholars under the leadership of Hayashi Jussai (1768-1841) were engaged in the project. The chronicle covered the political annals from the first Tokugawa shogun, Ieyasu, to the tenth, Ieharu (r. 1760-86). A later *Zoku Tokugawa jikki*, written in the Meiji era, covered the chronicles of the last five shoguns. Thus, the vigorous interest in history continued unabated to the end of the Tokugawa era and in the following times of modernization.

8. Kaibara Ekken (Ekiken) (1630-1714)

K aibara Ekken represents one of the pivots in Neo-Confucian learning at the turn of the eighteenth century, parallel with the *kogaku* philosophers. He learned in Kyoto from Matsunaga Sekigo, Kinoshita Jun'an and Yamazaki Ansai, but living afterwards as a physician on Kyushu, he was able to develop his ideas independently during a long life. He never rejected Neo-Confucianism or Heaven as the source of everything, but towards the end of his life espoused a ki thinking that has been termed a moderate criticism of the Chu Hsi orthodoxy.[333] This was in his *Taigiroku, Record of Grave Doubts* which was written about the time of his death in 1714 but published later (1766). Ri did not take precedence over ki as in orthodox thought, but was found within ki. Generally, he evinced a neutral Chu Hsi stance through his many scriptures – 110 according to one list – for example, in the botanical work, *Yamato Honzō* (1708), *Botany of Japan*, his most famous work. As a true scholar, he doubted but did not reject.

As the material world became his dominant interest, Kaibara turned to actual observation of nature. Thus, unlike Yamasaki Ansai whose focus was on developing spiritual life and moral practice, he tended to be more concerned with the ample evidence of the ri-ki amalgam in things. He writes: 'Those desirous of extending knowledge are to proceed to things. One makes one's mind clear through knowing the ri of things. To be unable to investigate things and therefore to focus only on one's mind is absolute stupidity. How is intelligence to be developed? One must surely extend his knowledge.'[334] 'Ekken applied this understanding of knowledge very concretely in his broad methodological investigation of the flora of nature. In this manner he carried the concept of useful learning (*jitsugaku*) one step further to worldly learning than had existed to date in Japan.'[335]

Ekken did, however, never despise the correspondence between the inner mind and outer things. It was essential not to forget the cultivation of the moral mind while one 'investigated the ri of all things'.[336] The equilibrium of the mind must come before all else, before the extension of knowledge can be undertaken. As he says: 'In the effort of extending knowledge one begins within oneself and proceeds to the principles of all things. If one is diligent in one's efforts, never avoiding what is troublesome or difficult, one will achieve true perception naturally and quite suddenly. Such is the effort of investigating things and exploring ri.'[337] The education of man comes first, the education of skills later.

Ekken was close to the Chu Hsi school and opposed to Lu Hsiang-shan's and Wang Yang-ming. Prompted by Lo Ch'in-shun's stress on the ki in things, he sought a study of nature that was unfettered by the restrictions of sacred morals, imagining a sole 'principle of life' (*seiri*) running through all beings and all reality.[338]

The ri in us is the ri in all things. He divided the ri into a 'constant ri' (*tsune no ri*) and 'changing ri' (*hen no ri*). Turning to the 'changing ri', his curiosity and eagerness led him deeper and deeper into an empiricism which made him conclude that: 'Abundant are the events and things which fill the world, and inexhaustible are their ri. It is through study that one grasps the ri of each. . . . This is the greatest happiness in life. Boundless is one's pleasure.'[339]

This meant: 'in some cases a pantheistic ki, by asserting the ultimate identity of ri and ki'.[340] The study of things came to be as in the present age of modern science.[341] The comprehension of nature and its operations were the proper way to serve the world and benefit the people – more so than the learning of history and meditative quiet sitting. Because nature did not reflect heavenly timeless norms, as posited in Neo-Confucian thought, but underwent constant change, it was imperative that man had it under continuous examination.

Ekken was inspired by a feeling of closeness to the whole of creation, to Heaven and Earth, and he recognized the importance of the reverence of the universe. Since nature is the source and sustainer of life, one should respond to it as to one's parents. A person must serve nature and his parents in order to repay the debt for the gift of life. 'Ekken's thought may best be summarized as a religious humanism based on a vitalistic naturalism that found expression in practical empiricism.' This was the motivating force behind his outlook.[342]

He was anchored to Chu Hsi through 'wide learning', and acknowledged that the 'changing principle' is limitless. The deeper one penetrates into ri, the better one understands Heaven's perspective, that is, its ri, both in its heavenly unitary original and its worldly dispersions. It is a *jōri* approach and an empiricism which, working to exhaust the pattern of order found within oneself and in the world, has the consequence of loosening the ties between the realm of ethics and intellectual sense perception. The interpretation of ri, emphasizing its immanent and tentative aspect, was an new beginning in Japanese Chu Hsi scholarship.

Ekken is perhaps mostly remembered as a popularizer of Confucian education and, supposedly, wrote works on women's duties in *Onna Daigaku* (1716), *Great Learning for Women*, and on children's morals and duties in *Dōjikyō* (1715), *Teachings for Children*.[343] Learning until the end of one's life was recommended in the *Yamato Zokkun*, '*The Pursuit of Learning*' (no date),[344] an admonition followed by many scholars. He became one of the most widely read Confucian writers during the Tokugawa era – and, afterwards, until 1945.

Ekken was close to the *I Ching*, which celebrates life as the 'begetter of all begetting'.[345] He was still firmly based in (Neo-) Confucianism when he wrote the *Taigiroku*, in which he emphasizes that all things link together in the unity of ri and ki. He says in the last chapter of the work which bears the title Ri-ki fukabun-ron, 'The Doctrine about the Indivisibility of ki and ri':

> The Way of Heaven and Earth began originally with the two ki not being separated. It was an unfragmented One-Ki Chaos (*ikki-konton*). This is the highest ri state, when the forms of the yin and yang are not yet manifest. . . . The Great Ultimate is the origin of the Way and the source of all the ten thousand things (*banbutsu*). All ri are jointly designated the Great Ultimate. The 'One Ki' (*ikki*) moves and this is called yang. This is the Great Ultimate in action; it moves and then is still. It turns still and condenses and this is called yin. It moves and then is still; there is an endless circulation of motion and stillness. That the One Ki is divided into the yin and yang, however, does not mean that there are two ki. It means that yang is the dispersal of the One Ki, and yin the condensation of the One Ki and that they represent the perpetual motion and stillness of the Great Ultimate.
>
> In Confucius' *I Ching* we find that the Great Ultimate generates the two dimensions of movement and stillness (yin and yang). . . . The Way of yin and yang constitutes the acting of the Great Ultimate. The Great Ultimate and the yin and yang are named differently due to what comes before and after. . . . Now, the Great Ultimate equals the One Ki and the konton – and the yin and yang are names

of what comes subsequently. Then follow the fluctuations of yin and yang and times for action and times for quiescence. . . .

The *I Ching* states that yin and yang together form the Way. Now, the way is a road that is trafficked and ki, like the traffic, goes back and forth. Therefore it is called the Way. Thus, the ki in motion or stillness is, on the one hand, yin and, on the other hand, yang. The yin and yang alternate endlessly. Therefore in the cosmic process they are called the Great Ultimate. Consequently, the Great Ultimate and the Way function in tandem, the Way being the Great Ultimate in yin and yang interaction. With one [kind of] ki the Great Ultimate does not move; there must be the two ki. Now, when the two ki move, it is done according to the *jōri* and is called the Way. This is the basic nature of the two ki. If things are not in proper order, this cannot be considered the Way. Then it is not true nature. Spring is refreshing, summer is warm, autumn is cool and winter is cold; they are constant and correct. A wrong yin and a wrong yang have lost their constants and are not the Way. When the equilibrium of yin and yang is right, it corresponds to the Way and is attuned to nature. The so-called Heaven's Way is yin and yang. During the year growth and harvest take place orderly. This fluctuation is the yin and yang and the Way in operation. In these operations there is nothing that does not correspond to the Way. . . .

Heaven and Earth are ki and their movements are the yin and yang. And all growth (*sei-sei*) without end is called life. Therefore the *I Ching* says, 'The great virtue of Heaven and Earth is life. Its fluctuations, the one being yin and the other yang, are called the Way'. . . . The balance of yin and yang is the Way. . . . When ri and ki agree, this is one thing (mono). They cannot be divided and be two because there is no ri without ki and no ki without ri. . . . One cannot say that the ri comes first and then the ki. . . . Thus ri and ki are not two things. They are inseparable.

The ri cannot be a separate thing. There is only the ri in ki. The ki in its right fluctuations is the Way. When there is order, it is called ri. The truth is that the Way and ri are one. If you perceive ri as something separate from what resides in ki, how does it differ from Lao Tzu who says that all things were produced before Heaven and Earth, or Shaka who said that something existed before Heaven and Earth? . . . The great harmony of the ki of the world functions in the manifestations of yin and yang, and the yin and yang have the ability to produce and reproduce and be the source of all things. Ri should not be disdained as being just vessels of the *keijika* world. . . .

Now, the endless growth of life (*sei-sei*) and change is called ki. Order and law from birth to death, this is ri. Ki and ri truly form one thing (mono). The laws are ri. When ri are followed, things are in perfect order and exude goodness and do not distance themselves from what is normal. . . . Since, on the other hand, ki can cause disorder, accidents happen and the right course is lost. This means that the right correspondence is lost between stillness and motion. However, this is not the true nature of yin and yang. . . .

If one compares this with water: water is originally pure, but in contact with mud, it gets turbid and loses its purity. It cannot be said, however, that this turbidity belongs to water's true nature. The ki has the faculty to generate all things (*banbutsu*), and ri can be said, likewise, to have the ability to generate all things. . . . The ri is, however, the ri of the ki and the two cannot be described as root and branches (*honmatsu*) or as before and after. This is because the two are one and neither is before the other nor the source of the other.

Chu Hsi stated in a reply to a letter . . . that ri and ki are two things (*nibutsu*). He repeats the same thing often in other writings. . . . This contradicts the sages who say that 'one yin and one yang constitute the Way' (*ichiin ichiyō dō*). Other sayings go in the same direction. This I do not understand and it makes me doubtful' (*yo no tokoro mayorite wakarazu nari*).[346]

Ekken displayed, thus, a cautious scepticism but does not deny the frontiers of the Chu Hsi thought. He brought the ki and ri together in an amalgam where the ki was dominant. It was the ri regularities in the ki 'stuff' that became of interest in his endeavours. In the spirited network of thought in the second half of the seventeenth century one wonders whether Ekken had both heard of and read Yamaga Sokō and Itō Jinsai and was motivated by them. His curiosity set the tone for Confucian rhetoric in years to come and his methodology, which involved a systematic study of regularities and correspondences of the universe, brought the outer half of Sung thought to the fore. Even if he doubted Chu Hsi, his scepticism was Confucian in outlook. Neo-Confucianism was converted into 'a reverent study of nature'[347] which included not only human relationships, but also flowers and bees.

9. The Ancient School Thinkers

As a reaction to the overwhelming Neo-Confucian thought came the *kogaku* thinkers. It was recognized that the teaching by Chu Hsi and other Sung scholars did not correspond to the indubitable truth in the Chinese canon which should be the ultimate law for all times. The scholars had been frivolous in their interpretation of the sacred heritage and had added to it as it suited them. Even worse, they had been influenced by Buddhism (also Taoism), which made their message unsavoury. Necessity demanded a return to the undiluted classical scriptures which should be understood in direct reading. The *kogaku* reaction has been interpreted as 'a philosophical metamorphosis in the history of Japanese Neo-Confucian studies'.[348]

Three scholars are mainly connected with this Renaissance. Yamaga Sokō is the earliest among them, soon followed by Itō

Jinsai. They both returned to Confucius and Mencius in their search for the truth in the 1660s. The third was Ogyū Sorai who did not stop with Confucius and Mencius but went further back to the early Five (Six) Classics for classical corroboration. These three protagonists were not linked and there was considerable divergence between their opinions. They resembled each other, however, in rejecting the Chu Hsi and resorting to the original classical texts in search of the undistorted truth. A later age brought them together under the name of kogaku school.

9.1 Yamaga Sokō (1622-85)

The *kogaku* 'ancient studies' school can be dated from 1665, the year that Yamaga Sokō[349] published the *Seikyō Yōroku, Essential Teachings of the Sages*. In this work he relates how he turned from Chu Hsi to Confucius and other classics in the early 1660s. He studied, as he says, day and night and finally understood the message of the sages. There was no need for exegetical works. As a result, he lost interest not only in Buddha, Zen, Lao Tzu and Chuang Tzu but also in Chu Hsi. A new outlook on human nature was born. He rejected the Neo-Confucian pursuit of self-transcendence and condemned 'the scholars of empty words for their entire ignorance of the affairs of everyday life and for their absorption in sterile literary pursuits'.[350] The *Seikyō Yōroku* was mainly a lexical exposition of Confucian terms, and it can imediately be difficult to understand why Hoshina Masayuki (1609-72) found it offensive and had Sokō exiled to Akō in 1666.

In a later essay, *Haisho Zanpitsu, Random Writings in Exile* (1675),[351] Sokō described his intellectual development. He was the child prodigy who had read the Confucian Books, the Early Five (Six) Classics and other Chinese writings by the age of eight. At nine he attended the Hayashi school and at only fifteen he lectured on the *Ta Hsüeh* and by sixteen on the *Meng Tzu* and the *Lun Yü*. Then followed studies which comprised Chu Hsi and other Confucian works. He became engrossed in those and he was, for the better part of his life, a Neo-Confucian believer. His wide reading also included *Lao Tzu, Chuang Tzu* and Japanese literature, such as the *Genji Monogatari, Ise Monogatari, Manyōshū* and *Makura No Sōshi*. He studied Japanese poetry and wrote waka poems. Further, he took an interest in military science from his young years and in the Shinto religion in his teens. He had accordingly a broad and well-rounded education which led to doubts about the Neo-Confucian canon. Then, about 1661 he cast aside Chu Hsi and turned to Confucius and the sages. Among the Confucian books he acknowledged the *Lun Yü* and the *Ta Hsüeh* but not the *Meng Tzu* and the *Chung Yung*. He found Mencius argumentative and the Chung Yung close to Buddhism and Taoism. These convictions eventually prompted the writing of the *Seikyō Yōroku*.[352]

Neo-Confucianism was for him in the end nothing but Buddhism. His firm belief in practical affairs was the result. He expressed the opinion that 'anyone who represses desire is not a human being'. Man becomes like 'dead bones' or 'a rotten tree', if he curbs his desires and subdues his passions, that is, the ki side of his nature. Or as he also said, 'He who flees from desire is not a man.'[353] The ideal personality combines the dignity of the interior with the strength of the exterior. He nurtures his ki (*yōki*) and steels his will (*gōsō*) and is capable of leading others. Instead of a Heaven of immutable and perpetual ri he saw the more classical Heaven of Will, determining man's fate and destiny. The ri was certainly there, but it was the ki energy, valour, the foremost virtue of the samurai, that should come primarily in a bushi's life.[354] So he became the creator of military Confucianism, the *shidō*, later *bushidō*, the 'Warrior's Way', which he presented in essays like *Bukyō Yōroku, Military Way Delineated*, and *Bukyō Zensho, All about the Military Way*.

In the *Yamaga Gorui, Yamaga Discourses* (1665?), he equates thinking wisely (as a sage) *seigaku* with useful action, not least samurai life. In one chapter that carries the title *shidō*, he speaks about the duties of the samurai, the loyalty towards his lord, the trustworthiness towards one's friends and military ethics generally. The samurai should practise both the literary and martial arts, letters being his left arm and military matters his right arm; neither must be neglected. He should look to the surrounding socio-political spectrum, be conscious of his duties, always cultivate his bravery, loyalty and integrity (*kisetsu*) and by all means avoid becoming a 'straw-mat (*tatami*) samurai'. As he said: 'The samurai keeps to the ways of peace, but keeps his weapons ready for use.'[355]

Cultivating his ki nature, the samurai actualizes his ri, which is the *jōri* inscape. The transcendence is achieved by rites and ceremonies which concern every aspect of life. Sokō's kogaku creed was based on the Confucian canon and the Sages' Way and the objective of his message was the correct life of the samurai in a world of peace. His military interest took shape in military ideas which are referred to as the Yamaga-ryū, the Yamaga School of Military Thought, which included teppō warfare. His interest in the past led to an ethnocentrism which put Japan side by side with the land of Confucius and was close to the nativist thought of the following century. The tendency to compete with and attempt to surpass the Chinese model was of an old date and continued until a new challenge derived from the West.[356]

It has been said that one finds the oldest intellectual basis of emperor worship in Sokō's thought.[357] This is possible, but the question is whether Yamazaki Ansai, perhaps even Nakae Tōju and Kumazawa Banzan, did not offer this intellectual basis before him. When Ansai concluded that the Ways of Shinto and Confucianism were 'naturally and mysteriously the same', he was forthwith elevating the Imperial Court and the emperor to the same level as the Confucian heaven – or above. Already Fujiwara Seika and Hayashi Razan expressed the idea that the Way of the Gods (*kami*) and the Way of the sages in China were the same. Sokō's turn to the indigenous culture was therefore in keeping with a general tendency in Tokugawa Confucian thought. This came in clear words when he declared in the Haishi ∠anpitsu that all emperors had been virtuous and that Japan was superior to China and all other countries.[358] Japan excelled because of its unbroken lineage of emperors and cultural uniqueness. Japan, not China, should be called the Middle Kingdom! All the norms found in Confucius' *Lun Yü* were fashioned independently in Japan, and, as a whole, formed the 'way of the warrior' (*bushidō*). This was not far from the *kokutai* thinking of the Mito school and to the nationalist consciousness of the nativists, first among them Keichū (1640-1701) who proclaimed 'Japan to be the land of the Gods'.[359]

Sokō finished his lectures, compiled as the *Yamaga Gorui*, when he was forty-three (about 1664). His popularity was rising among students who counted in the thousands. A year later, in 1665, he published the *Seikyō Yōroku*, and Hoshina Masayuki who was both a high official and a Chu Hsi believer had him banished to Akō from where he was pardoned nine years later in 1675 after Hoshina had died. He never retracted the *kogaku* beliefs he had pronounced in the *Seikyō Yōroku*, and continued to reject the Chu Hsi *ri* thought and propounded that Heaven and Earth was a 'wondrous amalgam' (*myōgō*) of the 'Two ki' (*niki*), that is, the negative yin ki and the positive yang ki.[360] He was allowed to give lectures in Edo until his death there in 1685.

9.2 Itō Jinsai (1627-1705)

Itō Jinsai went farther when, in the maturity of his thought, he considered life spontaneous, ki and not ri, when he stated that 'all between Heaven and Earth is the one original ki' (*tenchi no aida wa ichi-genki nomi*) and that 'Heaven and Earth are one enormous living organism' (*tada tenchi wa ichidai katsubutsu*).[361] Viewing the universe as a living thing (*katsubutsu*) without beginning or end, he expressed a one-dimensional ki monism and was close to the original Chinese mode of thought. The Way of Heaven and Earth is the timeless interaction of yin and yang energy (ki), and all things originate from the Five Elements. One should not go further and found the yin and yang on ri. Then one lands in the 'empty nothingness (*kyomu*) of Buddhism and Chuang Tzu'.[362]

'The Way is Life; ri is death.' The ri principles are there but they are just like veins or texture on a piece of jade. They are just like 'dead words' (*shiji*) while ki is the living thing (*katsubutsu*). As he writes in his major work, the *Gomōjigi* (*Lexicography of the Analects and Mencius*, 1666),[363] 'It should be very clear that ri did not exist first, before ki. Instead "ri is simply the rationale existing within ki" (*ri wa kaette kore kichū no jōri nomi*).'[364] Famous is his ki 'box'. He says:

> Heaven and Earth are comparable to a gigantic box, with yin and yang acting as the internal generative force (ki) within it. The myriad things of the world are like the white mould and mites spontaneously arising inside the huge box. Generative force (ki) does not come from anything, nor from anywhere. Wherever boxes or enclosures exist, the generative force will exist also. If there were no such crucibles, the generative force would not exist. We can thus comprehend how this generative force exists within Heaven and Earth. It should be very clear that ri did not exist first, and then generative force. Instead ri is simply the rationale existing within generative force (*kichū no jōri*) . . .[365]

Thus, Itō Jinsai rested his entire doctrine on the priority of ki.

Heaven and Earth is a 'living organism' (*katsubutsu*), and Heaven's Way is like a frolicsome horse galloping in all directions without being spurred by a ri rider. He says: 'The Way unfolds the dynamics of Heaven as if to reveal the mystery of the transformational process occurring in all things.' He argues further: 'What makes Heaven a living thing is its constant energy (ki). That energy is as essential to Heaven as vitality is to man.' The nature is made up of a vital energy field that harmonizes the correlated forces, yin and yang, in perpetual creativity. Chu Hsi's *rigaku* was replaced by Itō Jinsai's *kigaku*. The ri is relegated to a posterior and secondary role: 'In living things, there is the principle (ri) of living things. In dead things there is the principle (ri) of dead things. But a single primal material force (ki) is the basis, and ri is posterior to ki.'[366] Ri exists only in ki. He adds an egalitarian element to this thought, when he says that: 'all men are equally men . . . no matter where under Heaven or where on

Earth [they may live], and enveloped in the same brother-hood'.[367]

Itō Jinsai also denounced the emphasis of the Neo-Confucian scholars on seriousness and earnestness, not least referring to his neighbour in Kyoto, Yamazaki Ansai,[368] when he attacked their 'deadening, life-denying ... and calculating attitude towards things'.[369] 'He tired of their moralizing that denied the validity of human feelings', and insisted that ninjō, 'human sentiments', were part and parcel of one's innate moral nature.[370]

When perceiving and apprehending all reality as a ki cosmic box, Itō Jinsai was certainly prompted by Ming thought and perhaps especially by the above-mentioned Lo Ch'in-shun. Lo's work K'un-chih Chi (Jap. Konchiki) was published in Kyoto in 1658. Itō Jinsai lent a copy of this work to his students and 'he must have read it himself since some of his main insights and his most quotable phrases are identical to Lo's'.[371] As has been elucidated by J. A. Tucker, Itō Jinsai was also certainly motivated by Confucian thinkers through the seventeenth century beginning with Hayashi Razan.[372] His message suited the situation in Kyoto among samurai and city people.

Until about the age of 37, Itō Jinsai embraced the Chu Hsi learning and used the pen name Keisai, the Reverent, which indicated his recognition of the ri-ki dualism and the authority of all the Confucian Four Books. He said then, 'If a scholar first establishes the sagely teaching in the Ta Hsüeh and the Lun Yü and thereupon reads the Chung Yung and the Meng Tzu, he need not go wrong.' His philological studies (kogigaku) convinced him, however, that the Ta Hsüeh differed on some ten points from the Lun Yü and the Meng Tzu, and could not be a book by Confucius. In the same manner he repudiated the Chung Yung, asserting that several chapters had been inserted. He ended accepting only the Lun Yü and Meng Tzu. This made him critical of Chu Hsi generally, he became a kogaku ki monist – and he changed his pen name to Jinsai, the Benevolent. Confucius took the place of Chu Hsi.

His Kogidō school (School of Ancient Meaning)[373] opened

about the same time that Yamaga Sokō's *kogaku* thinking also began (1662). There he taught that one cannot explain all phenomena in the the universe by means of a singular ri principle. As he said in the *Gomō Jigi*:

> The Sung Confucianists thought that they could explain all worldly things through ri. They were not aware that . . . one cannot judge things in the world solely on that basis. They nevertheless depended upon this concept alone to account for everything under Heaven. Rhetorically, their argument sounds reasonable, but when applied to reality, it cannot explain many things.[374]

Itō Jinsai's thought was accordingly a break with Sung thought. Like Nakae Tōju, Kumazawa Banzan and others he reflected Ming and and also Ch'ing thought. All cosmos is in constant motion, and all creation must be understood in terms of life and productive motion. In place of Chu Hsi's abstract ri-ki dualism, Itō Jinsai offers the Mencian 'flood-like ki' monism. Further, basing himself on the *I Ching*, he contrasts The Way of Heaven with the Way of Earth (*chidō*) and the Way of Man (*jindō*). Each Way has its qualities: yin and yang are the Way of Heaven, hard and soft are the Way of Earth and goodness and righteousness are the Way of man.[375]

Itō Jinsai thus rejected Chu Hsi's transcendental ri, advancing a one-dimensional vitalistic ki. A monism took the place of the Chu Hsi dualism. The world was not unchanging ri but dynamic ki. This made the way a 'ceaseless back-and-forth movement of the the two ki forces, yin and yang'.[376]

His kogaku emphasized the *Lun Yü*, which he marked out as 'the highest, the ultimate and the first book of the universe' (*saijō shigoku uchū daiittō no sho*). He saw the *Meng Tzu* as a necessary commentary to the *Lun Yü*. He wrote in the *Dōshimon, Children's Questions*: 'Confucius is my teacher. Anyone who claims to be a student must have the Sage (= Confucius) as his guide. He must not hastily follow the footsteps of later Confucian scholars who engage in obsessive hair-splitting arguments for an appropriate means of obtaining the Way. In the end, he accomplishes nothing. Students cannot take a single letter from the sayings of the Sage.'[377]

Itō Jinsai's thought runs as a paraphrase of Confucius and Mencius. Goodness (jin) is the cardinal virtue and synonymous with love (ai) and the Way combines jin and gi. Then follows the entire length of other virtues and ethical terms and doctrines. All people are good and should be loved equally. Unlike Kumazawa Banzan and Ogyū Sorai, Itō Jinsai took no interest in political affairs. He puts a strong emphasis on the virtue of truth and sincerity (sei, makoto) and regards it as the Way of Heaven rather than on the virtue of reverence and respect (kei). So far he runs parallel with the Neo-Confucians: like Chu Hsi he emphasizes a moral sense rooted in the heart of the person. Itō Jinsai did, however, not see the origin of ethics in a heavenly 'original nature' but meant that 'morality and ethics existed within society as the overall structure which subsumed the multiplicity of human relationships'[378] and 'must be translated into actual ethical behaviour'.[379] When it comes to nature he does not follow Chu Hsi but goes to the I Ching according to which the world is characterized by the flux and flow of life.

9.3 Itō Tōgai (1670-1736)

Itō Jinsai was blessed with several sons. Itō Tōgai took over where his father left off in 1705 and faithfully carried on his father's teachings. He managed the Kogidō private academy on Horikawa street in Kyoto and 'compiled a formidable library of his father's writings, prepared an intellectual biography of him and maintained the Kogidō as a bastion of Ancient Learning, thus preserving a remarkably complete legacy of Itō Jinsai's writings for future generations'.

9.4 Ogyū Sorai (1666-1728)

Ogyū Sorai, likewise, was aroused by Ming thought when he regarded a life of goodness (jin) as that of ki and not of ri. Further, whether he admitted it or not, he was greatly stimulated by Itō

Jinsai. The main difference between them was that while Itō Jinsai leaned on the 'inner' side, Sorai leaned on the 'outer' side, that is, Itō Jinsai was an idealist and Ogyū Sorai a realist. Jinsai believed in man's goodness, more so than Ogyū Sorai who certainly acknowledged that goodness was the primary virtue but did not trust its social efficacy.[380] He admits the Ming influence when he mentions that Wang Shih-chen (1526-90) and Li P'an-lung (1514-59) had aroused him.[381]

Ogyū Sorai only accepted the *kishitsu no sei*, the 'ki nature', a nature that was personal and unchangeable. As he said rhetorically in the Benmei: 'Can *kishitsu* possibly be changed?! (*kishitsu wa hen-zubekenya*).' Nature is a living thing (*katsubutsu*) and 'a mystery that cannot be fathomed'. The ki nature differs with each individual. The *rishitsu no sei*, the 'ri nature', was also for him only the *kishitsu no jōri*, that is, the texture of 'the one great living being' (*ichidai katsubutsu*). Sorai mentions both the tenri, the 'Heavenly Ri', and the chiri, the 'Earthly Ri', and did not deny the existence of ri in things and affairs but attacked the view that there was a ri universalism. He considered Chu Hsi's cosmic ri to be fruitless speculation; instead he recognized distinct minds, as many as 'there are faces'.

Every individual, accordingly, possessed his ki nature which could be refined for the sake of civilized society; it was not the question of ri endowed in each person alike but of personal natures. The standards of the human Way were found in the Five (Six) Classics (*rikkei*), where the '*dōri* of Heaven and Earth (*tenchi no dōri*)' was expounded. Introspection, as recommended by Sung and Ming thinkers, only led to subjective thoughts, not to definite criteria. What Sorai advocated was the thorough study of Five (Six) Classics to attain the truth. What the Neo-Confucian thinkers had achieved was only 'forced interpretations' (*kenkyō*) by *kakubutsu-chichi* and *kyūri*.

The backbone of scholarship was Chinese philology, his *kobunjigaku*, 'Ancient Philology'. This was the true way of learning and mainly limited to 'poetry, history, rites and music' (*shi-sho rei-gaku*). 'Heaven was something beyond our comprehension ... an object of worship, not of rational enquiry'. Scholars should keep to socio-political philosophy (*keizai*). An extensive knowledge of history was important because 'the old and new are continuous'.[382] Personally, he took an interest in practical skills, as when he worked with catapults and bows, medicine, military strategy and even mathematics.

Sorai took an interest in the four Confucian Books and wrote commentaries on them all. His commentary on the *Lun Yü* (*Rongo-chō*) is considered one of his great works. His other commentaries were *Daigaku-kai, Chūyō-kai* and *Mōshi-shiki*.[383] Sorai does not explicitly make a distinction between them, but he says in the *Bendō* that he finds Mencius argumentative and deviating from the sages. He apparently never finished the latter three commentaries.

Sorai's was most radical when he demythologized the sages and separated the Way of man from the Way of Heaven. In orthodox thought the human Way was seen as an extension or reflection of the Heavenly Way, a replica that was as eternal as the original itself. It was a *tenjin gōitsu*, 'heaven and man in union'. Similar to Hsün Tzu, however, Sorai distinguished between the Way of Heaven and the Way of man, and propounded that the human Way was a creation (*sakui*) by the sage kings, who had been inspired by Heaven, and not a 'thus by itself', as the Taoists would have it. We have to do with artifice. The world changes and the Way changes accordingly. There was therefore no natural law appropriate to all historical situations. The Tokugawa Way could not be a carbon copy of the preceding Muromachi Way; it should only mirror the early Three Dynasties in its contours, reflect them in spirit and display the same ideals. This meant that the Way became a relative reality, capable of being altered by new knowledge. The unity of nature was broken. Sorai did not, however, deny the Way of Heaven and Earth. He just cautiously enunciated (in the *Benmei*):

> There is that which we call the Way of Heaven (*tendō*) and that which we call the Way of Earth (*chidō*). ... What we

call the Way of Heaven is impenetrable in its depth and profundity and supreme in its mystery. The ten thousand things begin from it. . . . When we ponder it quietly, it is as if there is something from which these things derive. Therefore, I call it the Way of Heaven. What we call the Way of Earth bears up mountains but is not burdened. Making rivers and seas flow, it releases no water. It is so immense, that its end cannot be reached. When we carefully consider it, it is as if there is something from which these things derive. Therefore, I call it the Way of Earth. I call them this – the Way of Heaven and the Way of Earth – in analogy to the Way of the Sages.[384]

Rei-gaku-kei-sei (Ch. *li-yüeh-hsing-cheng*), 'rites, music, penal law and government' is a comprehensive term expressing the institutions of the sages' way. The term comes from *Hsün Tzu*. One can discern a parity between what is inner and personal and what is outer and social. Both sides are equally important. One would imagine that Sorai would put penal law and government beforehand, but revealing his basic Confucian bent, he places rites and music first.

Gi, 'righteousness', is no virtue for Sorai, but represents correct action and social duty in accordance with the Sages' Way. All virtues are strung on jin, which also Sorai acknowledges as the virtue of virtues. *Jin* displays itself primarily in social, not least official, compassion. To bring peace and well-being to the world, 'to be the father and mother of the people', was the first duty of the ruler. Also the rules of propriety are sagely creations (*sakui*) made for human conditions. They are not ri bestowed by Heaven. The Chinese sage kings had presented the model and standards for all times. They were 'raised to the level of religious absolutes'.[385] They were towering but not transcendent. Sorai's faith in them was total. As he says in the *Bendō*: 'The teachings of the sages are complete. . . . That which the sages did not express does not need to be expressed.' Ancient China was idealized, and Sorai came to be considered a Sinophile.

There was a touch of modernity in Sorai's thought when he externalized the Way and made it a relative, worldly construct.

He also showed a modern outlook when he maintained that all men differ as much in their hearts as in their faces. The individual was to perform his tenshoku and shokubun, his mission and duty according to social class and inborn talents. There was a Confucian Heaven above his ki-world, a Heaven that had a will and was the fountainhead of the Sages' Way. There was, however, also a Shintō Heaven and ancestors and kishin. He says, 'the way of the Gods of our land is the way of the Gods of Morokoshi (= China)'.[386] Thus, he did not deny the Shinto creed.

Sorai's overall cosmic thought is well declared in the *Seidan* III:12:

> Now the truth (*dōri*) of the *I Ching* that 'things grow up from below' is certainly no foolish fancy. In the course of the year, spring and summer are the seasons when the spirit (ki) of Heaven descends, the spirit (ki) of Earth rises, and the two unite harmoniously so that all things grow. In autumn and winter the spirit (ki) of Heaven rises and the spirit of Earth descends; Heaven and Earth separate and cease to be in accord with the result that all things wither and die. It is also like that in the human world.[387]

There is a fatalism in Sorai's thought concerning the cosmos as well as man. Everything exists by the grace of Heaven (*ten no chōrei*). 'Heaven creates, supports and enfolds the complex reality of life.'[388] He quotes Confucius who says, 'Without recognizing the ordinances of Heaven, it is impossible to be a superior man.'[389] He indicates that it is thanks to Heaven's grace that he himself has achieved things in life.

Sorai began as a Chu Hsi ri-ist. He turned a ki-ist rather late in life – at about fifty years of age. Afterwards he did not acknowledge timeless archetypes (ri) manifested in the world. In the maturity of his thought he realized that there were no sages in later ages but that there could be wise rulers. Such a later-age genius was Tokugawa Ieyasu. What such a wise later-age ruler needed to do was to study the thought of the sages and to apply the divine and timeless paradigm to the Tokugawa reality. The touchstone was whether the established system (*seido*) brought peace and common welfare, not strife and impoverishment.

As a political economist Sorai was not satisfied with the situation in the Kyōhō era (1716-35), as expressed in his major work, the *Seidan* (1727). With the models of sagely times in China in mind, he proposed a number of administrative reforms which were mostly ignored by the authorities.[390] He was especially worried about the samurai class, which had turned effeminate over a century of peace and city life. He recommended, like Kumazawa Banzan prior to him, that they be returned to the countryside and agricultural work. The population should also otherwise be strictly regulated.

Sorai seems close to Hsün Tzu with his emphasis on government. The emphasis on law is, however, matched by an equal emphasis on human capacity (*jinzai*) and education. One finds no anti-intellectualism in Sorai's message. On the contrary, he asks for an almost exaggerated devotion to literary pursuits. In Sorai's Ken'en School the stress was on thorough classical studies. His affinities with legalism did not go farther than to Hsün Tzu. The goal was public prosperity and the way was through intellectual training of the ruler and the ruling élite.[391] In the *Seidan*, we are told that the most important duty of the ruler is to search out truly able men for the offices.[392] If men of talent were found, it was not important if the laws were imperfect. Sorai did not, however, stand aloof from morals. He was strictly upright in his own deportment but did not wish morality to turn into rigorous austerity.

Personal behaviour was not enough for creating a vigorous society. To rule the land, relying on ethical effort was like riding a horse with rotten reins or building a house without a measure. There must be external, objective norms. Like Aristoteles, Sorai considered man a '*zōon politikon*', 'a political animal', who needed society to develop. It was a fallacy to give priority to ethics over politics. These socio-political ends were negatively referred to as being utilitarian by orthodox thinkers but Sorai held that their aim was the just social order asked for by the sages. In twentieth-century terms they would be called progressive and even socialist, aiming at the maximun prosperity for the maximum number of people.

The Sorai school enlivened intellectual life in the eighteenth century. The philosopher was rare who did not mention him either positively or negatively. So also today. He had himself a limited number of students, among whom Dazai Shundai is usually mentioned first.

9.5 Dazai Shundai (1680-1747)

Dazai Shundai is the best known among Ogyū Sorai's disciples. He followed Ogyū Sorai when he focused his attention on matters of political economy and his main work, *Keizai-roku, Account of Political Economy*, echoes Ogyū Sorai's work, the *Seidan*. He also saw history beginning with the sage kings in China and considered the norms emanating from the early dynasties adequate for any age. Like Ogyū Sorai, moreover, he considered the way of the sages to be the way to rule the realm. Truth must be sought in the early scriptures and not in nature or oneself. He was even closer to his teacher when he held the opinion that no two men are born alike. Nature can just be nourished in conformity with 'rites' and attain harmony by means of 'music'. He was, however, not optimistic as regards the validity of the sages' Way for all situations. He therefore adjoined a number of principles as a supplement for the everlasting reality of becoming and being. With an understanding of his specific time, the ruler would be able to formulate a policy in conformity with the historical reality. His conclusion was that to live in the world was to live in hierarchy; only in a state of 'nature' like birds and beasts are men equal to one another. All people had, besides, divergent talents and faculties. His seido for the political economy was therefore more variegated than that which Ogyū Sorai proposed in the *Seidan*. More than Ogyū Sorai he proposed that the bakufu fiscal policy should foster manufacture and trade and not rely wholly on agriculture. He shared, generally, Ogyū Sorai's pessimistic appraisal of the situation in Kyōhō times.

Like Ogyū Sorai, he was critical of Neo-Confucianism. He added, however, a transcendent sentiment to his message when he advised the ruler to identify with the Taoist ideal of 'non-action' (Keizai-roku, Account of Political Economy) began with Kumazawa Banzan and followed with works by Yamaga Sokō, Ogyū Sorai and Dazai Shundai among kogaku scholars. Afterwards, numerous scholars turned to this subject through later Tokugawa times. Affairs of government, except when holding office, had been tabu. Now, after the ice was broken, numerous scholars turned to political and economic matters. Perhaps the greatest among them was Arai Hakuseki. Human relationships was less focused on, as governance, production and soon even profit came into focus.

10. Arai Hakuseki (1657-1725)

A rai Hakuseki, Ogyū Sorai's great rival in the intellectual world, was Kinoshita Jun'an's disciple. He was close to power from 1694 when he entered the service as a Confucian scholar (jusha) of the lord of Kōfu who later became Shogun Ienobu (r. 1709-12). He later noted that he gave a total of 1299 (!) lectures to Ienobu. Displaying an unusual breadth of mind, he took an interest in a wide range of subjects, such as geography, botany and languages (even Dutch!) and gave history a novel chronological coherence. 'He distinguished between Western science and Western religion but argued that Western learning was only concerned with ki, and lacked the dimension of ri.' The reference was possibly to an early source, Kenkon Bensetsu, Explanation of the Cosmos (1658) by Mukai Genshō (1609-77)[393]

which says: 'The scholars of barbarian learning do no know the ri
of yin and yang; therefore they do not know why Heaven is
Heaven. They say that the four elements and not Heaven are the
origin of all things. This is like knowing the mother and not the
father'. This view typifies the early philosophical reaction to
modern science.[394]

Philosophically, Arai belonged firmly in the Neo-Confucian fold
and as a statesman he strove to accomplish the ideal of
benevolent government. The heavenly ri and one virtue, rites
(rei), was for him, as for orthodox Chu Hsi believers in general,
the life line between heaven, earth and man, thus also in the
centre of the socio-political structures. As he writes:

> Heaven and human beings are fundamentally of the same
> spiritual substance (ki) and the interaction between them is
> stronger than that between the moon and the tide. Thus,
> when there is order in the human realm, the spiritual
> essence of Heaven and Earth is naturally sustained and in
> proper symmetry. When there is disorder in the human
> realm, the inherent harmony of the universe cannot be
> sustained. . . . When the yin and yang are not in tune, the
> generation of the myriad things cannot follow its valid
> course. . . . What keeps Heaven above and Earth below is
> rites (rei). What brings yang and yin in harmony is music.
> Consequently, rites and music are not simply instruments
> used by the former kings to teach and transform the
> people. They are what keep Heaven and Earth in their
> proper positions and harmonize yin and yang.[395]

He belonged among the new breed of curious minds who
searched for the jōri in this world while less attention was
devoted to the (ri) metaphysics. The balance of virtue and
knowledge was, however, not forgotten. Reading, for example,
the above-mentioned Kenkon Bensetsu, Explanation of the
Cosmos the vicissitudes of this world loom in the foreground,
while Confucius, Chu Hsi, Heaven's Way yet lurk in the
background. The same can be said about his work on history, the
Tokushi Yoron (see above), which has been characterized as one

of the great scholastic achievements of the Tokugawa era. Among his numerous other writings we can note the *Hankanpu, Record of Feudal Domains* (1701), *Seiyō Kibun, Report on the Western World* (1715)[396] and *Sairan Igen, Languages, Customs and Other Things in Foreign Countries* (1713, revised 1725), the first work on the han fiefs, the second two works on the arrival of Giovanni Battisti Sidotti (1678-1715) and on Western matters, primarily geography. Arai is considered the spiritual father of *rangaku* scholarship that grew strong later in the eighteenth century.[397]

Arai was asked to interrogate Giovanni Battista Sidotti (1668-1715), the Jesuit priest, who smuggled himself into Japan in 1708. It took him no time to discover that Sidotti's thought had two distinct sides.[398] On one side he was the 'irrational' Christian, but on the other side he was the 'rational' thinker, who astounded Hakuseki with his excellent knowledge of natural science, a dichotomy that amazed a Neo-Confucian thinker.

One can understand that Arai was stunned, when he listened to Sidotti and heard of the Christian creed, for which he gave expression in the *Seiyō Kibun*. Being steeped in the Neo-Confucian doctrine, plenty in the Christian gospel must have appared illogical and even absurd. For example, when Sidotti declared that God (*Deusu*) had created Heaven and Earth but had himself come about of himself, Arai wondered why Heaven and Earth could not also have come about of themselves?[399] He believed, like other Confucian philosophers, that 'they (Heaven and Earth) are so because they are so'.[400] With sharp perspicacity Arai also questions why Sidotti's God had to send his son to be crucified when he could have handled mankind himself just by exercising his omnipotence!

11. Muro Kyūsō (1658-1734)

Another well-known Neo-Confucian scholar originating from Kinosita Jun'an and indirectly from Fujiwara Seika was Muro Kyūsō. Recommended by Arai Hakuseki, he entered shogunal service and served in an advisory capacity to Shogun Yoshimune. Kyūsō can be recognized as a *bushidō* scholar who steadfastly remained within the Chu Hsi wisdom. Not showing any deviation from the orthodoxy, he rejected the *kogaku* creeds of both Itō Jisai and Ogyū Sorai. Among his writings was the *Meikun Kakun* (1715), *The Precepts of the Wise Ruler*, a work that underlined the loyalty of the samurai class, admonishing them not to stray from the straight and narrow path of the service to the lord. Shogun Yoshimune appreciated the work, recommended it to his close associates with the result that it spread with great rapidity among his retainers.[401] His writings stimulated other philosophers, among them, Bitō Jisshū, later in the same century (see below).

12. Practical Studies in the Genroku Era

There were also others in the Genroku era who took a keen interest in the ri of things, but they are not mentioned as often as those who dealt with lofty philosophy. How many have, for example, heard of Inō (Inao) Jakusui (1655-1715) who investigated herbs for medicinal reasons and wrote works like *Shobutsu Ruisan, Classified Collection of Many Things,* and is rightly called the 'ancestor of herbal studies' in Japan.[402] He had studied under Kinoshita Jun'an, belonged among the orthodox Chu Hsi scholars and encouraged, among others, Kaibara Ekken, as a physician and botanist. Or who has heard about Miyazaki Yasusada (1623-97), who is known for the *Nōgyō Zensho, Complete Work on Agriculture* (ca. 1697) a work that was highly influential in agricultural activity? Then, there were the 'technologists', commoners, mostly farmers, who lived in villages and were never concerned with the problems of government. They were inventive and wrote about matters like agriculture, silkworm breeding, forestry and farming techniques. Thanks to them rural industry flourished. Much is not known about these people but we have enough literature by them to fill a library.[403] They meant much for the growth of the national economy in Tokugawa times and laid the groundwork for the rapid industrial development of the Meiji economy.

Ogyū Sorai is mentioned and honoured and every well-educated Japanese knows his name. Inō Jakusui, Miyazaki Yasusada and the 'technologists' are not, even though they meant more for the daily life of the Japanese than all the scholars who worked with philology and lofty philosophy. The fact is, however, that practical studies increased during the Genroku period, and advanced steadily in the following eighteenth century until they exploded in the nineteenth century. The world of man was slowly demystified and the Heavenly ri put apart while its stepchild, the *jōri*, came more and more into the centre of intellectual endeavour. Medicine, astronomy, botany, zoology and mathematics became popular fields of study. Later in the century, Dutch studies also began to exert an influence on Japanese proto-science and the gap between philosophy and technology was diminished. It must be considered a weakness on the part of Ogyū Sorai and other Confucian thinkers that they did not widen their horizons and actively recognize studies outside areas prescribed by the ancient sages.

13. *Setchū-ha* and Eighteenth-century Confucianism

Motivated by not least Ogyū Sorai's Ken'en School, Confucian thought went in various directions and a number of new schools were established. Most well-known among them was the Eclectic School (*setchū-ha*), a group of scholars who formulated fresh syntheses of orthodox Chu-Hsi ri-ki-ism and *kogaku* ki-ism. With one leg they stood in the historical realism of Ogyū Sorai thought and with the other in the Lu-Wang idealism. What side they belonged to was mainly decided by personal predilection. They arose mostly as a reaction and an antithesis to Ogyū Sorai's kogaku thought. They formed a sundry group and did not add greatly to Confucian discourse. M. Maruyama, for example, says that 'they showed little creativity'.[404] Whatever originality they evinced has not made them known until this day. Their activities reached their peak in the 1780s.

Among them were Katayama Kenzan (1730-82), Inoue Kinga (1732-84), Minagawa Kien (1734-1807), Hosoi Heishū (1728-1801) and Kameda Bōsai (1754-1826). Whether they were ri-ists or ki-ists may be difficult to discern and only a study of each can demonstrate where they stood within the bounds of ri and ki and *vis-à-vis* Chu Hsi and Ogyū Sorai. Katayama Kenzan, for example, did not reject the Chu Hsi's ri-ki synthesis even though he tended to *kogaku* thought. He echoes the views of Chu Hsi when he says that 'ki is everywhere dependent on ri and ri allows every thing to be the way it must be', and that 'for every person it should be possible to realize the ri and become a sage'. Thus he accepted Chu Hsi and differed from Ogyū Sorai, whom he disparaged for his repudiation of moral education.[405] On the whole, however, they attempted to look in two or more directions, disclosing signs of a weakening Chu Hsi domination.

Inoue Kinga, in T. Najita's words, 'provided a theory of flexible selection of historical ideologies, thus allowing the ideas of Ogyū Sorai and of Neo-Confucianism to coalesce within a broad framework in which, [depending on] the circumstances, one or the other could be given emphasis'.[406] Minagawa Kien was a Confucian erudite and *littérateur* who combined the ancient message and Chu Hsi in synthesis taught at his school in Kyoto, attended by numerous students.

Also other 'heterodox' schools arose. There were the 'Independent' (*dokuritsu*) school, the 'Ancient Commentaries' (*kochū*) school, the 'Philological' or 'Evidential Research' (*kōshō*) school, all inspired by Chinese thought. Scholars vied for originality and popularity. According to Professor T. Okada: 'they promoted their independent theories, rejected the restrictions imposed by their teachers, and became self-appointed authorities on Confucianism. As a result, the traditional tenor of Confucian studies was lost, and the intellectual atmosphere came to resemble that which had prevailed in China during the late Ming.'[407] Further, the Nativist Studies (*kokugaku*) arose as a reaction against the predominant Neo-Confucian studies. Close to the Nativist learning was the Mito school. Further, Western learning spread and academies opened, where the Dutch studies were in the centre. It was indeed a Babylonian ideological multiplicity, not just ethics and etiquette, that made the authorities nervous and made them act.

14. The Kaitokudō Scholars

Another group of scholars worth mentioning are those who formed the Kaitokudō school, the Merchant Academy at Osaka. Both the school and its scholars are not discussed as often as other schools and scholars of the Tokugawa era, but it is evident that they played an important role in the intellectual landscape of the era. From a modest start at the beginning of the eighteenth century (founded 1726) it became a thriving educational institution initially with the founders Miyake Sekian (1665-1730) and Nakai Chūan (1693-1758) and then with scholars and teachers such as Tominaga Nakamoto (1715-46), Goi Ranju (1697-1762), Nakai Chikuzan (1730-1804), Nakai Riken (1732-1817), Kusama Naokata (1753-1831) and Yamagata Bantō (1748-1821).

Situated in Osaka, the commercial centre of Tokugawa Japan, the school, through the above outstanding men of letters, gained a strong position in the second half of the eighteenth century, reaching its peak with Yamagata Bantō. The scholars often combined the studies at the school with business activities. Because of its location and commercial connections, the school had direct contact with the country both East and West. Well-known scholars from the East, like Kaiho Seiryō, and the equally well-known scholars from the West, such as Miura Baien, frequented the school. From the school originated the influential academy of Dutch studies, Tekijuku, founded by Ogata Kōan (1810-63) in 1838 and located nearby in Osaka. Thus, via Ogata Kōan and Fukuzawa Yukichi the Kaitokudō learning stretched from Tokugawa into modern times.

The title Kaitokudō can be interpreted as the 'Academy for the Search of Virtue'. The Search of Virtue can also be said to have been the emblem of the scholarly activities from the beginning.

Further, students of both low and high status were admitted. If 'virtue' was the first goal on the agenda, 'ordering the world and helping the people' (keisei-saimin) came next. Chinese learning was the mainstay of the teaching programme, beginning with Confucius and Mencius. It was Chinese humanism: how to practise good manners, how to promote the common good of society, how to forward justice. In other words, the concern focused on the present life, not on happiness and unhappiness after death. This was the original message delivered by Miyake Sekian in 1726. It was primarily directed to merchants but it did not deviate from the orthodox Confucian teaching, whether old or new.

It is in the second and third generations that we find thinkers within the Kaitokudō entourage who show distinctive profiles. The first is Tominaga Nakamoto, the second Goi Ranju, next the brothers Nakai Chikuzan and Nakai Riken, and finally, the greatest among them all, Yamagata Bantō.

14.1 Tominaga Nakamoto

Tominaga Nakamoto had a sceptical mind – and had to suffer for it. At only fifteen years of age, he had the audacity to challenge Ogyū Sorai's kogaku creed. He attacked the classical texts and rejected the idea that timeless norms were embedded in old Chinese writings only. These norms he found polemical and unsuitable for a later (st)age in history. In the works, Shutsujō Gogo, Interpretations Subsequent to Origination and Okina No Fumi, Jottings of an Old Man,[408] he asserts that works on olden times are generally rhetorical distortions of what they claim to describe, refer only to a specific time and land, and are deceptive. Each successive generation repeats these misrepresentations. They add to them and unsuspecting human beings are misled.

Religious accounts especially are guilty of such dishonesty. Being the keen observer, Tominaga found that all the major religions are open to the same charges. He was one of the first in Japanese civilization who recognized the geographical relativity of culture, religion and traditions, picturing wide vistas of history in integrated patterns. He regarded Buddhism, Confucianism, Shinto and other cults with a critical eye and finally rejected them all. He castigated Buddhism for its mystical unfounded speculations, and its use of devious intellectual techniques to deceive people and outdo rivals. At a time when nativist thought began to flourish, he accused Shinto of beguiling people with arcane transmissions and polemical distortions. With trenchant sharpness he proposed that theories about the Imperial Way did not derive from olden times. Somehow, however, he found the Shinto creed in keeping with the Tokugawa historical tradition and the spirit of the land.

He criticized Confucianism for bringing forth mistaken theses about antiquity and accused it of false rhetoric. His conclusion was that all history is contingent and unreliable as a source for political guidance. On the other hand, he owed considerably to Ogyū Sorai's writings when he found subjective morality as dependable as 'rotten reins' in private as well as in official pursuits. Even more sharply he noted how history became increasingly distorted when transferred from one country to another. This relativization of culture was later developed further by Yamagata Bantō.

Having denunciated all 'fabricated' religions and ideologies, he presented his own creed 'above all creeds', 'the Way of Ways', which is the 'Way of truth' (makoto no michi) to be practised in daily life. He emphasized that only direct experience leads to 'truth'. To be 'truthful' was the Way.[409]

Although being among the bright students at the Kaitokudō, he was expelled because of his deviating thought and never forgiven. His radical spirit might have led to governmental displeasure and the school was not ready to take the risk. In spite of his untimely death at 31, however, he had managed to be not only one among the few Tokugawa sceptics but also to bring forth his own creed.

14.2 Goi Ranju

Contemporary with Tominaga Nakatomo at the Kaitokudō was

Goi Ranju, a scholar not often mentioned in the literature. He had, however, his own profile and not least his attack on *kogaku* thought is worth mentioning. He was a Neo-Confucian believer, and from this posture he launched a severe attack on Ogyū Sorai in *Hi-Butsu Hen, Polemic against Ogyū Sorai*.[410] It was Goi Ranju's opinion that Ogyū Sorai's theories had caused extensive damage to Confucian ethical philosophy. Following Itō Jinsai, Ranju believed that morals arose from Confucius and Mencius. Ogyū Sorai had located the way and all socio-political norms in the Five (Six) Classics, and required that the olden texts be studied. This necessitated, in turn, that scholars painstakingly learned the ancient language. Ranju considered this to be snobbish elitism that hindered living beings from comprehending the Way. The Way was made for all humankind to act in ways that are socially beneficial and truthful. Thus Ranju did not accept Ogyū Sorai's pessimistic opinion that most people lacked the ability to fathom the norms of the way.

Ranju defended the common man and it was the common man who was educated at the Kaitokudō school. The extravagance of high-flown learning did not fit the programme which had Mencius and Confucius in the centre. Reason and pragmatism demanded simple rules in education.

Ranju was amenable to new knowledge. Osaka was conveniently located between Kyushu and Edo and travelling scholars brought the information and ideas of technological advances East and West. Ranju was in touch with Dutch scholars on their way to and from Nagasaki and, for one thing, curiously noted their command of astronomy. From the 1750s the Kaitokudō became an academy where the study of nature in the Confucian light was increasingly intertwined with new knowledge of Dutch origin. In this accessible atmosphere, scholars with a scientific spirit were welcome. Among them was Asada Gōryū (1734-99), who established a private academy, Senjikan, near the Kaitokudō school, where he studied Western astronomy and medicine.[411] Miura Baien's students Waki Guzan (1764-1814) and Hoashi Banri (1778-1852)[412] attended Ranju's lectures and Miura

Baien himself visited the school. We can imagine that there were many other visiting scholars in the mid-1750s. We can also assume that this traffic continued under Nakai Chikuzan and Nakai Riken. Ranju's unprejudiced search for knowledge was thus one of the routes that led from classical Chinese studies to more extensive natural studies. The Kaitokudō school never embarked upon Dutch studies as such, but, from Ranju, it opened its doors generously to new knowledge. Ranju can be considered an important link in the academic development to a new epistemology in Japan.

Ranju, like Nakatomo, criticized Ogyū Sorai's division of the Way into a Way of Heaven, a Way of Earth and a Way of man. He did not, however, join Nakamoto in reducing the importance of history. No matter how relative he found the historical texts, he never denied their usefulness in education. Ranju believed further in Chu Hsi's Heavenly ri for the same educational reason and accused Ogyū Sorai of having made access to the truth long and arduous. Chu Hsi's Way, based on the Four Confucian Books, was pedagogically simple and easy to convey while Ogyū Sorai's historicism, based on the Early Five (Six) Classics, was convoluted and difficult. Ranju thus defended Chu Hsi's ri-ki thought and Mencius' convictions about human goodness.[413]

14.3 Nakai Chikuzan and Nakai Riken

The brothers Nakai Chikuzan and Nakai Riken followed in the second generation. The Kaitokudō school reached its peak period during their forty-year long leadership. The elder Chikuzan was a balanced thinker who held moderate Neo-Confucian beliefs. He ventured, however, to be critical as he rejected superstition and turned against what was not grounded in actual facts. He was close to Confucius and Mencius and kept away from thinkers who propounded transcendental principles.

Like his teacher Goi, he rejected the historicist ideas advanced by Ogyū Sorai. To Goi's *Hi-Butsu-hen* he added his *Hi-Chō*, a critical review of Ogyū's commentary on Confucius' *Lun Yü*, that is, *Rongo-chō*, in 1785. Ogyū Sorai's faith in the Early Kings, he meant, was not original but drawn from Ming thinkers. He was also disdainful of Itō Jinsai's *kogaku* thought, but was in line with his belief in human (inner) sincerity (*sei*). Chikuzan, thus, held to the Mencian premise that all human beings have an innate potential to know the timeless norms of compassion and truthfulness. It was his optimistic doctrine that a national educational system would foster good manners and benefit the cultural unity of the nation.

His brother Riken was the 'dreamer' who preferred to keep away from official activities and be at a distance from the school. Chuang Tzu was his ideal. He enjoyed his Taoist retreat, his kingdom of 'dreams', immersed in uncovering the 'principles in nature' and pondering Taoist elixirs and the search for immortality. He was only forced back to the Kaitokudō, when Chikusan died, in 1804, to be the successor. He was not as ambitious as his older brother and the school slowly deteriorated under his leadership (1804-17).

After Riken's death in 1818, the Kaitokudō did not display its previous intellectual vigour. Its last great name, and its greatest, was Yamagata Bantō. His epoch-making work, *Yume No Shiro, In Place of Dreams* – a title reminiscent of his linkage with Goi Ranju, Nakai Chikuzan and Nakai Riken – was the crowning glory of the school. It continued to exist through the nineteenth century, was renovated in the 1910s and finally destroyed during the Pacific War. One can discern a continuity in the search of erudition that began with Goi Ranju and reached its climax with Yamagata Bantō, followed by Ogata Kōan and innumerable other scholars until this day. The link between the Kaitokudō and modern discourse should not be forgotten, nor be under-estimated.

14.4 Ogata Kōan and the Tekijuku School

When the Kaitokudō was on the decline in the early nineteenth century, a new school, Tekijuku, was established by Ogata Kōan

(1810-63) in 1838. Ogata had studied Dutch medicine and the Tekijuku became a school of Dutch learning. There students studied medicine, navigation, engineering, chemistry, mathematics and other new fields. Dutch, first, and later English and French, were learned at the school. Symptomatic of a new time, ethical studies came in second place. Little or no mention was made of Confucius and other Chinese philosophers, even though the students were expected to have a prior training in the Chinese language and Confucian ethical doctrines.

As it were, the 'investigation of ri' (*kyūri*), which had been honoured since Sung and Chu Hsi, took a new direction. Knowledge was increasingly acquired in a world without spiritual values. This was something new in the Eastern world – and only a recent phenomenon in the Western world.

By far the most distinguished and well-known alumnus of the Tekijuki school was Fukuzawa Yukichi (1834-1902).[414] This intellectual giant of the following era, who introduced European liberalism to Meiji Japan, had his education with Ogata Kōan. We can therefore follow the scholarly line from Yamagata's scientism to Fukuzawa's modernism and pragmatism – and all-out Western studies.

Fukuzawa can be mentioned as the principal name in this new vogue of epistemology but thereupon the list of scholars professing Western thinking can be made longer than the catalogue of Don Giovanni's conquests.[415]

15. Kokugaku (Nativism) and Confucian Thought

The thin line between Chu Hsi thought and Shinto was witnessed not only on the Confucian side but also on the Shinto side. If Yamazaki Ansai incorporated the *kami* gods in his *suika-shinto* creed, Kada no Azumamaro (1669-1736) drew upon the whole (Neo-)Confucian tradition when he formulated his Confucian-Shinto syncretism. It contains the Five Elements, the yin and yang, the ki and ri, reconciled with the cosmogonic myths of the *Kojiki* and *Nihongi*. Among them, the ki figures prominently. It fills Heaven, where it is non-material, and congeals on earth to form all things. In the Heavenly realm it is quiescent, while it is active, moving, and changing constantly in the material realm. Human nature is a mixture of good and bad elements, and in man's mind the Confucian ki and Shinto's *kami* are united. The mind (*kokoro*) rules over the body and depending on his ki endowment, man is able to distinguish between good and evil, right and wrong.

With his eclectic Confucian-Shinto thought, Kada no Azumamaro differed from Kamo no Mabuchi (1697-1769), Motoori Norinaga (1730-1801) and other nativists who became increasingly anti-Chinese. They denounced the *karagokoro*, 'the Chinese heart', and rejecting the Confucian way, they turned to the unblemished 'True Heart' (*magokoro*) of Shinto. Anthropomorphic *kami* gods became the heavenly ri of Japan, and all things occurred at their behest.[416] The nativist ki-ism ended up in a classicism (based on the *Kojiki* and *Nihongi*) and a religious doctrine which Chinese thought just cosmeticized with ethical terms and admonitions.[417]

In a sense, *kokugaku* began with Hayashi Razan, who abandoned Buddhism and idealized the teachings of early Shinto. After him it became the fashion for Confucian thinkers to criticize and discard Buddhist thought while they increasingly placed Shinto thought side by side with the (Neo-)Confucian credo. This is clearly demonstrated also in the writings of later philosophers, for example, in Yamagata Bantō's *Yume No Shiro*. This work palpably exhibits a Confucian stance while Buddhism is severely criticized. The *kokugaku* fundamentalists went farther, denouncing Confucianism alongside Buddhism. The Confucian ri was exchanged for Shinto *kami* and morality obtained an indigenous character.

One can go farther yet and say that while Confucian thinkers made attempts to demythologize religion and undo superstitious practices, the Nativist scholars went the other way and resacralized the olden myths and customs in a *kokugaku* synthesis, introducing a religious mysticism that would incite following generations. The most important scholar in this development was Motoori Norinaga who shaped the mystic discourse which exalted the sacred uniqueness of everything in the land, language, trees and mountains, glorifying the hylozoism of all creation. His revulsion *vis-à-vis* China and Confucianism intensified as he worked on the *Kojiki* for more than thirty years.[418] Hirata Atsutane (1776-1843) and others thereupon exhibited religious bigotry with their *tenshu* (emperor) monotheism.[419]

16. The Mito Thought

Close to the *kokugaku* was the Mito philosophy. It was also nationalist and patriotic, but perhaps more political than numinous in tone. It originated in the Mito domain, where the lord, Tokugawa Mitsukuni (1628-1700), Ieyasu's grandson, conceived the project of writing a new history of Japan on the model of Ssu-ma Ch'ien's *Shih Chi, Records of the Historian*. The work was begun in 1657, but was interrupted by 1740, and, begun again by 1804, was not finished until in the early twentieth century (see above). The inspiration came not only from Chu Hsi and China but also from Mitsukuni's feeling of loyalty to the emperor and imperial history. A Chinese refugee, Chu Shun-shui (Jpn. Shu Shunsui, 1600-82), participated in the project as did scholars from the Kimon school. During the early stage of the project, until 1740, the balance was kept and the bakufu did not feel threatened, but the second stage after 1800 with a new political and intellectual atmosphere, the weakening bakufu and *kokugaku* thought, created tensions and conflicts between Mito and Edo. Now the *kokutai* mystique as regards the divine spirit of the land of Japan was added to the equation.

The ethos inspired by the Chinese model altered under Fujita Yūkoku (1773-1826) when the national thought became as strident and patriotic as in the *kokugaku* movement. Fujita wrote, for example, that 'there has never yet been a land comparable to ours in the eternity of the Imperial line' and that 'majestic Japan, from the time the land was founded by its Imperial ancestors, with Heaven as their father and Earth as their Mother, ... have ruled all within the four seas in splendour'. The encroachments of the West were also keenly felt and a new aggressive attitude demanded that defences should be built and the foreigners be repulsed. Another Mito scholar, Aizawa Yasushi (Seishisai) (1782-1863) developed the *kokutai* line further, 'regarding the Japanese people as one great family of a particular and distinctive nature, whose emperor was father as well as lord'. His *Shinron*, written in 1825, was the pinnacle of the later Mito movement and was read widely. Fujita Tōko, Yukoku's son (1806-55), was the third and last great person in the new Mito movement. He espoused the central aim of the *kokutai* nationalism, that is, the return of power to the emperor. The Way of Confucius was identified with the Way of the Gods. Together, they developed the Way of the

Japanese, under Amaterasu, and the selfless devotion to the nation in the form of pure loyalty to the imperial house.[420] Irrationalism won over rationalism, Amaterasu over Chu Hsi.[421]

17. Rational Thought

If irrationalism gained in strength in *kokugaku* nativism and Mito nationalism, *shushigaku* displayed rationalism in propagating the investigation of things. The general Chu Hsi tendency was to inveigh against superstition while fostering its own ri-ki metaphysics.

It did not take long for Japanese thinkers to jolt the harmony of the Chinese Neo-Confucian structure questioning the neatness of the ri-ki equipoise and to move deeper into exterior examination. It probably began with Kaibara Ekken, whose studies evinced that the outer reality was richer than presented in the Sung symmetrical doctrine. His study of nature was a beginning of empirical learning. Utilitarian thought took new steps forward with the kogaku scholars, especially Ogyū Sorai, for whom social institutions, laws and customs became human inventions. From the 1720s, knowledge widened through Dutch studies. At first, these studies were modest and only concerned useful subjects such as astronomy, medicine and weaponry, not dealt with by Confucian philosophers. A crescendo took place, however, through the late eighteenth century and in the first half of the nineteenth century Dutch studies turned to ever new fields. At the Kangien school at Ōita, founded in 1817, the curriculum included mathematics, anatomy, medicine, astronomy, geography, physics, botany, geology, art and other recent advances in European learning –

and etiquette. What came first a century earlier in the Kaitokudō school is mentioned last!⁴²² These studies became a flood after 1853 when they became a source of learning for all Japanese and under the name of *yōgaku*, Western studies.

To sum up, the tendency among principal Confucian thinkers was, under Chinese encouragement, to leave ri-ki idealistic dualism and turn to ki-ri realistic monism. They moved, as it were, from Plato's world of ideal forms to Aristotle's world of entelecheia (entelechy), from ideas above to life within things. 'There is no doubt that Ogyū Sorai played an important role in the process of de-mystification of the Neo-Confucian system.' This is Katō Shūichi's judgement of this development.⁴²³ He ignores the fact that there were similar developments in China and that also other Japanese thinkers had advocated a return to pre-Chu Hsi thought. Be that as it may, 'a monistic ontology that recognized only a physical dimension' was acknowledged.⁴²⁴

17.1 Andō Shōeki

Among thinkers in the early eighteenth century who put emphasis on ki was Andō Shōeki (1703?-62?) who saw nature (*shizen*) as the 'advance and retreat of the One Ki' (*ikki no shintai*).⁴²⁵ Ki advances (*shinki*) and ki retreats (*taiki*) in an eternal circular perpetuum mobile.⁴²⁶ All dualism is rejected and kami and Buddha are only cultural creations, as also ethics. Heaven and Earth are a composite term for nature, and the ki encompasses the life-force in its wholeness. Nishikawa Fumio has in his article, *Andō Shōeki ni okeru shizen no gainen, The Concept of Nature in Andō Shōen*, demonstrated how Andō Shōeki was close to Schelling in European nineteenth-century naturalism, while Jacques Joly in his *Le Naturel selon Andō Shōeki* has shown that he was close to the original Taoist thought in China.

He proved his originality when he exposed all thought systems, not least Confucianism, as schemes to rob the world, above all the peasants. Worst of all were the sage kings who cheated the people with the sacrosanct Way! He denounced scholars as a group, and further 'priests, physicians, samurai, prevailing creeds and the ruling order itself'. The only people who deserved respect were those who tilled the soil: 'Peasants who engage in direct cultivation and weaving, clothe and feed themselves happily are free of avarice and disorder and are the real children of nature.'[427] He was the first (and perhaps only) scholar who opposed the hierarchical Tokugawa social order – not even Tominaga Nakamoto went so far – and he got away with it probably because he lived anonymously and was not known in Edo.[428] Most other scholars, for example Ogyū Sorai, were staunch defenders of the hierarchical society.

Living among common people in the north, he developed the Utopian and egalitarian idealism which he expressed with words such as: 'In the way of nature, there is no superior and inferior ... no division between one and another.' Only selfish 'fabrications' (koshiraegoto) had created distinctions between high and low (jōge bunken) and abstract concepts that espoused the rigid class hierarchies – and justified poverty among the populace.[429] His ideal human society meant a community coexisting with nature and not poisoned by man-made 'civilization'.

17.2 Yamagata Daini (1725-67)

Another singular scholar in the mid-eighteenth century was Yamagata Daini.[430] He was, in the beginning, motivated by Itō Jinsai and Ogyū Sorai and like them he saw the operations of Heaven and Earth as an interplay of ki forces. Secondly, he was exposed to Kimon thought through Miyake Shōsai and Takeuchi Shikibu. Thirdly, his interest in national history led him to loyalism and Takeuchi Shikibu (1713-67), who advocated 'imperial restoration'. Together they became forerunners of the sonnō, 'Restoration of the Emperor', movement.

His loyalism and his thought generally were presented in his Ryū-shi Shinron, Ryūshi's New Doctrine (1759) (Ryūshi = Yamagata Daini). This was the first work that openly advocated the sonnōron, 'The Doctrine of Restoring the Emperor to Power'. Daini came to Edo as a rōnin about 1752 and opened a school. More than a thousand students are said to have studied with him between 1759 and 1767. Basing himself on Confucius, he expressed the idea that the emperor had been disavowed by the military shogunate and turning to Shinto, he espoused the *kokugaku* creed.

In his teaching, as a result, he advocated the restoration of imperial power. This was reported to the the authorities who concluded that he was plotting the overthrow of the bakufu. They reacted harshly. They had reason to be nervous, because loyalist thought began to be prevalent in the mid-eighteenth century. Ogyū Sorai had warned against a latent *sonnō* tendency already in the *Seidan* (1727) and now the authorities were faced with it openly in Daini's writing and teaching. This led to the Meiwa Incident and Daini's execution in 1767. Takeuchi Shikibu (1713-67) died on his way to deportation on Hachijōjima in the same year.

17.3 Miura Baien (1723-89)

Tokugawa *ki* thought perhaps reached its final and finest expression in Miura Baien's *Genkiron, On Primal Ki* and *Gengo, Mysterious Words*. In the *Gengo* – he rewrote the work no less than 23 times over a twenty-year period – ki is the supreme One Primal ki residing above as well as in things, equal to Heaven and Earth. The ki is diffused through yin-yang operations to become all things and all bodies. It is the ocean and totality of wholeness, it forms one body with Heaven and Earth and all things (*mono*) and in all life it is spirit (*kami*). Things are amalgams of *mono* and *kami*. With an often complex terminology, Miura registers symmetries of contrasting binary opposites in a union, germane to Heaven-Earth and yin-yang duality, ending up in the myriad forms of the world. All forces are ki, active or passive, waxing or waning, in dynamic flux or in static stillness, in becoming or in being. Above is the ki of Heaven, and below is the ki of Earth,

the ki of yin and the ki of yang, in *jōri* lines and patterns, in sets
of two. As Baien says: 'If one thinks carefully, it is obvious that ki,
or energy, fills up everything: the Earth with real-body-forms as
well as Heaven which is void of body and form, leaving no space
that is not penetrated by it. All things follow their ri textures
(*jōri*).'[431] 'We have again the 'ri-ki' harmony of things – but in a
new dinner jacket.'[432] This ki is Miura's Heaven in the upper
sphere while it exists antithetically in the lower sphere, acting
through yin and yang in expansion and dispersion, descending or
ascending – 'without beginning, without end' (*mushi-mushū*). In
summary, Miura presents a ki monism, comprising both Heaven
and Earth. This is, in one sense, a Taoist monism which has its
beginning in the One Primordial Energy (*ichi-genki*) and the
original Explosion – not unlike the Big Bang in recent scientific
theory.

Baien wrote that: 'at the age of thirty I recognized that Heaven
and Earth are ki; further, that Heaven and Earth possess *jōri*'.[433]
Thereupon he spent the rest of his life conveying this *jōrigaku*,
'learning of *jōri*', to others. In the illumination of his mind he saw
the oneness of the world, a oneness that was summarized by the
two-letter word ki. This primal ki takes shape in *jōri*
configurations.[434] On first sight, it appears difficult to differentiate
between his *jōrigaku* and Chu Hsi's *ri-ki-gaku*. On deeper
reflection, however, the difference might be that Miura reflects
the Tokugawa atmosphere of outer realism, while Chu Hsi's *ri-ki-
gaku* mirrors the Sung inner idealism. Miura is close to Itō Jinsai,
when he proclaims a monistic *ichi-genki*, 'one original ki' of
Heaven and Earth, but some inspiration might also have derived
from the West. In the work *Kagen* he writes:

> The study of astronomy and geography are coarsest among
> Buddhists, finer among the Chinese but they speculate and
> grope and know little of experimental verification. The
> Westerners make instruments and use them in ships; there
> are no lands on which they have not set foot. Thus they
> look at Heaven and Earth as at the backs of their hands.
> This is indeed a great joy of a thousand years. The Western

doctors show the same exactness . . . .

Thus he recognized the Western superiority in science and deplored that Chinese learning has stifled in age-long stereotypes. 'Westerners discover and measure and their experimentations become more and more clear', he says. Baien rejected the thought of the 'Five Elements' and doubted the existence of ghosts and spirits (*kishin*). He was either prompted by Nakai Chikuzan and Nakai Riken – or he prompted them; together, however, they motivated Yamagata Bantō and then Fukuzawa Yukichi.

Baien turned, thus, sceptical *vis-à-vis* a great deal of philosophical thought in the eighteenth century. He was, however, close to Kaibara Ekken's jōri-ism as presented in the *Taigi-roku* and aroused by the new learning brought by the Dutch. As early as 1745, at twenty-two years of age, he went to Nagasaki and learned about Western mathematics and astronomy and even acquired some knowledge of the Dutch language. Visiting Nagasaki again in 1778, he is said to have learned about the Copernican heliocentric theory.[435] Later, he also visited the Kaitokudō school in Osaka where he took an interest in the new knowledge emanating from Nagasaki.[436]

He learned to doubt and question things – also Westerners. He expressed the belief that Westerners should be kept out of Japan. He acknowledged their knowledge of material things, for example, astronomy – but 'there is nothing more to it than that'.[437] One wonders whether Yamagata Bantō had read what Miura Baien recommended in 1777[438] when he devoted the first chapter of the *Yume No Shiro* to just astronomy and made it the basis of the entire work. It remains to be added that Miura Baien, like Arai Hakuseki, was not impressed with Westerners' lack of understanding of the Way of Heaven!

Learning beyond *jōri* dialectics was unbecoming for a ki-ist philosopher like Miura Baien and left to 'practical' people. His study was the search for macrocosmic-microcosmic symmetries in the world. When he used a term like *hankan-gōitsu*, the 'oneness of opposite aspects' or 'synthesis of contraries', he expressed in

Hegelian terms how the balance works in dialectical manner. The human body is a case in point. It exemplifies the 'oneness of spirit and material matter' (dōitsu shinbutsu). This is 'viewing antithetical things in their synthetic unity'. The jōrigaku is rendered as 'study of dialectical logic' by G. K. Piovesana.[439] It is the creative operation, witnessed in its totality of successive manifestations of complementarities.[440]

He searched for the intrinsic harmony also in the political economy, and here the goal was the balance of resources and needs. Living as a doctor in a small community on Kyushu, he had first-hand insight into people's conditions which made him turn to making recommendations about the organisation of society.

Of interest is the warp and woof metaphor in his letter to Taga Bokkyō (1733-85).[441] The universe is a cloth of warp and woof with ki energy coming and going. As he says:

> After grasping the great warp and woof, we should come to understand that Heaven and Earth and all things are woven together similarly. . . . What operates endlessly is time and warp. . . . It is the route of all things. What fills up and envelops everything is space and woof. . . . It becomes the abode for all things. . . . Heaven and Earth take their respective places in the all-enveloping endless space, and with these, East and West, up and down, are determined. Consequently, with warp and woof understood as the origin, cannot we know about the warp and woof of small things? Certainly they are not woven by man, but they follow the law of nature. . . . For Heaven and Earth are the great organism and their creative energy keeps generating . . . and changing into endless variety of forms and features. The most complex comes into being from the most simple. . . . All things are woven together by warp and woof.[442]
>
> The best we can do is to start with small things and consider them and thereupon try to know the warp and woof of great things. After coming to grips with the great warp and woof, we should come to understand that Heaven and Earth and all things are woven together by warp and woof. To know directly what this universe is, we

should first perceive its warp and woof of Heaven and Earth and of fire and water.[443]

Miura used another image to describe the ki totality. The straight line coincides with the warp and the circle with the woof. The agent is the the ki energy. His entire ideology is comprised in the following poem:

A straight line, a circle, a warp, a woof.
Man, making things, has to tuck in
the material along the primordial ki.

(*itchoku-ichien-ikkei-ichii, jinzō shi ari, kore wo genki ni oru*).

This is close to Taoist thought. Everything has its balancing opposite. 'The arrow can fly leftwards only when the bowstring has been drawn far back rightwards.' 'The tree-trunk has roots below and branches above. The roots gradually divide into more roots, and the branches into more branches.' Throughout Miura's writings these doubles can be enumerated. They are coloured by his original revelation – all having its origin in Heaven and Earth and yin and yang, which 'contrast and oppose one another and, by opposition, combine in one'. Baien's correlative cosmological perspective forces everything to have a double – if needs be on a Procrustean bed.[444]

The full acceptance of the Western approach to learning, when only the parts of the whole are searched for, had to wait for another generation of scholars. As R. Mercer ends:

It is my conclusion that his (Baien's) philosophy is not, as is commonly said, to be judged as the prenatal stirring of the concepts of modern science, rather it should be interpreted as the highest culmination of late Confucian style natural philosophy.

She says later:

I am firmly convinced that Baien's philosophy belongs in the stream of philosophy of ki.[445]

This is Mercer's last word, and she appears right.

18. The *Rangaku* Scholars

In the Tokugawa period scholars turned more and more from moral philosophy to new knowledge about this world. This is already evinced in Kaibara Ekken's botanic studies, and Arai Hakuseki's interest in geography and numerous mundane subjects. This inclination gained in strength and was much stirred by the rangaku studies. It took Arai Hakuseki no time to understand that there was much to learn from Western scholarship while there was nothing to fear from a divided Europe. Therefore, beginning with him, not least inspired by what he had learned from Sidotti, a new interest was taken in Western scholarship from about 1720. Shogun Yoshimune, understanding the need for new knowledge, allowed Western books in Chinese dealing with astronomy, geography, medicine, weaponry, shipbuilding, food, clockwork and other fields. This was to develop into the rangaku studies later in the eighteenth century. Social utility and plain inquisitiveness came thereafter increasingly to require the recognition of Western thought until, with a scholar like Yamagata Bantō (1748-1821), it was the West that came gradually to be the centre of interest. Over the eighteenth century an intellectual revolution took place from the beginning with Arai Hakuseki to the acceptance of Western learning as witnessed in Yamagata Bantō's *Yume No Shiro* which combined utilitarian thinking with the *jōri* inscapes in things rather than the ri patterns beyond things, as it were, moving from virtue to true science. What a world of difference over a few decades!

The beneficence of Western medicine captured the curiosity of entrepreneurial physicians after 1770. Sugita Genpaku (1733-1817) is representative of these pioneering scholars who turned to 'Dutch studies'; that is, to studies with little heavenly reference. No vision of the absolute was needed, only a pure search for knowledge, as in Europe. Now the truth was no longer looked for in China, but in Europe, and forward-thinking scholars undertook to learn Dutch. The language studies came first. Already Arai Hakuseki had a list of 340 Dutch words. Early studies of Dutch were undertaken officially by Aoki Kon'yō (1698-1769) and Noro Genjō (1693-1761) in the 1740s.

The studies were originally directed to medicine, just like in the preceding nanbangaku[446] studies. Now it was not Portuguese but Dutch that had to be mastered. Painstaking language studies preceded the translation of the Dutch work on human anatomy, Anatomische Tabellen, which in Japanese received the title Kaitai Shinsho, New Work on Anatomy (1774).[447] Sugita Genpaku was one of the translators; Maeno Ryōtaku (1723-1803) and others worked together with him. Ōtsuki Gentaku (1757-1827) revised the work and had it reprinted in 1826. The Kaitai Shinsho was not the first work in the rangaku literature, but it was a breakthrough and marked the definite beginning of a new epoch of Japanese learning and of a rich literature dealing first of all with medicine but also with other fields, such as physics and botany. A list by M. Sugimoto and D. L. Swain presents some twenty-seven titles of translations and almost as many translators covering the period between 1773 and the 1850s.[448]

The Kansei Prohibition of Heterodox Studies (Kansei igaku no kin) in 1790 could only slow down this development but not suppress it. Confucian scholars who were hostile to the influx of Western learning and saw the danger of the new ideas to the Confucian ethos, could not hinder the spread of the new thought. The same had happened earlier in Europe where the conservative church had resisted the new erudition that undermined its power.

Sugita Genpaku was only one of the innovators of the new studies which would become fully-fledged Westernization in the nineteenth century.[449] A scholar who stood in both worlds, on the one side, in the old wisdom and, on the other, in rangaku learning, was Hiraga Gennai (1728-79). He went to Nagasaki in 1752 and learned about Western botany and pharmacology and thereupon to Edo in 1756 for studies in the Hayashi school and the study of herbal medicine. He made inventions, learned Dutch pottery, and even produced an electric motor. He also wrote fiction and drama – and ended a turbulent life by dying in prison. He was a true pioneer in a time when old values and institutions interwove with new ideas of utility and economic practicality. One can understand that the authorities were disturbed and wished to keep the monolithic system intact within an unchanging, Confucian framework. One early scholar, Hayashi Shihei (1738-93), was imprisoned when he turned to military matters and wrote the *Kaikoku Heidan, Discussion about the Defence of a Sea Nation*, in 1786.

19. The Confucian Schools in the Late Tokugawa Era

There were thousands who sided with the Chu Hsi orthodoxy throughout the Tokugawa era. Statistics illustrate that there were about 2000 students in the Chu Hsi schools, about 300 in the Ansai school and less than 200 in the Ogyū Sorai school in the early eighteenth century. The school system expanded rapidly in the second half of the Tokugawa era, when the great majority of the domains established schools.[450] These schools manifested no coherent pattern but, whether official or private, had Chinese learning as the necessary basis. The whole samurai class and common people, too, became literate and acquired the Confucian moral attitudes.

Because education became a routine matter, originality was rare and the names of both teachers and students have mostly fallen into oblivion. Those who broke with orthodoxy are, however, often noted in the annals. Among the private schools, the one mentioned most often was the Kimon School, because it brandished Yamazaki Ansai's belligerant spirit, attacking vehemently other schools and scholars.[451] It is of interest that it prospered with a great number of students a century after the death of the founder.

The School or Academy that was set up by the fifth shogun, Tsunayoshi (r.1680-1709), in 1691, the Shōheikō, 'The School of Prosperous Peace', became the bulwark of Neo-Confucian Chu Hsi orthodoxy. Hayashi Razan's grandson Hōkō (1644-1732) became the first rector of the school with the title *daigaku no kami* and was the eldest among ten Hayashi generations to head the school. As encouraged by Tsunayoshi it was the main centre of orthodox Confucian learning throughout the Tokugawa period.[452] It has been observed, however, that it fell into institutional conservatism by the nineteenth century. This might be true, but the fact is that it held a central role in education until the end of Tokugawa. Furthermore, scholars whether to the left or the right of the orthodoxy, were in the last analysis originally and primarily schooled in the orthodoxy of (Neo-) Confucianism. Most scholars remained also in the mainstream of Chu Hsi thought. Until the Meiji era (1868-1912) it took courage to change horses and turn to 'modern' studies.[453]

Towards the end of the eighteenth century the Neo-Confucian schools were challenged by the *kogaku* and eclectic schools. The eclectic scholars especially increased in number, and Hirose Tansō could note that 'out of ten scholars seven or eight belonged to the Eclectic School'.[454] These scholars dominated thirty-seven of the existing ninety-three domain schools. The eclectic schools did not always concentrate on moral education to the same extent as the Neo-Confucian schools. Heterodoxy was rampant and 'correct' learning (*seigaku*) vanished. Kameda Bōsai's eclectic school is said to have been attended by one thousand *hatamoto* disciples. This made the authorities anxious and a reaction was inevitable. Orthodox Chu Hsi Schools were established in Osaka,

Hiroshima and Saga between 1764 and 1781. In these schools any thought that was considered heteredox was rejected, including Ogyū Sorai, the eclectics and Yōmeigaku. The reason was later well formulated by Matsudaira Sadanobu (1758-1829):

> In Neo-Confucianism there are few things that one can doubt. Now, however, there are dozens of ideas – cartloads of them – and dozens of scholars abusing each other. Someone had to unify this. These scholars are like the bubbles of boiling water or the entangled strands of threads. Someone had to support scholarship. . . . In this, Ieyasu showed us the example by appointing Hayashi Razan, whose teachings, in contrast to all other theories, have not changed over the years.[455]

This was the political reason for the reform to come. The Chu Hsi creed stood for permanence and stability since Tokugawa Iesyasu's days. It should be saved – in its purity. In 1790, Matsudaira Sadanobu, head of the Council of Elders, issued an edict known as the Kansei Prohibition of Heterodox Studies (*Kansei igaku no kin*). This edict called upon Hayashi Kinpō (1733-92), the fifth rector of the Shōheikō, to reinforce Neo-Confucian teachings and to curb 'subversive doctrines'. The following sixth rector of the Shōheikō School, Hayashi Jussai, was thereupon functioning when heterodox studies were banned at domain schools (1795). Primarily the *kogaku* studies propounded by Ogyū Sorai and Itō Jinsai and the studies identified with the Yōmeigaku were targeted. It was an attempt to bring the intellectual world back to Chu Hsi and Confucius – and to the good days of Ieyasu. It should be ri-ki studies as begun by Hayashi Razan and continued by his school. At the same time, the Shōheikō school was rebuilt and reorganized. The reform aimed at revitalizing Neo-Confucian studies and strengthening popular education.[456] A primary scholar in the renovation was Satō Issai (1772-1859), a famous Confucian scholar of the era. Others were Bitō Nishū (1745-1813), Koga Seiri (1750-1817) and Shibano Ritsuzan (1736-1807). Two others were Okada Kanzen (1740-1816), who came from the Kimon School, and Nishiyama Sessai (1735-98), who originated from *kogaku* studies.

Thus, *rikigaku* won and Neo-Confucian thought remained the official creed until the end of the Tokugawa era. Virtually all scholars mentioned in the last century of Tokugawa rule belonged to the Chu Hsi school. When they deviated, they turned mostly to *rangaku* studies.

19.1 Matsudaira Sadanobu

Matsudaira Sadanobu was the true Neo-Confucian believer who recognized a Confucianism combined with martial arts. The school professed by him was the *Shinbu no michi*, 'The Way of Psychic and Martial Power', established by Suzuki Kunitaka (1722-90), a *jūjutsu* master. The martial arts were combined with a philosophy that sounds like a Chu Hsi primer. In this learning, man is conceived as a microcosm of Heaven and Earth (*shōtenchi*), filled with holy ki (*shinki*). Nature's macro-ki and man's micro-ki are identical. Where the celestial ki gathers, there is yang, and where the Earthly ki assembles there is yin. Man is the child of Heaven; and man and Heaven are one ri (*tenjin ichiri*). Man is however also the child of the terrestrial world and hampered by his animal nature which harbours the seven desires. Being responsible for the maintenance of the central harmony between Heaven and Earth, however, he must discipline his Earthly nature. All evil can be overcome, and the Shinbu no michi provided Sadanobu with the criteria for the pursuit of fulfilment and self-perfection. The military training aimed at easing the flow of the ki by means of bodily posture. Just as in Mencian thought, man's nature is essentially good. Man is originally not different from the sages and he should strive to attain sagehood. Heavenly virtue (*meitoku*) issues from Heaven and man's ethical task consists in sustaining this pristine virtue.

It became for him both a philosophy of life and a religion. In his later fifties, after some thirty years of inner cultivation, he felt that he had achieved his spiritual perfection – and was so convinced that he performed a rite to his deified self.[457] Sadanobu is an interesting case of a Neo-Confucian believer's way to self-realization and sagehood, and it is of special interest that he himself accounted for his progress in a Religious Record (*Shugyō-roku*). This record evinces that he attempted to live a Neo-Confucian life of simplicity and tranquillity, part of which was the rejection of all luxury in private life.[458]

19.2 Satō Issai (1772-1859)

Satō Issai was one of Hayashi Jussai's disciples who is worth special mention. Outwardly he professed to be a Neo-Confucian scholar, but in his *Genshi Shiroku* he is close to the *Lu-Wang* school. Like Nakae Tōju, he found the Heavenly ri contained in the kokoro to be the judge of right and wrong. He was thus, in the end, one of the exponents of the subjective side of Sung Confucianism, also referred to as *yuishinron*, 'only *kokoro* doctrine'. In his *Genshi Shiroku*[459] he fatalistically propounded that all life and death are pre-ordained.

His thought developed later in a Chu Hsi direction, perhaps motivated by the Prohibition of Heterodox Studies. He was an important scholar at the end of the eighteenth century and during the first half of the nineteenth century. He taught Chu Hsi at the Shōheikō but at his own private school he rather lectured on the Yōmeigaku idealism and subjectivism. It was said that he was 'Chu [Hsi] on the outside and Lu [Hsiang-shan] on the inside'. He is, thus, remembered for both his – private – Yōmeigaku and his – official – Chu Hsi devotion.[460] In his ri-ki thought he was clearly on the Chu Hsi side, as expressed in the *Genshi Shiroku*.

Reflecting the epoque, he was well aware of the new learning in his time and was critical of the materialism that it represented. He said:

> The ultimate truths of the West are the mathematical principles of the material world, while the truths of the *I Ching* are the principles of the metaphysical world. Take these principles, for example, as the root and trunk [of a tree], and take the mathematical principles as the branches, and leaves will follow. Ultimate truths should be derived from the principles of the *I Ching*.[461]

19.3 Bitō Nishū

Bitō Nishū was another leading Chu Hsi scholar at the time of the Prohibition of Heterodox Studies. He began as a student of kogaku but then turned to Chu Hsi under the guidance of, among others, the writings of Muro Kyūsō. He had already in 1772 written about the need to unify intellectuality and scholarship around Neo-Confucianism.

In the maturity of his thought he interpreted the relationship between ri and ki in this clear fashion:

> Fathers and sons are ki. Love on the part of the father and filial piety on the part of the lord and respect on the part of the vassal are ri. By inference we find that among all the myriad affairs and things there is not one which is not like that. If we were to discard filial piety, parental love and human respect and say that fathers and sons, lords and vassals are identical with the Way, would that really be acceptable? All that which has form and appearance – such as Heaven and Earth, yin and yang, wind and rain, cold and heat – is ki. Because they are ki, they have ri. The fact is that ki has form and appearance and is therefore easy to know. Ri, on the other hand, has neither sound nor smell and is therefore hard to put into words. For that reason the mass of men know what fathers and sons, lords and vassals are, but do not know what the Way of father and son, lord and vassal is; they know what Heaven and Earth and yin and yang are, but do not know the Way of Heaven and Earth and the Way of yin and yang.[462]

The list can be expanded to many other scholars in the late eighteenth century who belonged to the circle of orthodox Chu Hsi Confucianists, and who learned from each other and broadened their horizons with wide-ranging studies. Another among them was Matsumiya Kanzan (1686-1780) who combined Confucian education with military studies (heigaku), kokugaku studies and waka poetry.

19.4 Ōhashi Junzō (1816-62)

Satō Issai was not the only one to deplore the invasion of Western ideas. Another was Ōhashi Junzō who was one of the major Chu Hsi *rigaku* thinkers in the early nineteenth century and a staunch adversary of the opening of the country to foreigners. He fought against the increasing inflow of Western knowledge, which he correctly found to undermine the Confucian cosmology. He wrote in the *Hekija Shōgen, Short Words about Heterodoxy*[463] as late as in 1857:

> Followers of the Western learning steal the illustrious designation and call themselves natural philosophers, shamelessly saying that the West knows the laws of the universe.... True disciples of Confucius and Mencius should raise their banner, and destroy these false scholars, that they may get their just reward from the spirits of the former sages dwelling in Heaven.... Fire and water are ki; and their burning and flowing too are ki. But that water being water flows and does not burn, and that fire being fire burns and does not move, that such is the decreed nature of the two, this is their ri.... The adherents of the Western learning indeed study carefully the outward appearances, but have no right to steal the honoured name of natural philosophy. As when ki is destroyed, ri too disappears, so with their analysis of ki, they destroy ri and thus their learning brings benevolence, righteousness, trust and truth to naught.... The foreigners are like brutes. Not reverent of Heaven and ignorant of the purpose of the sages, they follow the custom of their land and study all the details, measure distances, observe the stars and make astronomy a toy.... Lights, comets and shooting stars are ordinary things and not the reproofs of Heaven to the Westerners, who will not stand in awe of them.
>
> ... Medicine in the barbarous countries of the West considers the dissection of the human entrails to be of the vital importance. This suffices to depict what brutal customs prevail there! ...
>
> ... Such is the learning of the West. It knows only ki and deals with what is perceptible. Analysis and the

microscope increase its minuteness but display no ri. . . . It can never learn that the egg enfolds an immutable ri, be its microscope ever so powerful. . . . The West knows not the ri of the virtues of the heart which are in all men unchangeably the same and it knows not benevolence and righteousness. . . . It studies only what comes into view and takes Heaven for a dead unmoving thing. . . . Heaven and man are of the same ri. . . . There is one ri in all the universe, one lord and ruler, the great parent of us all, called Heaven. '. . . The West thinks Heaven a dead thing not connected with portents. . . . When the rulers are virtueless and the ruled lawless, then Heaven and Earth feel their wickedness, . . . then come the Northern lights, comets, thunder in winter, snow in summer, earthquakes and famines. . . . When signs appear let us examine with all care. . . . Calamities and portents are for our sins and crimes. . . To separate man and Heaven and to cease to fear the signs, what folly is this! What blindness! . . . When an eclipse occurs, he who reverences Heaven beats a drum, makes his offering, fasts, stops all music as did the sages in pristine days, but nowadays all say that eclipses are ordinary things, not to be feared. . . The evil comes from measuring Heaven and not knowing its heart. . . '[464]

Ōhashi Junsō found that the Christian Bible, as he wrote in a letter, was 'shallow, narrow, mysterious and false' and that it lacked the Oriental reverence for Heaven.

This was in the limbo period between the Tokugawa and Meiji eras. Ōhashi Junsō bears witness that the orthodox Chu Hsi Neo-Confucian thought remained the dominant intellectual and philosophical discourse to the very end of the Tokugawa era. The 'one-dimensional' rationalism was not enough for scholars who had their roots in the complexity of Confucian metaphysics which included comets and shooting stars. They were not ready to leave the grand design of the cosmos and nature inherited from Sung scholars for ungodly scientism. As Ōhashi says, echoing Neo-Confucian thought, the universe is ki, the human body is ki, and ri is the heavenly tao and law that rule both universe and body. One is reminded of the saying in the *I Li*: 'To know the mother (ki) and not the father (ri) that is the way of the beasts!' To be fair, however, it must be added that Christianity always had a Heaven and a Heavenly Father above things.

20. Yamagata Bantō

A special position among the late Confucian scholars is held by Yamagata Bantō. He represents both an end and a beginning. With him the old Confucian thinking finishes and a new intellectual age starts. He stands with one leg in the age-long heritage originating in China and with the other in the learning springing from the West, indicating the way into the age to come, as it were, Janus-faced while solidly on national soil.

Yamagata Bantō was born in the Osaka area and was a student at the Kaitokudō school, where he was taught by the brothers Nakai Chikuzan and Nakai Riken. He combined study with business activities but luckily did not allow business to disrupt his scholarship. Under the encouragement of, among others, the Nakai brothers, he compiled his masterpiece, *Yume No Shiro, In Place of Dreams*, which remains one of the great works in Japanese intellectual history. It was submitted to Nakai Chikuzan in 1804. Weakened with age, Chikuzan handed it over to his brother Riken, who criticized the work, asking Bantō to rework and retitle it. It was completed between 1805 and 1807, but there might have been revisions until his death 1821. It is a massive work, consisting of twelve chapters and comprising 472 pages in a modern edition.[465] One is impressed with the wide reading and studies which preceded the undertaking. He must have had a huge library at his disposal, for example, at the Kaitokudō school.

He himself deplored that time did not allow him to polish the work. However, it is perhaps better to have it in unpolished form. If he had had time to edit it, it might have lost a great deal of the directness and lustre that it evinces today. In its totality it is a gold mine for anyone who wants to survey the intellectual situation in Japan at its Tokugawa maturity around 1800 before the full impact of the West later in the same century.

Bantō was fundamentally a Neo-Confucian scholar, who revered the Way of the sages, Chu Hsi and the ethical kyūri Way to wisdom. He never refuted the Neo-Confucian vision of the world, of nature and of man; he only wanted it to be decoded in the light of new knowledge. This approach was combined with *rangaku* studies. He was taught astronomy through Asada Gōryū. Under *rangaku* influence he imposed categories of scholarship arranged from the universal to the particular. All knowledge must be tested with reference to the all-inclusive science, this being astronomy. All other fields were in one way or another correlative, whether geography, history, economy and so on. He proved himself a sceptic with 'a distinctive materialistic world view'.[466]

A new universe had appeared with the *rangaku* studies. The telescope and the microscope had arrived, the theory of gravity had been introduced, and the Earth been found to revolve around the Sun. If the new learning from Dutch sources was recognized, the errors of the past could be corrected. Yamagata was well acquainted with primary European scholars in the astronomical and other fields. He refers to Nicolaus Copernicus (1473-1543), Tycho Brahe (1546-1601), Isaac Newton (1642-1727) and others. He was also generally well informed about Western culture and notices, for example, how practical the Western lineal chronology was in comparison with the stages of Chinese historiography. And he deplored that Japanese must have all the Chinese kanji. The Europeans could learn their 'a, b, c' alphabet of 26 letters in no time, while a Chinese would die without having learned his script! Above all, however, he was thoroughly acquainted with the Japanese culture and had encyclopaedic knowledge of religion, philosophy, literature, economy and more. He had covered the entire tradition by the time he wrote the *Yume No Shiro*. The Japanese scholars he mostly refers to are the Nakai brothers, to whom he gives credit for abundant erudition.

Bantō may be considered a turning point on the Japanese road to modernity. 'With him the study of the order of nature could no longer be kept within the boundaries of inhibitory ri thought but had to refer directly to the *jōri* patterns'[467] of things as in Western learning. The empirical method of Western praxis came to be considered to be the correct tradition. As he writes in the *Yume No Shiro*:

> Westerners have accumulated discovery upon discovery. And as the Japanese and Chinese too have begun to adopt their approaches, the errors of the ancients can now be exposed through actual experimentation. Moreover, as knowledge not yet known is continuously uncovered in the future, the errors of today will be made clear. And people beyond that will in turn do likewise of the errors they receive. What then can be the advantage of extolling the ancients? – *Inishie wo ronjite nan'no eki zo ya?*[468]

From astronomy – 73 pages – Bantō turns to geography – 45 pages – and displays an amazing familiarity with the world, not least Europe. His knowledge is, however, fragmentary and the global maps are quite fanciful. We are told that while Eastern people eat rice, Americans eat maize and Western people eat wheat. In some lands people eat only meat and there are further lands where people are cannibals. We are told that the Spanish discovered America in 1497(!), first South America and later North America. South America was colonized at the outset, and a great deal of gold, silver and other riches were brought to Europe from there. Europeans conquer and colonize lands around the globe, and they put profit first and the Christian faith (*jashū*: 'evil creed') next. Following chapters are mostly shorter: Chapter 3, *Shindai*, 'Age of Gods', 31 pages; Chapter 4, *Rekidai*, 'Ages of History', 28 pages; Chapter 5, *Seido*, 'Political System', 32 pages; Chapter 6, *Keizai*, 'Political Economy', 39 pages;

Chapter 7, *Keiron*, 'Classical Thought', 26 pages; Chapter 8, *Zassho*, 'Various Scriptures', 18 pages; Chapter 9, *Itan*, 'Unorthodox Creed(s)', 34 pages; Chapter 10, *Mukijō*, 'Non-existing Spirits, First Part', 32 pages; Chapter 11, *Mukika*, 'Non-existing Spirits, Second Part, 63 pages; Chapter 12, *Zatsuron*, 'Various Isms', 30 pages.

Bantō acclaims the Western way. He writes: 'Westerners base their thought on minute observation.' Also: 'They do not make maps of places where they have not been.' The Chinese on the other hand 'carelessly say things riddled with error without checking them and India and Japan accept them'.[469] Chinese sources are therefore not to be trusted. They are full of lies and fabrications.

European navigators have circled the globe, explored lands and waters, and Bantō finds it embarrassing that they claim all geographical discoveries and name them without regard to existing indigenous appellations. Only names introduced by the Western discoverers are used: Asia, Africa, America, Australia and so on! Even the Great Japan (*Dai-Nihon*) is named *Yāpan*! He bursts out.[470, 471] The resentment towards the European expansionism is understandable. He could also not help resenting the fact that Japan was reduced to being just a miniscule island on a round globe from having been a central land in the Eastern world, proudly considering itself the 'land of the rising sun'.[472] Like Tominaga Nakamato prior to him he recognizes the contingency and relativity of culture in a world filled with differing religions, creeds and habits and Japan is not special in this world of diversification. When he lists the lands and geographical locations on the five continents he begins with Asia and *Dai-nihon*, 'Great Japan'. Then follow Europe, Africa, South America and North America.[473]

After astronomy and geography, Bantō turns to history and refuses to mystify the historical beginnings. This concerns not only Japan but also China. Early studies regarding both countries, he does not acknowledge. Consequently, he is as critical of Ogyū Sorai as he is of the Japanese nativists and their attempts to 'beautify the origins'. He agrees with Ogyū Sorai, however, that each age must differ and create its specific system of institutions (*seido*). Before the written word there was mythology and after the written word there is history. All the pre-historical myths are 'fabrications', in the East as in the West. Like Arai Hakuseki, Goi Ranju, and Nakai Chikuzan earlier, he depicts an evolutionary Japanese history with crucial turning points, ending up with the Tokugawa feudal society. Thereupon he discusses the political economy, classical literature, unorthodox creeds, gods, spirits and medical matters. He examines the present situation, both analysing and defending the Tokugawa rule, and brings forth proposals for the material well-being of the nation.

His learning reflects Mencius and, quoting Goi Ranju and Nakai Chikuzan, he attacks the kogaku faith of Ogyū Sorai and Itō Jinsai. In the end, he finds most Chinese thought useless (*mueki no koto*). He debunks all mystifications and irrational beliefs and refers to Confucius who 'when asked about death, talked about life, and when asked about spirits, discussed human affairs'. Superstitions are foolish 'dreams' (as perhaps alluded to in the title of the work) – the Sun Goddess in Shinto, the Buddhist pantheon of gods, Christian thought about salvation in heaven, ghosts and spirits as well as popular folk faith. He discards them all and ends his great work with the following stoic words:

> In this world there are neither Gods or Buddhas (*shinbutsu*), nor monsters (*kemono*); still less are there strange and marvellous things.[474]

And

> After death there is neither hell nor heaven nor self. There is only humankind and the ten thousand things. In a universe without gods, buddhas and demons, there are surely no mysterious and miraculous happenings.[475]

His *Yume No Shiro, In Place of Dreams* (1802-20), has rightly been described as 'an intellectual guide for future generations' and the line between 'pre-Copernican' and 'post-Copernican' studies in Japan – between past and future. It anticipated what was to come. The time of the telescope and the microscope had arrived, and of the systematic observation, calculation and collection of data that had begun already earlier under the sway of Sung thought. An axis of scholarship leads up to Yamagata Bantō, from Kaibara Ekken, and a network of original thinkers, such as Miura Baien, who was also acquainted with Copernican thought. When Yamagata Bantō dichotomized knowledge into pre- and post-astronomy, he was an important link in this development. The world view, centring on the plain sense of things, had arrived. It must yet be emphasized that even Yamagata Bantō saw his studies taking place within a ri-ki reality consisting of matter in motion.[476] His *kyūri*, too, was utilized to reveal new vistas of moral *jōri* in the ki universe.

One is tempted to conclude that the Great Ultimate *(taikyoku)* was exchanged for astronomy in Yamagata's stance. His discussion begins in the astronomical totality and also ends there. This shows how flexible the Neo-Confucian ri-ki-ism could be. Western astronomy reaches out into a gigantic cosmos, today into an even more gigantic cyberspace, and from there all things can be traced, according to Chinese thought, no matter whether it is a *genri* or a *genki*. As he says in another context: 'All is based on a unitary principle', with reference to ri. As T. Najita puts it:

> To Yamagata ... phenomena close at hand, inclusive of natural and social objects, must first be located in relation to a prior universal 'centre' that could not be grasped through common sense 'observation'. Plants, animals, creatures, the physical landscape, history, social classes, all must be reinterpreted or recentred in accordance with an ultimate first principle of the universe.[477]

21. Political and Economic Thought in Late Tokugawa

The nineteenth century after Yamagata Bantō presents a long series of scholars who, without leaving the Confucian moral philosophy, presented innovative and spasmodic proposals for the alleviation of the political and economic situation. We need only name a few: (1) Kaiho Seiryō (1755-1817) (see below); (2) Ninomiya Sontoku (1787-1856), who proposed comprehensive reforms in agriculture; (3) Honda Toshiaki (1744-1821) (see below); (4) Kusama Naokata (1753-1831) (see below); (5) Satō Nobuhiro (1769-1850) (see below); (6) Hirose Tansō (1782-1856) (see below); (7) Hoashi Banri (1778-1852) and (8) Ōshio Heihachirō (1793-1837), who went so far as to begin a revolt in order to improve the world.

21.1 Kaiho Seiryō (1755-1817)

Among the political economists around the beginning of the nineteenth century Kaiho Seiryō was the earliest. This was a new age with increasing signs of national weakness and anxious Confucian thinkers turned more and more to political matters without being punished for it. Kaiho Seiryō came from the Ogyū Sorai school via the latter's disciple Usami Shinsui (1710-76). It is probable that he was acquainted with Ogyū Sorai's works on political economy, expecially his last work on the subject, the Seidan, and also with the work of the latter's disciple Dazai Shundai, the *Keizai-roku*. The subjects already presented in the Seidan are mostly repeated in the *Keizai-roku*, and they are again repeated in Kaiho Seiryō's most important work, the *Keiko-dan, Discourse on the Present and the Past* (1813).[478] He was impressed with the realists among the Confucian scholars, such as Arai Hakuseki, while he denounced the orthodox Chu Hsi-ists as 'parasites of the world'. He referred to them as 'rotten Confucians' (*kusare jusha*), in a way reminiscent of Andō Shōeki. Heaven receded and gave way to a new conceptual perspective.

In his philosophy he demonstrated an independent stand within Confucian parameters. Although aroused by Ogyū Sorai's *kogaku* thought, he put his trust in the heavenly principle (*tenri*) that causes everything to come into being and also determines the nature of all existing things. One even discerns Taoist influence, when he discusses the nothingness of things. He admits the ri principle as a rule of constant and neverending change and growth. The *keijijō* creed became, however, only a convenient backdrop for his *keijika* interests, where ri became the *jōri* in a ki economic world. The 'ri patterns' became money in circulation, the market of buying and selling and the production of commodities; they were the true standards of the world. He wished for the betterment of the world in accord with the principles of economic life and the principles of the merchant. The *tenri* acquired a pecuniary interpretation, suiting a new historical situation. He would have been punished for such thought a few decades earlier.

Seiryō left the samurai way of life and immersed himself in the commercial world of Osaka. The life in a merchant's house made him intensely aware of the distinction between the heavenly principle and the ways of man and made him modify his creed and infuse into the Neo-Confucian 'principle'(ri) the connotation of 'profit'. Principle and profit are two terms which in Sino-Japanese pronunciation are the same, ri (principle) and ri (profit). For the merchant the second ri accorded with the Heavenly ri. He deviated then from the Mencian conviction that profit was a social sin. Thus, realizing that society was more economic than moral he introduced a 'principle of profit' which suited the times better when merchants and peasants became increasingly important while the ruling samurai class was steadily losing its power.

21.2 Honda Toshiaki (1744-1821)

That the truth could be discovered in new directions was amply demonstrated by Honda Toshiaki whose thought turned to and advocated overseas expansion, colonization, shipping and trade. In the *Keisei Hisaku, Secret Plan for Government* (1798), and other works, he advocated international trade as the basis of 'good government' (*jinsei*). He proposed that foreign trade be allowed to improve the stagnant economy and that shipping and trade be taken away from the merchants and handled by the central government. Echoing Ogyū Sorai, he declared that the *seido* (system) was not correctly established and that the country suffered for this reason. Thus, he wished for the right institutions to be set up. 'These institutions would represent the natural way of government', that is, be in tune with Heaven and its *dōri*. Not surprisingly, he praised both Kumazawa Banzan and Ogyū Sorai. He must have been familiar with Ogyū Sorai's Seidan when he wrote the *Keizai Hōgen, Random Talk about Political Economy*. Reflecting a new time, he sees the solution of the crisis and poverty not within Japan alone but in overseas expansion – not heard of since Ieyasu. He takes England, 'a wasteland . . . with nothing of value', as the superb example of how the 'system' should be ordered. If the English example were followed, there would be a 'great island of Japan in the East comparable with the island of England in the West'. He proposed the establishment of colonies in the Pacific and North America and envisaged a Japanese North Pacific with the capital on Kamchatka (*sic*).

21.3 Kusama Naokata (1753-1831)

Kusama Naokata was a scholar from the Kaitokudō school who took a special interest in economics and human relations. These were appropriate subjects for him as a successful banker in Osaka. He wrote the enormous *Sanka Zu'i*, two volumes of 500 pages each, which he modestly titled an *Outline of the History of Money* with illustrations. It was finished in 1815 after twenty years of work. Like Ogyū Sorai he considered the money economy to fall within the vision of the ancient sages. He was also unhappy with the political situation and with the Bakufu that did not live up to the Confucian ethics that asked for 'ordering the world and benefiting the people'.[479]

21.4 Satō Nobuhiro (1769?-1850)

Satō Nobuhiro was also worried about the economic stagnation. Basing himself on the Chinese canon, he asked for political and economic reforms. Reflecting Ogyū Sorai, he also finds the existing seido to be defective and is pessimistic about the future. His proposals, found in the *Suitōhō, Method of Social Control*, are wider than those found in Ogyū Sorai's *Seidan*, and have been expounded as a programme for 'state socialism'. The Tokugawa feudal state was to be replaced with a totalitarian and centralized system which would control all economic and political activities. It was, as such, Utopian and, of course, never enacted. What is of special interest is that both the Confucian Heaven and the native Shinto Heaven are taken as justification for programmes, which were all impossible to carry out. He wished further for an empire which was to include China, South-East Asia, India and Central Asia, with the aim of making Japan the premier nation of the world. It is tempting to think that some leaders of the following modern revolution were acquainted with his ideas when they began the expansion on the Asian mainland.

21.5 Hirose Tansō (1782-1856)

Hirose Tansō is one of the well-known scholars from the time after the prohibition act of 1790 and can be taken as an example of the many who followed in the wake of enforced orthodoxy. His Kangien school in Ōita was opened in 1817. He was basically a Confucian scholar but described himself as an eclectic.[480] His studies were wide-ranging and he was familiar with not only Chinese literature, but also Japanese history and poetry. Like other scholars in his time, he studied the *kogaku* doctrine and expressed his admiration for both Itō Jinsai and Ogyū Sorai. Like them, he relied on the original classics and only later turned to the Chu Hsi commentaries and adopted a stance of *setchū-ha* syncretism.

From these studies coalesced his creed of reverence for Heaven (*keiten*), which conferred on man his spiritual nature. Heaven appeared as an anthropomorphic or anthropopathic essence and as the Way which commands life on Earth. He believed in Chu Hsi but did not stress the *kyūri* investigation of things. Close to the Lu-Wang school he rather emphasized that reverence and practical action must combine. The aim was to resolve the inherent problems of life by learning incessantly about the world, while turning the heart towards Heaven and displaying benevolence as a member of civilized society.

21.6 Hoashi Banri (1778-1852)

A learned scholar in the same late Tokugawa era was Hoashi Banri, one of very few intellectual samurai who made his way into official service. His studies embraced both Confucian studies at the Kaitokudō school with Nakai Chikusan, eclectic studies with Minagawa Kien (1734-1807), literary studies with Kamei Nanmei (1743-1814) and wide-ranging Dutch studies. He was an advocate of overseas trade and colonization and military defences, as expressed in *Tōsenpuron, Treatise about Hidden Affairs in the East* (1844) and in the *Kyūritsū, General Investigation of Truth* (1836). In these works he also openly advocated political reforms in support of the market-oriented industry that daring entrepreneurs had started in his time, not least in rural areas.[481]

22. 'Open Country Compromisers' – Late Tokugawa Reformists

P rogressive scholars in the nineteenth century favoured a positive response to foreign pressure and wished Japan to be opened to limited outside intercourse. They envisioned a balance between Eastern morality and Western knowledge, and a coalescence of the Neo-Confucian ethical *kyūri* and Western non-ethical *kyūri*. They were the *kaikoku*, 'open the country',[482] thinkers. Among them were Yokoi Shōnan (1809-69), Sakuma Shōzan (1811-64) and Yoshida Shōin (1830-59). They argued that, in the face of a shrinking world and unrelenting external pressure, it was impossible to be secluded and to refuse diplomatic and commercial relations. At the same time, they entertained a national consciousness: they desired a rich country (*fukoku*) and a strong army (*kyōhei*), in order to make Japan a global power that, financially and militarily, could stand up to the great powers of Europe.

Yokoi Shōnan originated from Kumamoto and was known for his liberal scheme asking for a synthesis of Confucian and Western learning. He came to Edo in 1839 and studied at the Mito School under Fujita Tōko. Later, he was in close cooperation with Motoda Eifu (1818-91) when he advocated the opening of the country, advancing his own international Confucianism. He was murdered by opponents of the Meiji reforms in 1869.

Sakuma Shōzan worried about the coastal defences and submitted propoals about building forts and ships, proposals which were disregarded by the shogunal authorities. He expounded that 'the learning of the West is science, [while] the teaching of Confucius is morality'[483] and that they complemented each other. He landed in prison in 1854 and was finally assassinated by conservatives in 1864.

23. The Meiji Era and the Twentieth Century

A mong the many scholars who continued the Confucian tradition at the end of the Tokugawa era and into the Meiji era, the two brothers Kusumoto Tanzan (1828-84) and Kusumoto Sekisui (1832-1916) are representative. They were close to the Yōmeigaku learning and lamented the waste of time on exegesis and broad learning.[484] Kusumoto Tanzan concentrated on meditative contemplation at Satō Issai's school and his younger brother Kusumoto Sekisui, likewise, took an interest in the interiorization of learning. Self-cultivation should come before practical and meritorious work.

From the Kusumoto brothers and others follows the late Confucian tradition that leads to our day. With the end of the Tokugawa era Confucian thought was no longer the centre of the intellectual world. Its decline was rapid and its schools and academies languished and disappeared. Most notably, the shogunal Shōheizaka institute was abolished. Like Buddhism earlier, it came to sink into the background while Western studies in all fields proliferated rapidly. The Western scholars were many and they paved the way into the following era. No modernizer, however, was devoid of a basic Confucian training and with this first education it was easy for him to turn to new learning.

Scholars like Fukuzawa Yukichi (1835-1901) found Confucian learning worthless in the new Meiji era and encouraged full-blown Westernization in works like *Seiyō Jijō* (*Conditions in the West*) (1866) and *Gakumon No Susume* (*Encouragement of Learning*) (1872). The Confucian values suffered an eclipse immediately after the Restoration (1868) but were not forgotten in the laws of the new education which were issued in the early 1870s. In the 1890s strenuous efforts were thereupon made to revitalize social virtues related to man's civil duties. We meet with names of scholars who took a stand for a new 'state' Confucianism. Perhaps the most well-known among them was Motoda Eifu (1818-91), who was Emperor Meiji's Confucian tutor and advisor. In an essay addressed to the emperor, he emphasized the importance of Confucius and the virtues of goodness, righeousness, loyalty and filial piety. The Japanese spirit should remain intact, and the Confucian virtues were an important component of this spirit. The slogan was 'Eastern morality and Western technology' (*Tōyō dōtoku, Seiyō gijutsu*). In a reaction to the dominance of Western learning, a number of high-ranking military men, statesmen and noted scholars backed the new Confucian trend, for example, Iwakura Tomomi (1825-83), and societies were formed to enhance the Confucian ethics. The thinkers who championed this policy came to be known under the designation of *kokumin dōtoku ronsha*, 'Theorists of the National Morality'. Japan was threatened by the intrusion of a material civilization; a solid ethical structure was needed. This came out clearly in the Imperial Rescript on Education (*Kyōiku chokugo*, 1890) in which the Confucian ideas corresponded to the Heavenly ri and constituted the moral standard of the Japanese people. It became a doctrine for a time of national crisis.[485]

Among the 'Theorists of the National Morality' was also Katō Hiroyuki (1836-1916), one of the most influential scholars and statesmen of the Meiji era. He began in Confucian studies and was inspired by Ogyū Sorai's ideas of benevolent government. Living at a time when the country was swamped with new thought from the West, he went through several 'conversions' under the direction of German legal thought, Darwin's theory of evolution, Spencer's positivism, Mill's utilitarianism, Locke's liberalism and Rousseau's naturalism. His basis remained, however, Confucian and he expressed that his respect for Confucius was 'unconditional'. Benevolent government could be combined with the forms of a constitutional government by consent. By establishing 'public assemblies' in which 'the sentiments of ruler and ruled were brought into accord', the lower classes would have a voice in administering the realm. Both

Heaven and Heaven's ri were referred to and showed that his underlying thought was linked to Confucius more so than to Locke and Rousseau. The rulers rule and the people obey. The constitution of 1889 was based on the Confucian thinking that natural rights come from above. The new 'seido' was decreed, autocratically, and no universal franchise was enjoined. The Lockian natural rights which dictate that the people rule and the rulers obey had to wait until 1945 to be attained.[486]

It was in the middle years of the Meiji era that Western philosophy was introduced by thinkers like Nishi Amane (1829-85)[487] to the extent that it became a compulsory subject in the universities. A term was invented and adopted for 'philosophy', that is, *tetsugaku*, by Nishi Amane in 1774. Since *kakubutsu* is related to the Way of Heaven and Earth (*tenchi no dōri*), it is not surprising that when a term was to be found for modern physics, it became *butsuri*, a term already used as a short form for *kakubutsu-kyūri*. From then onwards Western philosophy came to be at the forefront while Confucian thought became only a side subject.

Confucian learning was, however, re-established. After Motoda Eifu, Inoue Tetsujirō (1856-1944) led Japanese Confucianism into the twentieth century with works like *Nippon Yōmei-gakuha No Tetsugaku, The Philosophy of the Japanese Yōmei School* (1900), *Nihon Kogakuha No Tetsugaku, The Philosophy of the Japanese School of Ancient Learning* (1902) and *Nihon Shushi Gakuha No Tetsugaku, The Philosophy of the Japanese Chu Hsi School* (1905). His life was long, spanning the Meiji, the Taishō and the Shōwa eras. His writings were prolific.[488] He was opposed to the oncoming mechanistic view of life and its evil impact upon old Japanese traditions. The nationalized Confucianism can be followed from the 1870s; it was accentuated during the militarism from the early 1930s until 1945.

24. Okada Takehiko (1908-)

O kada Takehiko can be mentioned as a representative of the present-day Confucian thinkers who live in the shadow of the materialist predominance. He belongs to the Wang Yang-ming school and staunchly gives voice to the importance of contemplation in a number of works. Perhaps best known among these works is *Zazen To Seiza, Buddhist and Confucian meditation* (1972).[489]

Part III

CONCLUSIONS

Conclusion I

A long way led from the early socio-political Confucianism to
the later reverent Confucianism. Confucius took little interest
in spiritual matters while Chu Hsi, on the other hand, spent the
better part of the day pondering supernatural questions. The
simple ki world emphasis of olden times changed to ri-ki dualism
with emphsis on ri as Heaven's rationale. The other-worldly stance
of Sung thought did not mean, however, that this world had fallen
into abeyance. The better part of, for example, Chu Hsi's *Chin-ssu
Lu* (Jpn. *Kinshiroku*) deals with social and ethical life in this world.
The cosmological introduction of the work can be regarded as the
Heavenly umbrella for the work as a whole.

In the emphasis on the essential harmony between Heaven
and Earth, ancient and Sung Confucianism joined under the same
roof. The ri-ki dualism that dominated from the thirteenth
century and through the Ming and Ch'ing eras until modern times
avowed the same Heaven and Earth as the ancient monistic
thought. The cosmic view remained the same. It was only the
emphasis that shifted from age to age so that the stress was on
the Heavenly side of the axis in Sung, while moving via emphasis
on the human ki life in Ming to more and more on the Earthly
side of the axis during Ch'ing. Also under foreign pressure the
trend was away from dualism to monism. In Japan we can follow
the same trend during the Tokugawa era. The Ming thought
inspired thinkers in the seventeenth century while Ch'ing thought
turned important in the eighteenth century as intellectuality
inclined towards secular rationality. The development went from
ri-ki dualism to ki and *jōri* monism, preceding the fully-fledged
modern science and technology towards the end of the age –
however, never losing the original balance of the whole, the
Heaven above and the Earth below.

Classical Confucianism arrived in Japan in the fourth century and this meant that the Japanese islands left pre-history and entered history. The early annals evince that it became the backbone of the Yamato culture and the ethico-political philosophy of the imperial state that was established in the sixth and seventh centuries and found its initial expression in Prince Shōtoku's (572-621) constitution of 604, the first important literary work of Japan. It manifests the influence of Confucian culture in 16 of its 17 injunctions with Buddhism distinctly mentioned in one injunction. The tendency to use Confucianism for a unifying purpose characterized Japan thereafter and played a central role in all eras from Nara (710-84) and Heian (794-ca.1200). Continuous visits to China added to the Chinese learning. One of the earliest universities of the world was established in Nara where the Chinese wisdom and thought were predominant. Hereditary families became the teachers of this academy which existed through the medieval era until the Tokugawa age. In this academy, the new Confucianism was also introduced and studied.

The Japanese began to take an earnest interest in Neo-Confucian humanism just as the Tokugawa era commenced. The Sung synthesis was accepted just as Chou Tun-i, Chang Tsai, the Ch'eng Brothers and Chu Hsi had delineated it. The Japanese thinkers were, however, not so docile as their Korean brothers who mostly kept on the straight and narrow path of the Chu Hsi gospel subsequent to the inception of the Yi dynasty in 1392.

The age had hardly begun, and Confucianism become an ideology appealing to scholars, before the overall structure of the creed turned Japanese and indigenous. Already Fujiwara Seika, the first in the line of Tokugawa Neo-Confucian philosophers, combined the Chu Hsi philosophy with the native Shinto religion. Hayashi Razan followed the same line and afterwards there was hardly a Confucian scholar who did not mix Chu Hsi and Shinto. Somehow, there was room for both Amaterasu's Heaven and Chu Hsi's Heaven. The souls had space for both. In the present study only a single Confucian scholar is mentioned who rejected Shinto.

New independent thought came early when Nakae Tōju curtailed the Chu Hsi creed with the emphasis on individual conscience and action. This individualism was repeated by Kumazawa Banzan and became thereupon part and parcel of kogaku Confucianism. The Way was modified in accordance with changing circumstances.

This was not a serious infringement on Confucian values and customary institutions. Also Chu Hsi had been pragmatic and skeptical. A radical break with the unitary Chu Hsi thought came, however, when ki monists challenged the central structure of the Chu Hsi ri-ki dualism. The ri dimension of the Heavenly Way was greatly substituted by an all-embracing ki concept. Tendency in this direction is detected already in Kaibara Ekken who stretched Chu Hsi's *rikigaku* into acknowledging change and variety in nature. He represents an increasing number of inquisitive thinkers who researched the patterns of terrestrial phenomena, mapped them and registered them painstakingly, with pictures if necessary. He never left the Chu Hsi paradigm but, in the name of new knowledge, did not allow Heavenly ri to interfere with his ki studies – just as happened with God in Europe where Heaven's rôle in things was reduced with new discoveries. Ekken's work was empirical in nature but, as it were, not empirical enough to qualify as modern science.[490]

The altered ki thought was thereupon clearly expressed by Yamaga Sokō, Itō Jinsai, Ogyū Sorai and fully ideologized by Miura Baien in his jōrigaku. Itō Jinsai and Ogyū Sorai bisected the sacrosanct Way into a Heavenly Way and a separate human Way. The Way of man contrasted with the way of Heaven and Chu Hsi was, as it were, split in two. The most radical among them was Ogyū Sorai who declared that while the principles of Heaven were always the same, the Way of man was a human construct, consisting of man-made institutions and customs that shifted in accordance with historical circumstances.

Reality inclined to be a ki monism with ri as the ordering law within matter. The ri became the *jōri* – lines and veins – within the ki, like in early Chinese thought. The *jōri* was accepted also by orthodox Chu Hsi believers. They remained ri-ki-ists, regarding ri as archetypal on the *keijijō* side and as *jōri* on the *keijika* side.[491]

The *jōri* opened the way for the students who wished to be attached to antiquity and concurrently be involved in novel studies. They could classify, map and catalogue things and make discoveries. The way to modern science was, however, long. The *jōri* learning reached, as it were, deductive nominalism but not inductive science.[492]

The *jōri* approach could apply to all reality and focus on any new subject. Kumazawa Banzan and Ogyū Sorai adapted it to social matters and political economy. Also the political economy was via the sage kings anchored in the eternal tao and in accord with moral and spiritual principles. Yamagata Bantō actualized the *jōri* in astronomy, Kaiho Seiryō in monetary law and Honda Toshiaki and Satō Nobuhiro in colonial expansion. In the same manner the feudal class system was also bereaved of its Heavenly origin and declared to be man-made. Customs were similarly declared to be created by man. A priori social ideas were rejected.

Japan was quicker to transform than China. The proverbial Japanese openness to innovations could be one reason. Another reason could be that Japanese were free to develop their thoughts more so than their Chinese colleagues who were closely connected with state and power. Lastly, the Chinese cultural inertia, not to mention pride, probably stymied rapid modernization.

Not least the Chinese seemingly impenetrable monolithic society suppressed swift transformation. Its cultural continuity sustained a sense of superiority that barred modernizing and innovation. China had a two-thousand-year-long tradition with a stable internal order that changed little from 221 B.C. until 1911(!). It had always been the Central Kingdom and it was still the biggest empire of the world at the time that the Europeans arrived. It had everything it needed in its cyclical process from dynasty to dynasty, even a convincing ideology that declared it to be the only civilization of the world with Heaven above and barbarians around. It could look millennia back, admired and copied by neighbours. Uncivilized European upstarts made no impression on the emperor and the traditionalistic mandarin class and the inroads by the early Jesuit missionaries did not shake them in their conviction of superiority. Imported things, for example, astronomical instruments, could always be adopted as useful artifacts. This had been done during earlier dynasties and was done as easily during the Ch'ing era.

The problem was, however, that the Europeans came in Ch'ing times (1644-1912) with a culture and especially a technology that was equal to and eventually superior at a time that the Great Ch'ing dynasty showed signs of weakening and cultural stagnation, nothing unusual in a dynasty's second century. Now the challenge came from a civilization that was equal to and touched the essence and core of the Chinese way of life. It hurt the Chinese pride to discover that there was another civilization with other values that could measure up to theirs. It is reported that there were Chinese who were so appalled by this discovery that they cried and vomited.

This was easier for the Japanese for the reason that that they had already lived in the shadow of a great civilization for more than a millennium both ideologically and politically. The state structure was a mélange of Tokugawa power and some 250 independent domains among which the Tokugawa domain was *primus inter pares* – a feudal centralism while China was a centralized empire. It took some time but via the *jōri* compromise they moved first to early deductive science and then to inductive science and eventually to the modern state with all the attributes of the West grafted to the paradigm of the East – ahead of the Chinese. This was in itself not easy to recognize by the Chinese who were in the habit of referring to the Japanese islands as the land of dwarfs – (also today).

Conclusion II

When the Europeans came in the Muromachi era, the Earth turned from flat to round. With *rangaku* it shifted to revolving around the Sun. Scientific inquiry converted truth from absolute to relative, to change with every new discovery. Intellectuals turned from Chinese to European erudition and a new epistemology and cosmology emerged to capture the minds. For fourteen hundred years thinkers had embraced an ancient universal truth embedded in the Chinese classics and mediated by Confucius and Chu Hsi. Now it was Nicolaus Copernicus (1473-1543), Tycho Brahe (1546-1601), Galileo Galilei (1564-1642), Johann Kepler (1571-1630), Isaac Newton (1642-1727) and others who captivated them. Scholars began to study the world without connecting it with the search for 'sageliness within and kingliness without'. From now on, it gradually became knowledge for the sake of knowledge.

In the middle of the nineteenth century, the *rangaku* studies widened into *yōgaku* learning, rarely mentioning China and Confucius. The recognition of Western science and technology based on mathematical rigorism spelled a new intellectual world in which both ri and ki were interpreted with no need of a spiritual heaven beyond things . Heaven was discarded, and an automatic clockwork with no inherent moral laws and no absolute guidelines for human society took its place. The unitary *ten-dō-ri* system broke up, as *jōri* prepared the way for spiritless European learning that 'neglected man and speculated about nature'.[493] Earlier, a live Heaven and an equally live moral world had been primary; now, with a new mode of thought, the Confucian ethical *kyūri/jōri* inquiry was replaced by the non-ethical imported science and technology. This was associated with new epistemological perspectives, already accepted at the time of Yamagata Bantō.

This development could not be barred. A traditionalist and conservative like Matsudaira Sadanobu could only sigh and note that:

> ... the barbarian lands are proficient in science, which in the fields of astronomy, geography, arms and internal and external medicine are of considerable profit. But [*rangaku*] causes people to become curious, and makes them say unfavourable things. It should actually be forbidden, yet if we proscribe it, it will not disappear, but develop even stronger. It is therefore best to ensure that such books do not fall in the hands of the wrong people.[494]

Conclusion III

M ost scholars, however, did not willingly break away from the wisdom of remote antiquity. They never stopped harking back to the golden age where people lived in harmony and peace under the direction of Heaven and wise rulers and when all was perfection. When they directed their inquiries to worldly matters, they yet remained the children of Confucius and Chu Hsi. Nothing new should deviate from the ancient truth. What derived from the West went, protractedly, through the litmus test whether it fitted in with the age-old gospel. The idea that the Earth moved around the Sun had, to begin with, to be fallacious since it 'departed from the Classics and was contrary to the Way'.

The Tokugawa thinkers, like Yamagata Bantō, who recognized a wider world vision, generally did not feel in conflict with or discarded Chinese learning. They moved from 'virtue' to 'science' and, as it were, ended up with 'Copernicus in Confucius'. For a long time the European learning was put in a Confucian *ri* setting. *Ri* was still the rider on the horse. The natural order was not questioned, because there was, after all, a latent empiricism in Confucian rationalization. The new European technology was also *kyūri*, and however unethical, it could be accepted as *jōri*. One can follow the process from Yamagata Bantō's *jōri* scientism to Fukuzawa Yukichi's *keimō* 'enlightenment' philosophy: Unethical *kyūri* just replaced ethical *kyūri*. In this age of rapid change, we find the 'modernizers', for example, Fukuzawa Yukichi, side by side with conservatives, for example, Ōhashi Junzō, representing, respectively, the new and old 'enlightenment'.

The world governed by the Newton and Descartes had to wait for the twentieth century and new generations of scientists. The heavenly absolutes were dropped, and only relative knowledge remained. Thinkers became sceptics and atheists in the face of ever new discoveries about the material world. The cosmos became an evolution without need of a creator and spiritual values. Science, the new logos, took Heaven's place in the East as it had taken God's place in the West. A new era of knowledge unfolded, a life of thought without gods and buddhas (*mushin-mubutsu*).[495]

Conclusion IV

W as, then, the way so long from traditional *ri-ki* thought to today's science? Science and progress were disregarded and neglected by the Confucian élite for whom the truth existed already in the classics. Ethical consideration was always in the centre and moral insight was the prime goal of all endeavour. 'Interest was not directed in mastery of nature, but in self-mastery and the right ordering of life.' To settle one's mind, 'so that it becomes like still water or a clear mirror' and to know Heaven was the dictum since Mencius and Chu Hsi. Studies and inquiry should thus lead to personal wisdom (chie), first, and to the betterment of society, second. Knowledge for the sake of just knowledge was not appraised but the faiths and ideologies did not thwart change. No one was burned at the stake for his belief.

The ten-ri-dō thought could be seen as an impediment to modernization. Chu Hsi's kyūri contained, however, the potentiality for modern science. As Chu Hsi said: 'If we carry our knowledge to the utmost and investigate the ri of all things we come in contact with, . . . then the qualities of all things will be apprehended and the mind in its relation to things will be perfectly intelligent.'[496] Thus, Neo-Confucian learning enjoined rational enquiry!

This was not in the sense of modern theoretical science but it was nonetheless a quasi-scientific investigation of the external world.[497] The moral emphasis was always paramount. The kyūri was in the end a search for the truth, not a search for the laws of nature, even though consonant with the scientific spirit![498] And as the ri of the individual and the ri of nature were identical, the truth could be revealed in the ri of a tree, a blade of grass or an insect. The questions were just different, directed at sagehood and illumination, not at the galaxies and atoms.

Taoism was even less a hindrance. It had from early times been conducive to scientific breakthroughs.[499] J. Needham notes that Taoists originated 'chemistry, mineralogy, botany, zoology and pharmaceutics in East Asia' and that 'The philosophy of Taoism . . . developed many of the most important features of the scientific attitude' but concludes that 'they [the Chinese] failed to reach any precise definition of experimental reasoning or any systematization of their observations of nature'. Hence, both Taoism and Neo-Confucianism presented a scientific spirit 'extremely congruent with that of natural sciences'. On the other hand, Wang Yang-ming was 'most inimical to the development of natural science' and 'Buddhism was unfortunate for science'.[500]

The Eastern thought was synthetic, stretching into eternity, while the Western thought was analytic, and limited to this world only. We have an integrated indivisible whole in the East and a mass of segmented inert parts in the West.

Until the Renaissance European philosophy was also synthetic. Things went from the particular to the universal and the whole (God). It was thought that the planets were driven by souls and divine intelligence. The evolving analytical natural science bore a new paradigm, a Renaissance acceptance of early Greek atomism. The mathematical apprehension of the universe became the starting point of the following scientific expansion and the rise of the West. A unitary God was gradually left outside his clockwork – in time to the extent that the clock was considered without him. Man together with animals and plants became not different from machines. A Faustian heureka spirit and a Napoleonic hubris appeared: a will to master the world, to find out its secrets and aim at the endless unknown. A dividing line was placed between matter and spirit – and a new *Weltgeist*: 'the ordering power, the cognitive achievement, the scientific method, experiment and mathematics outside the whole: Galileo Galilei (1564-1642) did not only theorize about mechanical motions, the pendulum and the falling stone; he tried them out with experiments.'[501]

The past inspired the Confucian intellectual. He appealed to the golden age of the Three Dynasties when sage kings ruled and truth was known. In Europe, too, it was at first the footsteps of the past that counted and the Renaissance was, literally, an attempt to return to and revive the spirit of classical antiquity. Technological innovations were frowned upon as often in the West as in the East. The novel thinking that developed in the medieval universities from the thirteenth century was both a reaction against and a continuation of the scholasticism of the Middle Ages. Not so in the East where the reformation had to wait for the arrival of the *rangaku* and *yōgaku* to turn around and face the future rather than the past.

In the West, the transition from feudalism to modernism was further stimulated by the Bible's demand that man subdue nature in order to make it serve him. Scholars were inspired by this demand and felt that they were unmasking the great cryptogram of God's creation. Eastern peoples had no scriptural command-ment that encouraged similar progression. They kept within the confines of the ancient wisdom.[502]

In the West most early scientists were Christian, either Catholic or Protestant, and we do not hear that religion stood in their way. When they encountered persecution, it came from the church and its organs, for example, the inquisition. When Jan Hus (1372-1415) and Giordano Bruno (1548-1600) were burned at the stake, it was not religion that condemned them; it was the church. Scientists, including Descartes, Galileo, Newton and Kepler, were deeply religious and felt that they unravelled God's handiwork with their scientific efforts. It was the priests who engendered the conflict between science and religion and it was a later age, the Enlightenment, that turned atheistic and established the secularized world.[503]

Thus, a ki vitalism remained predominant in Chinese thought, both classical and Neo-Confucian, while cold, mathematical scientism surged into prominence in the West, where the Cartesian cleavage gradually limited inquisitiveness to the material world. While the intellectual paradigm stayed intact over millennia in China, it changed from age to age in Europe. Curiosity and the desire for knowledge moved in ever new directions, and change, considered a sin in pre-Renaissance times, became glorified and today afforded (Nobel) prizes for novelty.

Conclusion V

W ho were right, the ki-ists or the ri-ists? It appears that they were both right. Originally there was ki. Then came ri in Sung Confucianism, and over the following centuries we can follow a ri-ki dialectic, the ri being the rationalizing force of the ki world. The emphasis was on the ri in Chu Hsi's synthesis. In Ming and Ch'ing times the stress came gradually to be on the ki. In modern times the emphasis has again been on ki. First came Darwin who exhibited that all ri in evolution are contingent, and then came Einstein and set forth that all forms (ri) in space and time are relative. Their corresponding energy (ki) is conserved, never lost or destroyed, neither diminished nor increased.[504] Whatever happens and whatever is done, however many phenotypes are generated, energy and matter string together in harmony and remain the same, while the genotypes alter and adapt according to environment. Thus, there is no entropy in the ki; entropy is only found in the ri, within the constant, ongoing process of change.[505] No two ri constellations are ever the same; no two fingerprints; no two leaves of a tree. Neither are two days identical, nor two winters. The laws, whether they concern man, land or government, are never timeless, while the energy, the life-force of the universe, is conserved and indestructible and can only be manipulated. In science, Karl Popper says, truth is transient.[506] So, it seems, today, that the ki-ists were closer to the 'truth' than the ri-ists. They were the realists while the latter were the idealists. In this light, Miura Baien and others were correct when they put ki first and ri second. And Ogyū Sorai was right when he stated that the ri has no fixed criteria (*ri naru mono wa teijun naki mono nari*) whereas Chu Hsi was wrong when he stated that ri was immutable.

Chang Tsai and Einstein stand side by side when they express the equivalence of mass and energy and declare that ki and energy are the ultimate reality and indestructible (energy-matter = ki). Einstein's formula, $E = MC^2$, sums up all matter and creation in the universe and so does the Chinese word ki. Chang Tsai and Einstein stand side by side also in another respect. Chang Tsai acknowledges a Heaven above the ki totality that sets the ORDER and Einstein recognizes a GOD '*der würfelt nicht*' beyond his theory. Einstein's hypothesis and the ki postulation, both embracing everything, seem, identical. The difference is that while ki is a living reality with Heavenly connotations, Einstein's field of energy is free from otherworldly connotations: it is matter fettered in mathematical terms – even though a God '*der würfelt nicht*' is imagined.

God and the Way disappear in the new age of modern science and the phenomena of the world become but the temporary forms of integration and disintegration just like in Chinese ki monistic thought.[507] Taoist and Western thinking are in the end remarkably similar. Their world views coincide. But with a difference: the beyondness of a numinous Heaven and the complexity of the indivisible whole were never forgotten in Chinese thought. A God or a Heaven are rarely mentioned and the enigma of the total natural ORDER is mostly avoided. In Japan we find Miura Baien who declares that if ki energy goes out on the one side, it comes in from the other side. In other words, it stays intact. It is a (ki) field of life and energy; all matter in the universe is nothing but vital energy.

Amazing, is it not! The Taoist ki-ists three thousand years ago expressed, *mutatis mutandis*, the same thing as Einstein in our day!

It was scholars in the West who began to quantify and measure the phenomena both in their ri and ki dimensions in ways that were not done in the East. Galileo Galilei presented the motto, 'Measure everything that can be measured and make measurable what cannot yet be measured' and by Newton and others the brave new world of mechanistic science was created from the sixteenth century, which later reached Japan as *rangaku* and *yōgaku*. The East had its learning but it was the Western science and engineering that would create the confines of advanced studies – transcending all frontiers. This was the world dominated by inorganic rationalism which by means of mathematics started not only to map but also to control things. Both ri and ki have since been split apart, nature has been atomized, and the great cosmos has been traced back to a Big Bang at the beginning of time. The rapid modernization throughout the world has been based on a systematic study of all nature, organic as well as inorganic, spreading to ever more areas, even experimental psychology. The original thought of ri and ki has been lost in the cold logic of mathematical structures – with no heaven, only a blue sky, above. A Big Bang (*ein Urknall!*) and a long unfolding (today up to 16 billion years!) has replaced God, Heaven and a living nature. The dicta of natural science (and long series of zeros) have replaced subjective religion! At its very worst, unethical materialism has created a nihilism which has allowed world wars, mass destruction, the atomic bomb and genocide.

They are numerous, both East and West, who have not affirmed reality as a cold evolutionary machine, and there have been reactions against atheistic rationalism. William Blake (1757-1827), for example, reacted strongly against abstract thinking and baneful materialism. Another reaction came in the early nineteenth century Europe with the Romantic Movement. The 'dead nature' of cause and effect became again the 'organic and life-giving nature' and the one-dimensional mechanistic view of life was exchanged for an idealism that shimmered like an Indra's net of life. Friedrich Schelling (1775-1854) was perhaps the greatest among the Romantics and what he expressed is close to what a Japanese thinker such as Andō Shōeki said: 'Heaven and Earth are but the totality of nature' (*Sore tenchi wa shizen no zentai nari*). The Romantic Movement was mostly limited to poets, artists and philosophers in the nineteenth century, but in art and literature it has stayed alive until our day. A modern philosopher, Henri Bergson (1859-1941), has given expression to similar subjective thinking in works such as *L'être et le Néant* and *L'évolution Créatrice* (1907) and Alfred North Whitehead (1861-1947) has rejected the scientific atheism. Existentialism can also be seen as a revolt against the present materialistic ideas. Today, there is a tendency, even among leading scientists, to consider reality vital and organic, not just mathematical.

With the full-fledged acknowledgement of the West after 1868, Western thinking came to rule the Japanese intellectual world, while Confucian ri-ki thought receded as Confucian ethics was first modified and then discarded – although not entirely. When scholars like Nishi Amane (1829-97) and Nakae Chōmin (1847-1901) coined new words for this new cultural era, they again came to use ri and ki as the key terms, well aware of the basic meanings of ri and ki. Ri became a part of words like *ri-ka*, 'science', *butsuri-gaku*, 'natural science', *shinri-gaku*, 'psychology', *chiri-gaku*, 'geography', *shūri*, 'repair', *shori*, 'management', *kanri*, 'administration' and so on, words which deal with the form of things. On the other hand, ki came to be part of new words like *denki*, 'electricity', *kiatsu*, 'atmospheric pressure', *kishō*, 'weather conditions', *kishitsu*, 'character', 'disposition', *jiki*, 'magnetism' and hundreds of other terms which deal with life and energy. In this way one can discern a link between organic Neo-Confucian ri-ki thought and inorganic, mathematical knowledge, and a correlation between the earlier Chinese and later Western civilizations.

And what became of Confucianism? As Sung beliefs melted away after 1868, it returned to the original Confucius and became the morals of a new age, and as ethics it has served Japan and other East-Asian countries well and continues to do so today. And for many a Chinese and Japanese the universe is still a living ki reality.

Epilogue

In our shrinking world the East is on the rebound. It started in Japan and it did not take long before the rest of the East – not to mention the entire world – started to look to the Japanese example. Singapore, first, and soon country after country in the East applied the slogan 'Look Japan', at last even the giant among them all, China. The mechanisms of globalization bring the disparate parts of the world together. The lifestyles of such disparate countries as China and the United States begin to blend.

Not only the scientific orientation but also new political ideals have promoted this development. The Western democratic liberalism and egalitarian ideals, have come to form a new horizontal dimension, while Confucian ethical humanism has remained the vertical dimension. Where the two dimensions meet, the new symbiosis of East and West grows forth. It is a clash between old and new values that leads to the modernity in the East – as it does in the West.

It is noted that the Confucian ethics had to be modified since it was 'undemocratic'. However, the same can be said about the earlier European political philosophy, not to mention religion. A great deal had to change in the royal order of Europe before the parliamentary ideology could take root and the peoples could begin to rule with one vote per person. The Confucian countries were not less democratic than their Western counterparts a few hundred years back, when kings and emperors ruled. It was the Renaissance and thereupon the Reformation which put Europe on a new path away from despotic power.

Parliamentary democracy – the wonder of modern history – was only introduced recently and did not unfold in England until in the eighteenth century. It moved on to the United States and then to other European countries.[508] It was slowly forced upon existing political forms, for example, in Sweden in 1809 and in Denmark in 1849. Only a few countries had accepted parliamentary democracy prior to the Second World War. It is only after 1945 that it has spread to a majority of states and become the world's predominant political ideology. This means the world-wide affirmation of the secular multiparty rule and the people as the source of authority. Lightning-fast communications have eliminated all distances and we have become one single world. History need, however, not be finished with the dominance of the liberal-democratic principle and the elimination of distances. Over-population, poverty, religion, hatred, and recently terrorism cause new problems to arise. Francis Fukuyama's optimistic 'History is finished' was indeed premature.

Confucianism was not a greater obstacle to modernity than Christianity. Confucian culture had neither priests nor popes. It had its Heaven, its scriptures and statutes and it was incumbent upon every man to seek the truth, attain poise and serenity and serve the world. It had faith in human nature and perfectibility in a community of dynamic relationships stretching vertically from the ruler to the common man. Its basis was the belief in the oneness of Heaven and man and in the humanism that declared that all men are brothers and sisters, expressed by thinkers like Mencius and Chang Tsai. Absolute rulers reigned mercilessly, however, East and West, and governance was as harsh on the one side as on the other.

It is easy to blame Confucianism for the East lagging behind in science and technology. If the West had declined, the Christian religion would certainly have been blamed in the same manner. Therefore, the enigma does not lie in religion and philosophy. China had arrived at a high level of humanism early and it was technically, culturally and commercially superior until the seventeenth century – and no religious opposition is known.[509] When Europe moved ahead, it was in spite of the antagonism of the church. More important than religion, in Western Europe as in ancient Greece, was competition. It was greed that led to the technical and commercial revolutions and then to the cultural and scientific advances which took place in spite of the priests! Spirited intellects developed ideas which were transferred from country to country, thriving in rivalry and war, and only rarely stifled by religion which was itself in competition – Catholicism versus Protestantism. They took no account of national boundaries. The Dane, Tycho Brahe, could go to Johannes Kepler in Prague and exchange views on astronomy. Thomas Hobbes could – in political exile! – be in touch with René Descartes and visit Galileo Galilei. The views of Newton could arouse philosophers on the other side of the Dover Strait. Thus, the new ideas could interseminate from north to south, from West to East, and then over to America. Ideas spread and inventions radiated in the sundered West just as in the Greek antiquity. Similarly, Mammon and avidity brought the Europeans out on the oceans, discovering new lands. The Chinese evinced no similar attitude. They felt culturally superior and, moreover, were not challenged until the West appeared by the eighteenth century. Even Buddhism became Chinese in all appearances. Korea and Japan never rivalled the Chinese culture, and were never regarded as competitors, only as humble admirers – and behaved as such.

The technical revolution commenced in late medieval times, not least, in weaponry. The shotgun and the cannon meant all the differance in a time when the West European nations – in competition – went out to conquer the world. Without the gun, the Spaniards would have been helpless in America and the Portuguese likewise in India and Malacca. The compass and gunpowder – supposedly Chinese inventions – also made a difference. The merchants went first, in the name of profit, and religion and the church tagged along. Then came the industrial revolution, capitalism and rapid economic growth that put Europe decisively ahead. Religion itself had little or nothing to do with the rapid advances either economically or politically. It became a godly mask for blatant commercial imperialism.

When Japan first and China later decided to become 'modern', it meant political and military reforms in the light of the West. The slogan *fukoku kyōhei*, 'a rich country and a strong army', expressed these ambitions. The political reforms that came simultaneously meant the demolition of the feudal customs and the construction of modern centralized nations, organized on the European models of liberal democracy. In Japan this was done swiftly and the country learned fast to play the imperial game, faster than China that had a more persistent national orthodoxy to deal with. Japan's and China's rise to become major world powers in recent decades is impressive. This modernization and industrialization process is worth our consideration and observation. It is evident that an educated élite is at the forefront – and the uneducated majority willingly follows along.

Both church and political philosophy had to adjust to fit into a political spectrum where man voted and ruled. It took centuries for people in the West to turn from vertical to horizontal thinking and transform the love gospel to equal rights and parliamentary government. The East could hence not be asked to adopt it quickly either. The Confucian hierarchical view of society had to cede. This was not impossible. The uppermost virtue, *jen*, 'goodness', including all other virtues, can be taken in a horizontal sense as compassion and equality.

The potent combination of elected, democratic power and common education makes it possible for Eastern and Western peoples to fuse and create a global community. Scientific knowledge represents no hindrance. Science and technology talk the same language, East or West, and can be shared by all peoples of the world. Early Chinese technology, such as gunpowder, entered Europe early and Ricci and other Jesuits brought European astronomy, mathematics and other Western learning to China in the seventeenth century. The democratic ideology is, further, open, always amenable to transformation and never finalized. It can adapt to differing conditions. For example, the voting system can be altered again and again. Women who had no right to vote some decades ago, are now sharing the power with men on a more and more equal basis, West and East.

There are valuable nuggets of wisdom in every tradition which are worth being retained and included in our multiculturalism.

Chinese thought is one of the gold mines of humanism and we lose by neglecting its existence. In its Neo-Confucian garb it had to die, but it is now like a Phoenix rising from the ashes to new freshness. When the Western rationalization has run its course, showing limits and shortcomings in its one-sided emphasis on the mastery of nature, the Eastern – not least the Confucian – norms with their assertion on righteousness and serenity will make a contribution in the evolution of a inter-civilizational human order. The East has the old wisdom, the West the new knowledge, and both are equally needed. Western science paired with Chinese humanism could give impetus to new modes of living.[510] Together they might teach us to flow with nature rather than to subdue nature and to live with and treasure nature rather than to just use it as it suits us.[511] The pendulum swinging West might again be swinging East. We would learn sumultaneously to finish being 'professionals without spirit' and 'spiritual paupers in the midst of material affluence'.[512] And realize that 'Great knowledge sees all in one. Small knowledge breaks down into the many.'[513]

Bibliography

Abe, Yoshio, 'Development of Neo-Confucianism in Japan, Korea. and China: A Comparative Study', in *Acta Asiatica* vol. 19, Tokyo, (1970), pp. 16-39.

Ackroyd, Joyce, *Lessons from History: Arai Hakuseki's* Tokushi Yoron, University of Queensland, 1982.

Ames, Roger T. and Hall, David L., *Focusing the Familiar, A Translation and Philosophical Interpretation of the Zhongyong*, Honolulu, 2001.

Armstrong, Karen, *A History of God*, London, 1993.

Backus, Robert L, 'The Kansei Prohibition of Heterodoxy and Its Effects on Education', in *HJAS*, vol. 39: 1 (1979), pp. 55-106.

——, 'The Motivation of Confucian Orthodoxy in Tokugawa Japan', in *HJAS*, vol. 39: 2 (1979), pp. 275-338.

——, 'The Relationship of Confucianism to the Tokugawa Bakufu as Revealed in the Kansei Educational Reform', in *HJAS*, vol. 34 (1974), pp. 97-162.

Berling, Judith A., *The Syncretic Religion of Lin Chao-en*, New York, 1980.

Barthel, Manfred, *Die Jesuiten, Giftmischer oder Heilige?*, Gernsbach: Casimir Katz Verlag (Hamburg), 1991.

Bartholomew, James R., *The Formation of Science in Japan*, Yale, 1989.

Baskin, Wade, *Classics in Chinese Philosophy*, New York, 1972.

Berthrong, John H., *Transformations of the Confucian Way*, Westview Press, 1998.

Birdwhistell, Anne D., *Transition to Neo-Confucianism: Shao Yung on Knowledge and Symbols of Reality*, Stanford, 1989.

Bitō, Masahide, 'Thought and Religion, 1550-1700, in (ed.) J. Whitney Hall, *The Cambridge History of Japan, vol. 4, Early Modern Japan*, pp. 395-424.

Blacker, Carmen, *The Japanese Enlightenment. A Study of the Writings of Fukuzawa Yukichi*, Cambridge, UK, 1964.

Bloom, Irene, On the 'Abstraction' of Ming Thought: Some Concrete Evidence from the Philosophy of Lo Ch'in-shun, in *Principle and Practicality*, (eds.) Wm. T. de Bary and I. Bloom, New York, 1979.

Bodde, Derk, 'Evidence for 'Laws of Nature' in Chinese Thought', in *HJAS*, vol., 20 (1957), pp. 709-727.

Bolitho, Harold, *Bereavement and Consolation, Testimonies from Tokugawa Japan*, New Haven and London, 2003.

——, *Treasures among Men, The Fudai Daimyo in Tokugawa Japan*, New Haven and London, 1974.

Boot, W. J., *The Adoption and Adaptation of Neo-Confucianism in Japan: The Role of Fujiwara Seika and Hayashi Razan*, Leiden, 1992.

Bruce, J. Percy, *Chu Hsi and His Masters*, London, 1923.

Busch, Heinrich, 'The Tung-Lin Academy and its Political and Philosophical Significance', in *Monumenta Serica, Journal of Oriental Studies*, Vol. XIV (1949-1955), pp. 1-163.

Carter, Robert E., *Encounter with Enlightenment, A Study of Japanese Ethics*, New York, 2001.

Chamberlain, Basil Hall, 'Teachings for the Young, A Translation of the "Dou-zhi-keu" (Dōjikyō)', in *TASJ*, Vol. IX, Yokohama (1881), pp. 223-248.

Chan, Wing-tsit, (trans. and comp.), *A Source Book in Chinese Philosophy*, Princeton, 1963.

——, 'The Ch'eng-Chu School of Early Ming', in (ed.) Wm. T. de Bary, *Self and Society in Ming Thought*, New York, 1970, pp. 29-51.

——, 'Chinese and Western Interpretations of jen (humanity), in *Journal of Chinese Philosophy*, 2: 2 (1975), pp. 107-129.

——, (ed.) *Chu Hsi and Neo-Confucianism*, Honolulu, 1986.

——, *Chu Hsi, Life and Thought*, New York, 1987.

——, 'The Concept of Man in Chinese Thought', in *Neo-Confucianism, Etc.: Essays by Wing-tsit Chan*, (ed.) Harvard University (Oriental Society), Hong Kong, 1969, pp. 117-185.

——, 'The Evolution of the Confucian Concept Jen', in *Philosophy East and West*, 4: 1 (1955), pp. 295-319.

——, 'The Evoluion of the Neo-Confucian Concept Li as Principle', *Neo-Confucianism, Etc.: Essays by Wing-tsit Chan*, (ed.) Harvard University (Oriental Society), Hong Kong, 1969, pp. 45-87.

——, 'How Buddhistic Is Wang Yang-ming?', *Philosophy East and West*, 12: 3 (1962), pp. 203-315.

——, *Neo-Confucian Terms Explained (The Pei-hsi tzu–i)* by Ch'en Ch'un, 1159-1223, Columbia, New York, 1986.

——, *Reflections on Things at Hand*, tr. Chin-ssu lu, (The Neo-Confucian Anthology Compiled by Chu Hsi and Lü Tsu-ch'ien), New York and London, 1967.

Chang, Carsun, *The Development of Neo-Confucian Thought*, New York, 1957.

——, *Wang Yang-ming, The Idealist philosopher of 16th-Century China*, New York, 1962.

Cheng, Chung-ying, *Tai Chên's Inquiry into Goodness*, Honolulu, 1971.

Chin, Ann-ping and Freeman, Mansfeld, *Tai Chen on Mencius, Explorations in Words and Meaning*, New Haven and London, 1990.

Ching, Julia, *Confucianism & Christianity, A Comparative Study*, Tokyo, 1977.

——, *The Religious Thought of Chu Hsi*, Oxford, 2000.

——, *To Acquire Wisdom, The Way of Wang Yang-ming*, New York and London, 1976.

Chinese Science, Explorations of an Ancient Tradition, (eds.) Shigeru Nakayama and Nathan Sivin, Cambridge, Mass., and London, 1973

Choi, Hae-Suk, *Spinoza und Chu Hsi, Europäische Hochschulschriften, Reihe XX, Philosophie*, vol. 573. Frankfurt am Main (Peter Lang), 1998.

Craig, Albert, 'Science and Confucianism in Tokugawa Japan', in Marius B. Jansen, *Changing Japanese Attitudes Toward Modernization*, Princeton, 1965, pp. 133-160.

de Bary, Wm. Theodore, 'Neo-Confucian Cultivation and Seventeenth-Century Enlightenment', in *The Unfolding of Neo-Confucianism*, (ed.) Wm. T. de Bary, New York, 1975, pp. 141-216.

——, 'Neo-Confucian Individualism and Holism', in *Individualism and Holism: Studies in Confucian and Taoist Values*, (ed.) Donald J. Munro, Ann Arbor, 1985.

——, *Neo-Confucian Orthodoxy and the Learning of the Mind-and-Heart*, Columbia, New York, 1981.

——, *The Liberal Tradition in China*, Hong Kong, 1983.

——, *The Trouble with Confucianism*, Harvard, 1991.

——, (ed.) *Self and Society in Ming Thought*, New York, 1970.

de Bary, Wm. Theodore, et al., (eds.) *The Unfolding of Neo-Confucianism*, New York and London, 1975.

de Bary, Wm. Theodore and Bloom, Irene T.,(eds.) *Principle and Practicality*, New York, 1979.

Chow, Kai-wing, Ng, On-cho and Henderson, John B., *Imagining Boundaries, Changing Confucian Doctrines, Texts, and Hermaneutics*, New York, 1999.

Conte-Helm, Marie, *The Japanese and Europe, Economic and Cultural Encounters*, London, 1996.

Cooper, J. C., *Yin & Yang, The Taoist Harmony of Opposities*, Wellingborough, Northamptonshire, 1981.

Cooper, Michael, (ed.) *The Southern Barbarians, The First Europeans in Japan*, Tokyo, 1971.

Craig, Albert M., 'Science and Confucianism in Tokugawa Japan', in Marius B. Jansen, *Changing Japanese Attitudes Toward Modernization*, Princeton, 1965, pp. 133-160.

Craig, Albert M. and Shively, Donald H., *Personality in Japanese History*, Berkeley, Los Angeles, London, 1970.

Day, Clarence Burton, *The Philosophers of China, Classical and Contemporary*, New York, 1962.

Deuchler, Martina, *Neo-Confucianism as a Social Ideology: the Case of Korea, Some Preliminary Thoughts*, unpublished paper.

Dobson, W. A. C. H., Mencius, *A New Translation Arranged and Annotated for the General Reader*, London, 1963.

Durant, Will, *The Story of Philosophy, The Lives and Opinions of the Greater Philosophers*, New York, 1953.

Durant, Will and Ariel, *The Lessons of History*, New York, 1968.

Earl, David Magarey, *Emperor and Nation in Japan, Political Thinkers of the Tokugawa Period*, Seattle, 1964.

Edo jidai no shisō, *Kindai Nihon no meicho*, vol. 1, (ed.) Naramoto Tatsuya and Kinukasa Yasuki, Tokyo, 1966.

Eichhorn, Werner, *Die Westinschrift des Chang Tsai, Ein Beitrag zur Geistesgeschichte der nördlichen Sung*, Leipzig, 1937.

Eliot, Charles, *Japanese Buddhism*, London,1935.

Elison, George, *Deus Destroyed, The Image of Christianity in Early Modern Japan*, Harvard, 1973.

Fang, Thomé H., Chinese Philosophy: Its Spirit and Its Development, Taipei, 1981.

——, *The Chinese View of Life*, Hong Kong, 1957.

Ferguson, J. C., Political Parties of the Northern Sung Dynasty, in *Journal of the China Branch of the Royal Asiatic Society*, Vol. LVIII (1927), London,

1927, pp. 36-56.

——, Wang An-shih, in *Journal of the China Branch of the Royal Asiatic Society*, vol. XXXV (1903-1904), London 1904, pp. 65-75.

Field, Stephen L., 'Yi Jing (I Ching) Book of Changes', in *Great Thinkers of the Eastern World*, pp. 60-66.

Fingarette, Herbert, *Confucius – the Secular as Sacred*, New York, 1972.

Fisher, Galen M., 'Dai Gaku Wakumon, A Discussion of Public Questions in the Light of the Great Learning', in *TASJ*, vol. 16 (1938), pp. 259-356.

——, 'Kumazawa Banzan, His Life and Ideas', *TASJ*, vol. 16 (1938), pp. 223-258.

——, The Life and Teaching of Nakae Tōju, the Sage of Omi, in *TASJ*, vol. 36.1 (1908), pp. 24-96.

Forke, Alfred, *Geschichte der alten chinesischen Philosophie*, Hamberg, 1964.

Fróis, P. Luís, *Historia de Japam*, (ed.) José Wicki, Lisbon, tr. G. Schurhammer and E. A. Voretzsch with the title, *Die Geschichte Japans (1549-1578)*, Leipzig, 1926.

Fujita, Neil S., *Japan's Encounter with Christianity, The Catholic Mission in Pre-modern Japan*, New York, 1991.

Fukuzawa Yukichi on Education, *Selected Works*, tr. Eiichi Kiyooka, Tokyo, 1985.

Fung Yu-lan, *A History of Chinese Philosophy* (2 vols.), tr. D. Bodde, Princeton, 1952.

——, *A Short History of Chinese Philosophy*, (ed.) D. Bodde, New York, 1960.

——, 'The Philosophy of Chu Hsi', tr. D. Bodde, in *Harvard Journal of Asiatic Studies*, vol. 7 (1942-1943).

——, 'The Rise of Neo-Confucianism and its Borrowings from Buddhism and Taoism', tr. D. Bodde, in *HJAS*, vol. 7 (1942-43), pp. 89-125,

——, *The Spirit of Chinese Philosophy*, tr. E. R. Hughes, Boston, 1947.

Gardner, Daniel K., *Chu Hsi and the Ta Hsüeh*, Harvard, 1986.

——, 'Confucian Commentary and Chinese Intellectual History', in *The Journal of Asian Studies*, vol. 57: 2 (1998), pp. 397-422.

——, *Learning to be a Sage, Selections from the Conversations of Master Chu, Arranged Topically*, Berkeley, Los Angeles, Oxford, 1990.

——, 'Transmitting the Way: Chu Hsi and His Program of Learning, *HJAS*, vol 49: 1 (1989), pp. 141-172.

Geldsetzer, Lutz, *Grundlagen der chinesischen Philosophie*, Stuttgart, 1988.

Girardot, Norman J., Behaving Cosmogonically in Early Taoism, in (eds.) R. W. Lovin and F. E. Reynolds, *Cosmology and Ethical Order, New Studies in Comparative Ethics*, Chicago and London, 1985, pp. 67-97.

Goodman, Grant K., *Japan and the Dutch 1600-1853*, London, 2000.

——, *Japan: The Dutch Experience*, London, 1986.

Graham, A(ngus) C(harles), *The Book of Lieh-tzü*, A new translation. London, 1960.

——, *Disputers of the TAO*, La Salle, Illinois, 1989.

——, *Studies in Chinese Philosophy & Philosophical Literature*, Singapore, 1986.

——, *Two Chinese Philosophers: Ch'eng Ming-tao and Ch'eng Yi-ch'uan*, London, 1958.

Great Thinkers of the Eastern World, (ed.) Ian P. McGreal, New York, 1995.

Hall, John Whitney, (ed.), *The Cambridge History of Japan, Volume Four, Early Modern Japan*, Cambridge, 1981.

Hall, David L. and Ames Roger T., *Thinking Through Confucius*, New York, 1987.

Hane, Mikiso, *Japan, A Historical Survey*, Knox College, 1972.

Hansen, Chad, 'Individualism in Chinese Thought', in (ed.) D. J. Munro, *Individualism and Holism: Studies in Confucian and Taoist Values*, pp. 35-56.

Havens, Thomas R. H., *Nishi Amane and Modern Japanese Thought*, Princeton, New Jersey, 1970.

Heisenberg, Werner, *Across the Frontiers*, (World Perspectives, vol. 48), New York, 1974.

——, *Physics and Philosophy, The Revolution in Modern Science*, London 1958.

Hiraishi, Naoaki, *The Classics, the Interpreter, and his World: the Case of Ogyū Sorai, a Japanese Confucianist*, London (LSE), 1988.

HJAS: Harvard Journal of Asiatic Studies

Hocking, William Ernest, 'Chu Hsi's Theory of Knowledge', in *HJAS*, vol. I (1936), pp. 109-127.

Holcombe, Charles, 'Ritsuryō Confucianism', in *MN* 57: 2 (1997), pp. 543-573.

Hosuck, Kang Thomas, *The Making of Confucian Societies in Tokugawa Japan and Yi Korea: A Comparative Analysis of the Behavior Patterns in*

Accepting the Foreign Ideology, Neo-Confucianism, University Microfilms International, Ann Arbor, 1971.

Hucker, Charles O., *China's Imperial Past, An Introduction to Chinese History and Culture*, London, 1975.

Imanaka Kanshi, 'Jokyō shisō tenkai', in *Nihon shisō-shi kōza 4* (Kinsei no shisō 1), pp. 86-106, Tokyo, 1977.

——, *Soraigaku no kisoteki kenkyū*, Tokyo, 1966.

Ivanhoe, Philip J., *Confucian Moral Self Cultivation*, New York, 1993.

——, *Ethics in the Confucian Tradition: The Thought of Mengzi and Wang Yangming*, Indianapolis and Cambridge, 2002.

Jansen, Marius B., *Changing Japanese Attitudes Toward Modernization*, Princeton, 1965.

Japan and Korea, Contemporary Studies, (eds.) B. Frellesvig and R. Starrs, Aarhus University Press, 1997.

Japanese Religion, A Survey by the Agency for Cultural Affairs, Kodansha, Tokyo, 1972 and 1974.

Joly, Jacques, *Le Naturel selon Andō Shōeki*, Paris, 1996.

Jones, Eric L., *Growth Recurring, Economic Change in World History*, Oxford, 1988.

——, *The European Miracle*, Cambridge, 2003

Kaibara, Ekken, *Ekken zenshū*, 8 vols, Tokyo, 1910-1911.

——, *Yōjōkun, Japanese Secret of Good Health*, Tokyo, 1974.

——, *Yōjōkun no sekai, NHK kōza* (Tachikawa Shōji), Tokyo, 2001.

Kasaya, Kazuhiko, 'The Identity of Samurai in the Tokugawa World', in *Two Faces of the Early Modern World: The Netherlands and Japan in the 17th and 18th Centuries*, (ed.) International Research Center for Japanese Studies, Tokyo 2001, pp. 165-180.

Kasoff, Ira E., *The Thought of Chang Tsai (1020-1077)*, Cambridge, U.K., 1984.

Kassel, Marleen, *Tokugawa Confucian Education, The Kangien Academy of Hirose Tansō (1782-1856)*, New York, 1996.

Katō, Shūichi, *A History of Japanese Literature, vol. 2, The Years of Isolation*, tr. D. Sanderson, Tokyo, 1983.

——, 'Tominaga Nakamoto, 1715-46, A Tokugawa Iconoclast', in *MN*, XXII, 1-2, pp. 177-193.

Keene, Donald, 'Characteristic Responses to Confucianism in Tokugawa Literature', in (ed.) P. Nosco, *Confucianism and Tokugawa Culture*,

Princeton (1984), pp. 120-137.

Kim, Ha Tai, 'Transcendence Without and Within: The Concept of T'ien in Confucianism', in *International Journal of Philosophy of Religion*, III: 3 (1972), pp. 146-160.

Kim, Yung-sik, *The Natural Philosophy of Chu Hsi (1130-1200)*, Princeton, 1979.

Kinski, Michael, *Knochen des Weges, Katayama Kenzan als Vertreter des eklektischen Konfuzianismus im Japan des 18. Jahrhunderts*, Izumi 4, Wiesbaden, 1996.

——, 'Takai Ranzan's Shokuji kai, Introduction, Transcription and Translation. Part One (Admonitions Regarding Food Consumption)', in *Japonica Humboldtiana, Yearbook of the Mori Ōgai Memorial Hall Berlin Humboldt University*, vol. 7 (2003), pp. 123-178).

——, 'Talks about Teachings of the Past, Translation of the First Part of Kaiho Seiryō's Keiko dan with a Short Introduction', in *Japonica Humboldtiana, Jahrbuch der Mori-Ogai-Gedenkstätte Humboldt-Universität zu Berlin*, vol. 1 (1997), pp. 115-198.

——, 'Talks about Teachings of the Past, Translation of the Second Part of Kaiho Seiryō's Keiko dan', in *Japonica Humboldtiana, Jahrbuch der Mori-Ogai-Gedenkstätte Humboldt-Universität zu Berlin*, vol. 4 (2000), pp. 59-130.

Kitagawa, Joseph M., *Religion in Japanese History*, New York, 1966.

Knowledge Painfully Acquired, tr. of Lo Ch'in-shun, The K'un-chih chi by Irene Bloom, New York, 1987.

Knox, George Wm., 'Ki, Ri and Ten', in *TASJ*, 1st series, XX, pt. 1 (1892). pp. 157-177.

Koschmann, J. Victor, *The Mito Ideology, Discourse, Reform, and Insurrection in Late Tokugawa Japan, 1790-1864*, Berkeley, 1987.

Kracht, Klaus, *Studien zur Geschichte des Denkens im Japan des 17. bis 19. Jahrhunderts*, Chu-Hsi-konfuzianische Geist-Diskurse, Wiesbaden, 1986.

Kristensen, Roald E., 'Western Science and Japanese Neo-Confucianism: Interpreting a History of Interaction and Transformation'. Unpublished paper.

——, 'Western Science and Japanese Neo-Confucianism: A History of Their Interaction and Transformation', in *Japanese Religions*, vol. 21:2, July, 1966.

Kuwako, Toshio, *Kansei no tetsugaku*, Tokyo, 2001 (NHK Books, 914).

Lai, Whalen W., 'How Principle Rides on Ether: Chu Hsi's Non-Buddhistic Resolution of Nature and Emotion,' in *Journal of Chinese Philosophy* II (1984), pp. 31-65.

Lao, Yung-wei, 'On Harmony: The Confucian View', in S.-h Liu and R. E. Allinson, *Harmony and Strife, Contemporary Perspectives, East & West*, pp. 187-209.

Lau, D. C., *Introduction to translation of Mencius*, Harmondsworth, Penguin Books, 1970.

Le Blanc, Charles, Huai-nan Tzu, *Philosophical Synthesis in Early Han Thought*, Hong Kong, 1985.

Legge, James, tr. *The Yi Ching, vol. 16, The Sacred Books of the East*, Oxford, 1879.

Le Guin, Ursula K., Lao Tzu Tao Te Ching, *A Book about the Way and the Power of the Way*, Boston, 1997.

Leinss, Gerhard, *Japanische Anthropologie, Die Natur des Menschen in der konfuzianischen Neoklassik am Anfang des 18. Jahrhunderts Jinsai und Sorai*, Wiesbaden, 1995.

Levenson, Joseph R., *Confucian China and its Modern Fate, The Problem of Intellectual Continuity*, London, 1958, and University of California Press, 1964.

——, 'History and Value: The Tensions of Intellectual Choice in Modern China', in (ed.) Arthur F. Wright, *Studies in Chinese Thought*, No. 1, pp. 146-194.

——, *Modern China and Its Confucian Past*, Anchor Books, 1964.

——, 'The Abortiveness of Empiricism in Early Ch'ing Thought', in *Far Eastern Quarterly*, XIII, 2 (1954), pp. 155-165.

Lewin, Bruno, *Kleines Lexikon der Japanologie. Zur Kulturgeschichte Japans*, Wiesbaden, 1995.

Lidin, Olof G., *Distinguishing the Way, An Annotated Translation of Bendo*, Tokyo, 1970.

——, *Ogyū Sorai's Discourse on Government (Seidan), An Annotated Translation*, Wiesbaden, 1999.

——, *Tanegashima, The Arrival of Europe in Japan*, Copenhagen, 2002.

——, *The Life of Ogyū Sorai, a Tokugawa Confucian Philosopher*, Lund, 1973.

Li Suping, The Philosophical Concept of li in Chinese and Japanese Neo-Confucianism: A Comparative Study, in *The Japan Foundation Newsletter*, vol. XXIII/No. 4 (January 1996).

Liu Shu-hsien, *Understanding Confucian Philosophy, Classical and Sung-Ming*,

Westport (Connecticut) and London, 1998.

Liu Shu-hsien and Allinson, Robert E., *Harmony and Strife, Contemporary Perspectives, East & West*, Hong Kong, 1988.

Lloyd, Arthur, 'Historical Development of the Shushi Philosophy in Japan', in *TASJ*, vol. XXXIV, part IV (1907), pp. 1-40.

Lloyd, Geoffrey and Sivin, Nathan, *The Way and the Word. Science and Medicine in Early China and Greece*, New Haven, 2002.

Lo Ch'in-shun, K'un-chih chi, English tr., *Knowledge Painfully Acquired*, by Irene Bloom, New York, 1987.

Lu, David J., *Japan, A Documentary History*, New York and London, 1997.

——, *Sources of Japanese History*, New York, 1974.

Maruyama, Masao, *Studies in the Intellectual History of Tokugawa Japan*, tr. from Japanese by M. Hane (Hane, Mikiso), Tokyo, 1974.

Matsumoto, Sannosuke, 'The Idea of Heaven: A Tokugawa Foundation for Natural Rights', in T. Najita and I Scheiner, *Japanese Thought in the Tokugawa Period, Methods and Metaphors*, pp. 181-199

Matsuyama, Masao, *Nihon seiji shisō shi kenkyū*, Tokyo, 1952.

McClatchie, Canon, Rev., *A Translation of the Confucian 'Classic of Change'* with Notes and Appendix, London, 1876; reprint, Taipei, 1973.

McGreal, Ian P., (ed.) *Great Thinkers of the Eastern World, The Major Thinkers and the Philosophical and Religious Classics of China, India, Japan, Korea and the World of Islam*, New York, 1995.

McMorran, Ian, *The Passionate Realist, An Introduction to the Life and Political Thought of Wang Fuzhi (1619-1692)*, Hong Kong, 1992.

——, 'Wang Fu-chih and the Neo-Confucian Tradition', in *The Unfolding of Neo-Confucianism*, New York and London 1975, pp. 413-468.

McMullen, I. J., *Idealism, Protest, and the Tale of Genji, The Confucianism of Kumazawa Banzan (1619-1691)*, Oxford, 1999.

——, *Rulers or Fathers: A question of Casuistry in Tokugawa Japan*, unpublished paper.

Mehl, Margaret, *Private Academies of Chinese Learning in Meiji Japan*, Copenhagen, 2003.

Mercer, Rosemary, *Deep Words, Miura Baien's System of Natural Philosophy*, Leiden, 1991.

Merton, Thomas, *The Way of Chuang Tzu*, New York, 1965.

Milton, Giles, *Nathaniel's Nutmeg*, London, 1999.

Minamoto, Ryōen, '"Jitsugaku" and Empirical Rationalism', in (eds.) Wm. T.

de Bary and I. Bloom, *Principle and Practicality*, pp. 375-469.

——, *Tokugawa shisōshi*, Tokyo, 1973.

Minear, Richard H., *Japanese Tradition and Western Law, Emperor, State, and Law, in the Thought of Hozumi Yatsuka*, Cambridge, Mass., 1970.

——. 'Ogyu Sorai's Instructions for Students: A Translation and Commentary', in *HJAS*, vol. 36 (1976), pp. 5-81.

Miura, Baien, 'Taga Bokkyō kun ni kotauru sho', translation by G. K. Piovesana under the title of 'An Answer to Taga Bokkyō', *MN*, Vol. XX, No. 4, (1665), pp. 422-443.

Miyake, Masahiko, 'Jukyō ni okeru gōrishisō', in *Nihon shisō-shi kōza* 4, (Kinsei no shisō, 1), pp. 128-156.

MN: Monumenta Nipponica

Moore, Charles A., *The Japanese Mind, Essentials of Japanese Philosophy and Culture*, Honolulu, 1967.

Mugitani, Kunio, 'What is the Core of Taoist Thought? The Meaning of the Trinity: Tao, Ch'i and God', in *Dōkyō to Higashi-Ajia bunka, International Symposium*, no. 13, International Research Center for Japanese Studies, Kyoto, 1999, pp. 213-215. Abstract. Original in Japanese, 'Dōkyō kyōri shisō no kakushin wa nani ka', in the same volume, pp. 55-59.

Müller, Hans, Hai-Yaso-Anti-Jesus, Hayashi Razan's antichristlicher Bericht über eine konfuzianisch-christliche Disputation aus dem Jahre 1606, *MN* 2 (1939), pp. 268-275.

Munro, Donald J., *The Concept of Man in Early China*, Stanford, 1969.

——, (ed.) *Individualism and Holism: Studies in Confucian and Taoist Values*, Ann Arbor, 1985.

——, 'The Family Network, the Stream of Water, and the Plant', in (ed.) Donald J. Munro, *Individualism and Holism: Studies in Confucian and Taoist Values*, pp. 259-291.

Murakami, Kyōichi, *Andō Shêki no sekai, 18-seiki no yuibutsuronsha*, Tokyo, 1982.

——, *Rinrigaku*, Tokyo, 2001.

Murdoch, James, *A History of Japan, Vol. III, The Tokugawa Epoch, 1652-1868*, London, 1926.

Najita, Tetsuo, 'History and Nature in Eighteenth-century Tokugawa Japan', in *The Cambridge History of Japan, Volume 4, Early Modern Japan*, (ed.) J. W. Hall (1981), pp. 596-656.

——, 'Method and Analysis in the Conceptual Portrayal of Tokugawa

Intellectual History', in (eds.) T. Najita and I. Scheiner, *Japanese Thought in the Tokugawa Period*, Chicago and London, 1978, pp. 3-38.

——, 'Political Economism in the Thought of Dazai Shundai (1680-1747)', in *TJAS*, vol. XXXI, No. 4 (1972), pp. 821-830.

——, 'Restorationism in the Political Thought of Yamagata Daini (1725-1767)', in *The Journal of Asian Studies*, vol. XXXI, no. 1 (1971), pp. 17-31.

——, *Visions of Virtue in Tokugawa Japan*, Chicago, 1987.

Najita, Tetsuo and Scheiner, Irvin, *Japanese Thought in the Tokugawa Period, Methods and Metaphors*, Chicago and London, 1978.

Nakai, Wildman Kate, *Shogunal Politics, Arai Hakuseki and the Premises of Tokugawa Rule*, Cambridge, Mass., and London, 1988.

——, 'Tokugawa Confucian Historiography: The Hayashi, Early Mito School and Arai Hakuseki', in (ed.) P. Nosco, *Confucianism and Tokugawa Culture*, pp. 62-91.

Nakamura, Hajime, *A History of the Development of Japanese Thought from A.D. 592 to 1868*, Tokyo, 1969.

Nakamura, Yoshihiko, 'Itō Jinsai', in Y. Nakamura et al., *Kinsei no shisō*, Tokyo, 1969, pp. 1-41.

Nakayama, Shigeru, *A History of Japanese Astronomy, Chinese Background and Western Impact*, Cambridge, Mass., 1969.

Needham, Joseph, *Within the Four Seas*, London, 1969.

——, *Science and Civilization in China, vol II*, Cambridge University Press, 1956.

Neo-Confucianism, Etc.: Essays by Wing-tsit Chan, (ed.) Harvard University (Oriental Society), Hong Kong, 1969.

Nihon no shisō, vol. 17. (ed.) T. Nishida, Tokyo, 1970.

Nihon rinri ihen, (ed.) T. Inoue and Y. Kanie, Tokyo, 1901-1903.

Nihon shisōshi jiten, Dictionary of Japanese Intellectual History, (ed.) N. Koyasu (Koyasu Nobukuni), Tokyo, 2001.

Nishikawa Fumio, *Andō Shōeki ni okeru shizen no gainen*, unpublished paper.

Norman, E. Herbert, 'Andō Shōeki and the Anatomy of Japanese Feudalism', in *TASJ*, 3rd ser., vol. 2, Tokyo, 1949.

——, *Japan's Emergence as a Modern State*, New York, 1940

Nosco, Peter (ed.), *Confucianism and Tokugawa Culture*, Princeton, 1984.

——, *Remembering Paradise, Nativism and Nostalgia in Eighteenth-Century Japan*, Cambridge, Mass., and London, 1990.

Ogyū, Sorai, see *Nihon shisō taikei*, vol. 36.

Numata, Jirō, *Western Learning*, Tokyo, 1989.

Okada, Takehiko, 'Neo-Confucian Thinkers in the Nineteenth Century', in P. Nosco (ed.), *Confucianism and Tokugawa Culture*, pp. 215-250.

——, 'Practical Learning in the Chu Hsi School: Yamazaki Ansai and Kaibara Ekken', in *Principle and Practicality*, (eds.), W. T. de Bary and I. Bloom, New York, 1979, pp. 231-305.

——, *Zazen to Seiza*, Tokyo, 1972.

Ooms, Herman, *Charismatic Bureaucrat, A Political Biography of Matsudaira Sadanobu Tokugawa Ideology, 1758-1826*, Chicago and London, 1975.

——, 'Hakuseki's Reading of History', *MN*, 39: 3 (1984), pp. 333-350.

——, 'Neo-Confucianism and the Formation of Early Tokugawa Ideology: Contours of a Problem', in (ed.) P. Nosco, *Confucianism and Tokugawa Culture*, pp. 27-61.

——, *Tokugawa Ideology, Early Constructs, 1570-1680*, Princeton, 1985.

Ozawa, Eiichi, 'Juke no rekishi shiso' – ryūshigaku kara buke shiron e', in *Nihon shisō-shi kōza 5*, (Kinsei no shisō 2), Tokyo, 1975, pp. 87-94.

Passin, Herbert, 'Modernization and the Japanese Intellectual: Some comparative Observations', Marius B. Jansen, (ed.) *Changing Japanese Attitudes Toward Modernization*, pp. 447-487.

Petersen, Willard J., 'Another Look at Li óù', in *The Bulletin of Sung-Yüan Studies*, no. 18 (1986), pp. 13-31, Cornell University, 1986.

——, Fang I-chih: 'Western Learning and the "Investigation of Things"', in *The Unfolding of Neo-Confucianism*, (ed.) Wm. T. de Bary, New York and London, 1975, pp. 369-412.

——, 'Making Connections: Commentary on the Attached Verbalizations' of the Book of Changes', in *HJAS*, vol. 42: 1 (1982), pp. 67-116.

——, 'The Life of Ku Yen-wu (1613-1582)', in *HJAS*, vol. 29: 1 and vol. 30: 2 (1968 and 1969).

Piovesana, Gino K., 'Miura Baien, 1723-1789, and His Dialectic & Political Ideas', in *MN*, vol. XX, No. 4 (1965), pp. 389-443.

——, *Recent Japanese Philosophical Thought 1862-1996, A Survey*, London, 1997,

Pollack, David, *The Fracture og Meaning, Japan's Synthesis of China from the Eighth through the Eighteenth Centuries*, Princeton, 1986.

Popper, Karl R., *The Open Society and Its Enemies*, vol. 2, New York, 1962 (paperback edition).

Porkert, Manfred, *Theoretical Foundations of Chinese Medicine*, Cambridge, MIT Press, 1974, and in *HJAS*, vol. 51: 2 (1991). (Die theoretischen Grundlagen der chinesischen Medizin, Wiesbaden, 1973).

Principle and Practicality, Essays in Neo-Confucianism and Practical Learning, (eds.) Wm. T. de Bary and I. Bloom, New York, 1979.

Provine, W., 'Evolution and the Foundation of Ethics', in *MBL Science 3*, 1988.

Pye, Michael, Aufklärung and Religion in Europe and Japan, in *Religious Studies 9* (1973).

——, *Emerging from Meditation*, London, 1990.

——, Religion and Reason in the Japanese experience, in *King's Theological Review*, spring 1982.

——, 'Tominaga Nakamoto (1715-1746) and Religious Pluralism', in G. Daniels (ed.), *Europe Interprets Japan*, Tenterden (England), 1984, pp. 191-197.

Reasoner, Paul, 'Sincerity and Japanese Values,' in *Philosophy East and West*, 40, no. 4 (October, 1990), pp.471-488.

Rickett, W. Allyn, Guanzi, *Political, Economic, and Philosophical Essays from Early China, A Study and Translation by W. Allan Rickett*, vol. One and vol. Two, Princeton, 1985 and 1998.

——, *Kuan-tzu, A Repositary of Early Chinese Thought, A Translation and Study of Twelve Chapters*, Hong Kong, 1965.

Robinet, Isabelle, *Histoire du Taoïsme des origines au XIVe siècle*, tr. and adapted by Phyllis Brooks under the title *Taoism, Growth of a Religion*, Paris, 1992, and Stanford, 1997.

Roth, Harold David, 'Psychology and Self-Cultivation in Early Taoistic Thought', in *HJAS*, vol. 51: 2, pp. 599-652.

——, *The Textural History of the Huai-nan Tzu*, Ann Arbor, 1992.

Ronan, Colin A. and Needham J., *The Shorter Science & Civilization in China: 1*, Cambridge and London, 1978.

Rubinger, Richard, *Private Academies of Tokugawa Japan*, Princeton, 1984.

Rüttermann, Markus, 'Die Schreibregularien (Shorei kuketsu) des Kaibara Ekiken. Übersetzung und Kommentar.Erster Teil', in *Japonica Humboldtiana, Jahrbuch der Mori-Ogai-Gedenkstätte Humboldt-Universität zu Berlin*, vol. 2 (1998), pp. 103-163.

Sagara, Tōru, 'Kinsei jukyō no tokushoku-sei (makoto) no rinri' in *Nihon shisō-shi kōza 4* (Kinsei no shisō 1), pp. 55-86 ('Kohaku-ha'), Tokyo, 1977.

——, *Kinsei Nihon ni ukeru jukyō undō no keifu*, Tokyo, 1955.

Sansom, George, *A History of Japan 1334-1615*, Stanford, 1964.

Schirokauer, Conrad, *A Brief History of Japanese Civilization*, Harcourt Brace College Publishers, Fort Worth, 1993.

Schurhammer, Georg, S. J., *Die Disputationen des P. Cosme de Torres mit den Buddhisten in Yamaguchi im Jahre 1551, nach den Briefen des P. Torres und dem Protokoll seines Dolmetschers Br. Juan Fernandez S. J.* ('Mitteilungen' der deutschen Gesellshaft für Natur- und Völkerkunde Ostasiens, vol. XXIV), Tokyo, 1929.

——, *Gesammelte Studien, Herausggeben zum 80. Geburtstag des Verfassers, III*, Xaveriana, Rom, 1964.

Schwartz, Benjamin I., *The World of Thought in Ancient China*, Cambridge, Mass., and London, 1985.

Shryock, J. K., *The Study of Human Abilities, The Jen wu chih of Liu Shao*, New Haven, 1937, reprint New York, 1966. (*American Oriental Series*, vol. II, New Haven, 1937)

Shimada, Kenji, *Shushigaku to Yōmeigaku*, Tokyo, 2000.

Shively, Donald H., 'Tokugawa Tsunayoshi, the Genroku Shogun', in (eds.) A. M. Craig and D. H. Shively, *Personality in Japanese History*, pp. 85-126.

Sivin, Nathan, 'State, Cosmos, and Body in the Last Three Centuries B.C', in *MN* 55: 1 (1995), pp. 5-37.

Smith, D. Howard, *Chinese Religions*, London, 1968.

Smith, Thomas C., *Native Sources of Japanese Industrialization 1750-1920*, Berkeley, 1988.

——, 'Okura Nagatsune and The Technologists', in (eds.) A. M. Craig and D. H. Shively, *Personality in Japanese History*, pp. 127-154.

Smith, Warren W. Jr, *Confucianism in Modern Japan, A Study in Japanese Intellectual History*, Tokyo, 1973.

Solomon, Bernard S., '"One is No Number" in China and the West', in *HJAS*, vol. 17, pp. 253.260.

Sources of Chinese Tradition, vol. I, (eds.) Wm. Theodore de Bary, Wing-tsit Chan and Burton Watson et al., New York, 1960.

Sources of Japanese Tradition, (eds.) R. Tsunoda, Wm. T. de Bary and D. Keene, New York, 1958.

Spae, Joseph John, *Itō Jinsai. A Philosopher, Educator and Sinologist of the Tokugawa Period*, Peiping, 1948.

Stark, Rodney, *For the Glory of God*, Princeton and Oxford, 2003.

Steele, John, *The I-Li or Book of Etiquette and Ceremonial*, tr. from the Chinese, London, 1917.

Sugimoto, Masayoshi and Swain, David L., *Science & Culture in Traditional Japan*, Rutland and Tokyo, 1989 (Tuttle edition).

Sugita, Genpaku, *Dawn of Western Science in Japan, Rangaku Kotohajime*, tr. R. Matsumoto and E. Kiyooka, Tokyo, 1969.

Taira, Shigehide, 'Shintō shisō', in *Nihon shisō-shi kōza 4* (Kinsei no shisō 1), pp. 170-177.

TASJ = *Transactions of the Asiatic Society of Japan*.

Taylor, Rodney Leon, 'The Centered Self: Religious autobiography in the Neo-Confucian Tradition', in *History of Religion*, 17 (1977), Chicago, 1977, pp. 266-283.

——, 'Confucianism: Scripture and the Sage', in *The Holy Book in Comparative Perspective*, (eds.) Frederick M. Denny & Rodney L. Taylor, Univ. of South Carolina, 1985.

——, *The Confucian Way of Contemplation, Okada Takehiko and the Tradition of Quiet-Sitting*, South Carolina Press, 1988.

——, *The Cultivation of Sagehood as a Religious Goal in Neo-Confucianism, A. Study of Selected Writings of Kao P'an-lung*, Ann Arbor, 1978.

——, 'Neo-Confucianism, Sagehood and the Religious Dimension', in *Journal of Chinese Philosophy*, vol. 2, 1 (1974-1975), pp. 389-415.

——, *The Religious Dimensions of Confucianism*, Albany, N.Y., 1990.

——, 'The Sudden/gradual Paradigm and Neo-Confucian Mind-Cultivation', in *Philosophy East and West*, XXXIII, 1 (1983), Honolulu, 1983, pp. 17-34.

——, *The Way of Heaven*, Leiden, 1986.

The Cambridge History of Japan, Volume 4, Early Modern Japan, (ed.) J. W. Hall (1981), Cambridge, 1981.

The Kuan-tzu, a book written probably three centuries before Christ., tr. T'an Po-fu and Wen kung-wen, Carbpndale, Illinois, 1954.

Thompson, Kenneth F., Jr., *Whitehead's Philosophy of Religion*, The Hague, 1971.

Thornton, S. A., 'Yamaga Sokō' in *Great Thinkers of the Eastern World*, (ed.) I. P. McGreal, pp. 359-362.

Tillman, Hoyt Cleveland, 'Consciousness of T'ien in Chu Hsi's Thought,' in *HJAS*, vol. 47:1 (1987). pp. 31-50.

——, *The Idea and the Reality of the 'Thing' during the Sung: Philosophical Attitudes Toward WU*, Arizona State University, 1978.

—, *Utilitarian Confucianism, Ch'en Liang's Challenge to Chu Hsi*, Cambridge, Mass., and London, 1982.

Toby, Ronald P., 'Both a Borrower and a Lender Be', in *MN*, vol. 46, no. 4 (1991), pp. 483-512.

TASJ = *Transactions of the Asiatic Society of Japan*.

Totman, Conrad, *Early Modern Japan*, Berkeley, Los Angeles, London, 1993.

Tu, Wei-ming, *Confucian Thought: Selfhood as Creative Transformation*, New York, 1985.

——, 'Neo-Confucian Religiosity and Human-Relatedness', in *Confucian Thought: Selfhood as Creative Transformation*, (1985), pp. 131-148.

——, *Neo-Confucian Thought in Action, Wang Yang-ming's Youth (1472-1509)*, Berkeley and London, 1976.

——, 'Subjectivity in Liu-Tsung-chou's Philosophical Anthropology', in (ed.) D. J. Munro, *Individualism and Holism: Studies in Confucian and Taoist Values*, pp. 215-238.

——, 'Yen Yüan: From Inner Experience to Lived Concreteness', in (ed.) W. T. de Bary, *The Unfolding of Neo-Confucianism* (1975), pp. 511-541.

Tucker, John Allen, *Discerning the Meanings of the Sages' Concepts*, unpublished translation of Ogyū Sorai's Benmei.

——, *Itō Jinsai's Gomō jigi and the Philosophical definition of Early Modern Japan*, Leiden, Boston, Köln (Brill), 1998.

Tucker, Mary Evelyn, 'Kaibara Ekken', in I. P. McGreal, (ed.) *Great Thinkers of the Eastern World*, pp. 367-370.

——, *Moral and Spiritual Cultivation in Japanese Neo-Confucianism, The Life and Thought of Kaibara Ekken (1630-1714)*, New York, 1989.

Turnbull, Stephen R., *The Samurai: A Military History*, London, 1977.

Uenaka, Shuzo, Last Testament in Exile, Yamaga Sokō's Haisho Zampitsu, in *MN* 32, 2 (1977), pp. 125-150.

Ui, Hakuju, *Bukkyō jiten*, Tokyo, 1965.

Wach, Joachim, *The Comparative Study of Religions*, New York, 1958.

——, *Types of Religious Experience, Chrisitian and Non-Christian*, London, 1951.

Wachutka, Michael, *Arai Hakuseki*, unpublished seminar paper, University of Tübingen, 1997.

Waley, Arthur, *The Analects of Confucius*, New York, 1938.

——, *The Way and Its Power*, New York, 1958.

Wallacker, Benjamin E., *The Huai-nan-tzu, Book Eleven: Behavior, Culture, and the Cosmos*, New Haven, 1962.

Wang Pi, Commentary on the Lao Tzu, tr. by Ariane Rump in collaboration with Wing-tsit Chan, *Monographs of the Society for Asian and Comparative Philosophy*, No. 6, The University Press of Hawaii, 1979.

Watanabe, Hiroshi, 'Rituals of the Tokugawa Shogunate and Confucianism', in *Courtiers and Warriors, Comparative Historical Perspectives on Ruling Authority and Civilization*, International Research Center for Japanese Studies, Kyoto, 2003, pp. 167-174.

Watsuji, Tetsurō, *Rinrigaku, Ethics in Japan*, tr. by Yamamoto Seisaku and Robert E. Carter, New York, 1996.

Welch, Holmes and Seidel, Anna, *Facets of Taoism, Essays in Chinese Religion*, New Haven and London, 1979.

Whitehead, Alfred North, *Science and the Modern World*, Cambridge, 1925.

Wildman Sakai, Kate, 'The Naturaliszation of Confucianism in Tokugawa Japan: The Problem of Sinocentrism', in *HJAS*, vol. 40: 1, pp. 157-199.

Wilhelm, Richard, trans. *The Book of the Changes: The Richard Wilhelm Translation rendered into English by Cary F. Baynes*, Princeton, 1967.

Williamson, H. R., *Wang An Shih, a Chinese Statesman and Educationalist of the Sung Dynasty*, 2 vols., London, 1935.

Wittenborn, Allen, *Further Reflections on Things at Hand, A Reader Chu Hsi, Translation and Commentary by Allen Wittenborn*, Lanham, New York and London, 1991.

Wright, W. B., 'The Capture and Captivity of Père Giovanni Batista Sidotti in Japan from 1709 to 1715'. in the *TASJ*, vol. IX (1881), pp. 156-172.

Wyatt, Don J., 'Chu Hsi's Critique of Shao Yung: One Instance of the Stand Against Fatalism'. in *HJAS*, vol. 45.2 (1985) pp. 649-665.

Yamagata, Daini, Yanagi-shi shinron, in *Nihon no shisō*, vol. 17, pp. 343-428.

Yamamoto, Makoto, *Nakae Tōju no jugaku, sono keiseishiteki kenkyū*, Tokyo 1977.

Yamaori, Tetsuo, *Nihon no kokoro, Nihonjin no kokoro, NHK Rajio dai-ni hōsō*, no. 2, Tokyo 2004.

Yamashita, Samuel Hideo, 'The Early Life and Thought of Itō Jinsai', in

HJAS, pp.453-480.

——, *Master Sorai's Responsals, An Annotated Translation of Sorai sensei tōmonsho*, Honolulu, 1994.

——, 'Nature and Artifice in the Writings of Ogyū Sorai', in P. Nosco (ed.), *Confucianism and Tokugawa Culture*, pp. 138-165.

——, Reading the New Intellectual Histories, in *The Journal of Japanese Studies*, vol. 22, no. 1 (1996), pp. 1-48.

Yanagizawa, Minami, 'Miura Baien to sono shūhen', in *Nihon shisō-shi kōza 4* (Kinsei no shisō 1), pp. 86-106 ('Kohaku-ha'), Tokyo, 1977.

Yasunaga, Toshinobu, *Ando Shoeki, Social and Ecological Philosopher in Eighteenth-Century Japan*, New York, 1992.

Yoshida, Mitsukuni, 'The Chinese Concept of Nature', in (eds.) Shigeru Nakayama and Nathan Sivin, *Chinese Science, Explorations of an Ancient Tradition*, pp. 71-89.

Yoshikawa, Kōjirō, *Jinsai, Sorai, Norinaga, Three Classical Philologists of Mid-Tokugawa Japan*, Tokyo, 1983.

Yü, Ying-shih, 'O Soul, Come back!' A Study in the Changing Conceptions of the Soul and Afterlife in Pre-Buddhist China, in *HJAS*, vol. 47: 2 (1987), pp. 363-395.

Yukawa, Hideki, 'Modern Trend of Western Civilization and Cultural Peculiarities in Japan', in (ed.) C. A. Moore, *The Japanese Mind, Essentials of Japanese Philosophy and Culture*, Honolulu, 1967, pp. 52-65.

Zee, A., *Einstein's Universe, Gravity at Work and Play*, Oxford, 1989.

Zierer, Otto, *Ideen bewegten die Welt, Die Höhepunkte der Geistesgeschichte aus zwei Jahrtausenden*, Wien 1978.

Notes

PART I

1   The term 'materialism' in this work refers to the modern (Western) materialism without the metaphysical connotation. Only important terms are given in both Chinese and Japanese; otherwise, depending on context, in either Chinese or Japanese.

2   See J. Legge, *The Yi King*, vol. 16 of the *Sacred Books of the East* (1879) and R. Wilhelm, trans. *The I Ching* or *Book of Changes* (1967) (original in German). For a short presentation, see S. L. Field, 'Yi Jing (I Ching) (Book of Changes)', in *Great Thinkers of the Eastern World*, New York, 1995, pp. 60-6. For the Five (or Six) Confucian Classics, see, for example, *Sources of Chinese Tradition*, vol. I, pp. 2-4. Western thought is often said to be nothing but footnotes to Plato. Chinese thought can likewise be seen as footnotes to the *I Ching*.

3   The *Tao Te Ching* (also *Daodejing*), 'Book of the Way and the Virtue'. 'Nothing about it is certain except that it's Chinese, and very old, and speaks to people everywhere as if it had been written yesterday.' U. K. Le Guin, *Lao Tzu Tao Te Ching. A Book about the Way and the Power of the Way*. p. ix. See also I. Robinet, *Histoire du Taoïsme des origines au XIVe siècle* (Taoism, Growth of a Religion), pp. 26-30, *et passim*. It was during the Han era that scholars 'collected and edited the texts of the Chinese tradition after the disasters of the Ch'in dynasty and the great civil wars'. J. H. Berthrong, *Transformations of the Confucian Way*. p. 35.

4   For these roots see B. I. Schwartz *The World of Thought in Ancient China*. pp. 16-39, *passim*.

5   The term 'Confucianism' is a later Western designation of the Chinese tradition of thought, as begun by Confucius. This tradition can be followed through the centuries and includes the Sung tradition, which became prominent from the eleventh century. First mainly ethical, later more metaphysical, it constitutes one of the longest traditions of thought in the world. See J. Ching, *Confucianism & Christianity*. pp. 7-12. The difference between Confucianism and Taoism is well described by A. C. Graham: 'Taoism represents everything which is spontaneous, imaginative, private, unconventional in Chinese society, Confucianism everything which is controlled, prosaic, public, respectable; the division runs through the whole of Chinese civilisation.' A. C. Graham, *The Book of Lieh-tzü*, p. 9.

6   It has been appropriate to capitalize the terms Way, Heaven and Earth, as they are so central in Confucian thought. Names are generally given with family names first and personal names second. Well-known scholars are often referred to by personal names in sequences where they are first presented with both family and personal names.

7   Statement by Satō Naokata around 1716. H. Ooms, *Tokugawa Ideology*, p.208.

8   As for the beginnings of Neo-Confucian thought in China, see, for example, Fung Yu-lan. 'The Rise of Neo-Confucianism and its Borrowings from Buddhism and Taoism', in *HJAS*, vol. 7 (1942-43), pp. 89-125.

9   For Neo-Confucian *seiza*, see T. Okada, *Zazen to Seiza*, R. L. Taylor, *The Confucian Way of Contemplation, Okada Takehiko and the Tradition of Quiet Sitting* and ibid., 'The Cultivation of Sagehood as a Religious Goal' in *Neo-Confucianism. A Study of Selected Writings of Kao P'an-lung*, pp. 77-88.

10   Y. Abe mentions that the monks Shunjō and Enji, returning from China in 1211 and in 1241, respectively, brought back Chu Hsi's writings. Abe indicates that Chu Hsi was introduced earlier in Japan than in Korea. Y. Abe, 'Development of Neo-Confucianism in Japan, Korea and Japan: A Comparative Study', in *Acta Asiatica*, No. 19 (1970), p. 17.

11   H. Ooms makes the period longer. 'For 500 years in Japan *ju* (i.e., Neo-Confucian studies and scholars) were housed within Zen.' In *Journal of Japanese Studies*, 26:2, p. 444.

12   So did the Abe, Ōe and Sugawara families.

13   P. Nosco, *Remembering Paradise. Nativism and Nostalgia in Eighteenth-Century Japan*, p. 33.

14   For a good review of Neo-Confucianism in China and Japan: Wm. T. de Bary, 'Sagehood as a Secular Ideal in Tokugawa Neo-Confucianism', in *Principle and Practicality*, pp. 127-88.

15   R. Tsunoda *et al.*, *Sources of Japanese Tradition*, pp. 335-52.

16   Chu Hsi said, 'Heaven equals *ri*' (Jpn., *ten soku ri nari*). It must always be remembered that in all Confucian thought, whether old or new, Heaven is both the top and bottom line.

17   Cf., for examples, Fung Yu-lan, *The Spirit of Chinese Philosophy*, pp. 185-9.

18   In Miura Baien's letter to Taga Bokkyō, 'Taga Bokkyō-kun ni kotauru sho, An Answer to Taga Bokkyō written by Miura Baien', translation by G. K. Piovesana, in *MN*, vol. XX, no. 4 (1965), p. 428. Taga Bokkyō was one of Miura Baien's students and friends. See below.

19   Translation by R. Mercer of letter to Taga Bokkyō, in *Deep Words* p. 161.

20   A Western equivalent would be Einstein's 'Unified Field'.

21   Miura Baien uses the same simile. He says, 'Veins of the human body are the carriers of energy (ki) and blood throughout the body'. See Miura's letter to Taga Bokkyō, 'Taga Bokkyō kun ni kotauru sho, An Answer to Taga Bokkyō written by Miura Baien' in *MN*, vol. XX, no. 4 (1965), pp. 429. Miura Baien. See below.

22   'The universe being like a beautifully woven cloth, everything in it is made up of a crosswork of threads similar to warp (*tate-ito*) and woof (*yoko-ito*).' This is said by G. K. Piovesana about Miura Baien's universe, but it applies equally to Chu Hsi's universe. G. K. Piovesana, *Miura Baien, 1723-1789*, p. 411.

23   See D. J. Munro, 'The Family Network, the Stream of Water, and the Plant: Picturing Persons in Sung Confucianism', in Donald J. Munro (ed.), *Individualism and Holism: Studies in Confucian and Taoist Values*. pp. 259-91. Cf., St Luke, 13: 18-21.

24   For discussions of the term *ri*, see W. Peterson, 'Another Look at li' in *The Bulletin of Sung-Yüan Studies*, No. 18 (1986), pp. 13-31 and D. K. Gardner, *Learning to Be a Sage*, pp. 90-2. *Ri* is left untranslated in this work. In Anglo-Saxon literature it

is mostly translated as 'principle', and no regard taken for its development over
many centuries. When this writer translated it as 'inscape' (under the influence of
Prof. P. Boodberg) in a work about Ogyū Sorai in the Kyōhō era (1716-35) it
referred to the later nuance of the term, synonomous with *jōri*. See below. NB.
The terms 'empiricism' and 'empirical' are not referring to observations based on
systematic theorizing as in modem science. They can be characterized as referring to
observations in a pre-modern-science as existed also in Greece and early Europe.
Cf., n. 266, below.

25   Needham expresses the same with the words, 'Principle (*ri*) means the intrinsic
organization of a thing . . .' Joseph Needham, *Science and Civilization in China*. II,
476 and 562-75.

26   Or as Chu Hsi says (in the *Chu-tzu yü-lei*, Book 94):'From the beginning to the
end *ri*, the only reality, is one, but millions of things share it in order to acquire
essence . . . It is just like the moon which is one, but which is reflected in many
rivers and lakes and is seen everywhere. One cannot say that the moon is split up.'
Quotation from C. Chang, *The Development of Neo-Confucian Thought*. p. 257. It is
close to Greek philosophy which speaks about the heavenly 'essence' (*ousia*) and its
'energies' (*energeiai*) or activities in the world. Quotation from K. Armstrong, *A
History of God*. p. 254. It is amazing how close a Christian could also be to Chu Hsi.
Listen to the way Francis Xavier describes God to Japanese Buddhist priests: 'About
all things which exist we know that they had a beginning. We know well that they
cannot have begun all by themselves. Therefore there exists a Principle that has
given them all their beginnings. This Principle had no beginning and will have no
end, and this principle we call God in our language.' Quotation from M. Barthel, *Die
Jesuiten, Giftmischer oder Heilige?*, p. 225.

27   Cf., *Kinshiroku* (*Chin-ssu lu*), III:50 and 53.

28   Fung yu-lan (Derk Bodde), *The Philosophy of Chu Hsi*, p. 7.

29   W.E. Hocking, *Chu Hsi's Theory of Knowledge*, pp. 113-5.

30   When the first missionaries (Francis Xavier and João Fernandez) came to Japan
and were asked, 'What is God', they answered: 'We know about all things which
exist that they have a beginning (*principio*). We know, however, well, that they did
not have a beginning by themselves. Therefore, there is a Principle that gives them
all a beginning. This (Principle) had no beginning and will have no end, and this
Principle we call in our language *Dios*, (that is, *God*).' Notice that the Latin term
'principio' is used for both 'beginning' and 'Principle'. It is amazing how close
Chinese *ri* thought and Christian thought is here.

31   One can also add *ming* (Jpn. *mei*. 'mandate, decree, order') to heaven and the
composite term will then be *ten(mei)-dō-ri*, 'heaven-decree-way-principle'. It is an
anthropopathic moral order directed towards the cosmos.

32   It is a matter of argument whether the cosmos shall be seen as a self-
generating, sponaneous *ch'i* (ki) organism, as described by Chang Tsai, or as an
ordered *li-ch'i* (ri-ki) organism, as suggested by Chu Hsi. In any case, it is an
organism for both of them, formed and developed within itself, no creator
mentioned. See, for example, J. Needham, *op. cit.*, pp. 472-85.

33   Or the 'ten thousand things', referring to all cosmic things.

34   Y. Abe, *op. cit.*, p. 28, passim.

35   W.-T. Chan, *Chu Hsi, Life and Thought*, p. 110 and J. R. Levenson, *Confucian China and its Modern Fate*. p. 66.

36   Y. Abe, *op. cit.*, pp. 28-9.

37   P. J. Ivanhoe, *Confucian Moral Self-Cultivation*, p.55. Ivanhoe's quotation, adapted from W.-t. Chan, *A Source Book of Chinese Philosophy*, p. 623.

38   Cf., K. Armstrong, *A History of God*, p. 46: 'Something that had true identity remained always the same, characterized by permanence and immutability.' Armstrong speaks about Plato and the ideas, but she could as well be speaking about the heavenly ri. K. Armstrong, *ibid.*, pp. 42-8.

39   D. K. Gardner, *op. cit.*, p. 53. Quotation adapted.

40   A. C. Graham, *Two Chinese Philosophers*. pp. 8-11, and J. H. Berthrong, *op. cit.*, p. 107.

41   'Oughtness', term used by C. O. Hucker, in *China's Imperial Past*, p. 92.

42   This thought is close to the Lotus Sutra and the T'ien-tai (Tendai) universalism.

43   *Ta Hsüeh*, 'Commentary of Tseng Tzu', 5; translation from D.K. Gardner, *Chu Hsi and the Ta-hsüeh*, pp. 104-5. See also D. K. Gardner, *Learning to be a Sage*, pp. 117-8.

44   From Chu Hsi's *Tu-shu lu* ('Notes on Reading'), quoted in W.-T. Chan, 'The Ch'eng-Chu School of Early Ming', in Wm. T. de Bary (ed.), *Self and Society in Ming Thought*, p. 34.

45   W.-t. Chan, *Chu Hsi and Neo-Confucianism*, p. 54.

46   See the *Kinshiroku* (*Chin-ssu lu*), III: 9-13, tr. in W.-t. Chan, *op. cit.*, pp. 91-93.

47   Ōhashi Junzō, quoted in G. Wm. Knox, 'Ki, ri and Ten', in *TASJ*, 1st series, XX, pt. I (1892), p. 168.

48   Quotation from Y.-S. Kim, *op. cit.*, p. 22.

49   This trinity is, *mutatis mutandis*, close to the Christian trinity with God = Heaven, Christ = Tao, and Holy Spirit = ri.

50   J. P. Bruce, *Chu Hsi and His Masters*, p. 101, p. 303 and p. 306.

51   Cf., Tai Chen's statement in his 'Fifteen Articles on the Meaning of Principle (ri)', in which he says, 'Ri is a name assigned to the arrangement of the parts of anything which gives the whole its distinctive property or characteristic, and which *can be observed by careful examination and analysis of the parts down to the minutest detail*' (emphasis added). Translation from A. Chin and M. Freeman, *Tai Chen on Mencius*, p. 69.

52   The quotations are from *Chu-tzu yü-lei* 12: 8b3-9ao and 11: 3a1. Tr. Y.-S. Kim, *The Natural Philosophy of Chu Hsi (1130-1200)*, p. 22. Y.-S. Kim's excellent chapter contains more apt quotations. As J. R. Levenson puts it: 'A thing exists as a complex of ri and ki, ideal form and mutable matter. To ki, which is perceptible, ri is the regulative principle: to li, which is intelligible, ki is the medium in which it manifests itself. Li is the universal which the intellect apprehends and the senses never reach, and the metaphysical order is from universal to particular, from Being to individual things.' J. R. Levenson, *Modern China and its Confucian Past*, p.3.

53   Quotation from K. F. Thompson, Jr., *Whitehead's Philosophy of Religion*, p. 18. See Whitehead's *Science and the Modern World* for his 'philosophy of organism'. Other European philosophers have been close to Chu Hsi, among them, Hobbes, Spinoza and Leibniz.

54   Quotation from C. A. Ronan and I. Needham, *The Shorter Science and Civilisation: I*, p. 246.

55   Another interpretation of the term is presented by P. Demiéville in the *Annuaire du Collège de France for 1947*. He traces the term to the *Book of Odes* (*Shu Ching*) and concludes that it originally referred to the division of land into plots. He ends with the translation 'un principe d'ordre, de bonne répartition des choses'. He adds that it was the Buddhists who made it into an 'absolu métaphysique' in opposition to the phenomenal and relative world. A. C. Graham, *op. cit.*, p. 21. Yet another translation of ri could be 'organization' 'since the universe can be described in terms of organized levels'. C. A. Ronan and J. Needham, *op. cit.*, p. 239.

56   K. Shimada, *Shushigaku to Yōmeigaku*, pp.91-2. It is tempting to compare the tao in Chinese thought with the 'unmoved mover' in Greek thought. There are similarities, but it has to be remembered that the 'unmoved mover' is indeed 'unmoved' while the tao implies constant 'movement'.

57   Ri is first found in the *I Ching* in the binomial word *kyūri* (*Ch. chiung li*), 'to probe and apprehend the ri [in things]'. Later, in the *Hou-nan-shu* and *Wei-shih* (AD 297), it refers to the study of the patterns and inscapes of things and not to any heavenly 'principle' in things and activities. D. K. Gardner, *op.cit.*, p. 12.

58   Ri has been decribed as a 'perplexing idea' (W. Peterson, *op. cit.*, p. 13) and it has been translated into English in various ways. As D. K. Gardner says, 'As there is no one English word that conveys the full sense of Chu Hsi's Neo-Confucian understanding of the term ri, rendered 'principle' here, one is tempted to leave it untranslated. But since over the years 'principle' has become the standard translation for ri, I will acquiesce to convention, trusting that the reader will not be deterred by the English 'principle' to gaining an understanding of the Chinese concept as he confronts the concept in Chu's numerous comments.' D. K. Gardner, *Chu Hsi and the* Ta Hsüeh, p. 104.

59   W.-t. Chan points out that the three latter cases is of a higher order, but still refers basically to order. W.-t. Chan, *The Evolution of the Neo-Confucian Concept* li *as Principle*, pp. 48-9.

60   H. Watanabe finds *li* (Jpn. *rei*) a difficult term to translate. He lists 'ritual, rites, manners, propriety, rules of proper conduct' as examples of English translation. The li according to Professor Watanabe, 'concretized forms of tao (the Heavenly Way) or *li* (the Heavenly Principle *ri*) which any human being should comply with as long as he or she wants to live in a civilized way'. H. Watanabe, 'Rituals of the Tokugawa Shogunate and Confucianism', in *Courtiers and Warriors*, pp. 167-74.

61   J. Needham, *op. cit.*, p. 27. D. J. Munro, *The Concept of Man in Early China*, pp. 23-9 *passim*.

62   Rendering kei and sei as (outer) and (inner) sincerity is an attempt to keep them apart. Kei also stretched inner and sei also outer. There was however a distinction, kei displaying 'outer' dignity and behaviour and sei showing an 'inner' state of tranquillity. When the Wang Yang-ming school equalled sei and ryōchi, sincerity was identified with the Way of Heaven. Cf., the *Chung Yung*: 'Sincerity is the beginning and end of things; without sincerity there would be nothing.' Thus, the inner state school equalled *sei* and *ryōchi*, sincerity was identified with the Way of Heaven. Cf., the *Chung Yung*: 'Sincerity is the beginning and end of things;

without sincerity there would be nothing.' Thus, the inner state of sincerity comes before outer behavioural sincerity. R. E. Carter, *Encounter with Enlightenment*, p. 70, with reference to P. Reasoner, 'Sincerity and Japanese Values', in *Philosophy East and West*, 40, no. 4, p.476.

63 This passage is based on J. Needham, *op. cit.*, p. 477.

64 As for Liu Shao and his thought, see J. K. Shryock, *The Study of Human Abilities. The Jen wu chih of Liu Shao*. New Haven, pp. 1-45, and *in toto*.

65 B. S. Solomon, '"One is No Number" in China and the West', in *HJAS*, vol. 17 (1954), p. 257, with reference to the *I Ching*, 7 (ts'e 2).9.a; 12b, and Legge, *Sacred Books of the East*. 16, p. 375.

66 *Chu-tzu yü-lei*, 94: 11a, quoted by W.-t. Chan, *Chu Hsi and Neo-Confucianism*, p. 104.

67 'It gives witness to the philosophical influences coming from Hua-yen and T'ien-t'ai Buddhism, with their teaching of one in all and all in one of the "Storehouse of the Absolute" in its totality, which has within itself the natures pertaining to all other things.' J. Ching, *Confucianism & Christianity*, p. 131. The unity in multiplicity need not be limited to eastern thought. It was likewise expressed by mystics in the West. For example, Nicholas of Cusa expressed the idea that God is revealed in everything, when he said, 'God is in all things in such a way that all things are in him.'

68 The term *taikyoku* (*t'ai-chi*) is derived from the Great Commentary of the *I Ching, The Book of Changes*. It says, 'In the Changes there is the Great Ultimate (*taikyoku*), which generates the primary forms (the *yin* and the *yang*) . . .' (*Sources of Chinese Tradition*, p. 196). The *taikyoku* may also be translated as the 'ultimate limit', with reference to the outer border of our cosmic reality.

69 This comes close to 'the Buddhist *tathāgata-garbha* (storehouse of the absolute) idea, which maintains that each thing is the *tathāgata-garbha* in its entirety while possessing within itself the natures of all other things.' Quotation from J. Ching, *The Religious Thought of Chu Hsi*, p.46. See also *Chu-tzu yü-lei* 94:35b.

70 H. C. Tillman, *Consciousness of t'ien in Chu Hsi*. pp.40-2, and C. Blacker, *The Japanese Enlightenment*, p. 44. Blacker continues: 'The li of a fish was the essence of its fishiness, that by which it was essentially a fish rather than a bird or a shapeless lump of matter. It was li therefore, which kept order in the universe. Were it not for li, a Japanese follower of Chu Hsi explained, eyes might be vertical and noses horizontal; people might walk on their heads and carry things with their feet; crows might hatch out from storks' eggs and willow trees might grow from peach seeds. Everything, including even dried and withered things and incorporal moral ideas, owed its distinct and separate nature to its li. One is reminded of Plato and his world of ideas and of the DNA in modern biology.

71 *Gogyō* is often translated as the 'Five Processes' (A. C. Graham) or the 'Five Phases' (W. A. Rickett), the reason being that *gogyō* denotes movement and change in contrast to the elements in Greek philosophy which rather denote *unchanging* substances. In this work the old translation 'element' is used.

72 J. R. Levenson, *Confucian China and its Modern Fate*, p. 4.

73 J. Ching, *op. cit.*, p. 28. Excellent definition of Chu Hsi's ri.

74 W.-m. Tu, 'Neo-Confucian Religiosity and Human-Relatedness', in *Confucian*

Thought: Selfhood as Creative Transformation, p. 132. W.-m. Tu is also quoted in M. E. Tucker, *Moral and Spiritual Cultivation in Japanese Neo-Confucianism, The Life and Thought of Kaiban Ekken (1630-1714)*, p. 8. Tucker's discussion of 'the religious dimensions of Neo-Confucianism' is enlightening (pp. 6-10).

75   K. Mugitani, 'What is the Core of Taoist Thought? The Meaning of the Trinity: Tao, Ch'i and God', in *Dōkyō to Higashia-Ajia bunka*, p. 213.

76   B. I. Schwartz, *The World of Thought in Ancient China*, pp. 179-82.

77   Y.-s. Yü, '"O Soul, Come Back!" A Study in the Changing Conceptions of the Soul and Afterlife in Pre-Buddhist China', in *HJAS*, vol. 47: 2, p. 376.

78   Mencius, 2A: 2.

79   Term borrowed from A. Wittenborn, *Further Reflections on Things at Hand, A Reader Chu Hsi*, p. 23.

80   Chu Hsi emphasized that ri has no visible forms or traces, whereas ki has. Y.-s Kim, *op. cit.*, p. 38. 'A thing exists as a complex of ri and ki, ideal form and mutable matter. To ki which is *perceptible*, ri is the regulative principle; to ri, which is *intelligible*, ki is the medium in which it manifests itself.' (emphasis added) J. R. Levenson, *Modern China and Its Confucian Past*, p. 3. New-fangled terms like 'materialism' and 'idealism' do not fit in.

81   A. Wittenborn, *op. cit.* p. 22.

82   See the *Lun Yü*, 3: 7; cf., the *Lun Yü*, 1: 1. The ideal man for Confucius was the virtuous man (*kunshi*, Ch. *chün-tzu* Jpn. *kunshi*) who had achieved the inner and outer balance. The sage, (*sheng-jen* Jpn. *seijin*), the semidivine man in the Chinese tradition, and the worthy (*hsien-jen*, Jpn. *kenjin*) were the nonpareil. The *seijin* were the inimitable early kings and almost saints, 'co-virtuous with Heaven and earth', while *kenjin*, the 'wise men', and the *kunshi* (*chün-tzu*), the virtuous men in the world. Among the sages 'Yao and Shun were the true paragons' (*Kinshiroku* XIV: 1). On the whole, however, they were all three ideals for the Confucian to emulate. For a discussion of the sage and sagehood, see J. Ching, *Confucianism & Christianity*, pp. 79-86.

83   J. C. Cooper, *Yin & Yang, The Taoist Harmony of Opposites*, p. 60.

84   See Y.-s Kim, *op. cit.*, p. 33. I have profited from Kim's work.

85   Y.-s. Yü, *op. cit.*, p. 376.

86   B. I. Schwartz, *op. cit.*, pp. 181-2, slightly adapted.

87   See Y.-s Kim, *op. cit.*, pp. 34-5.

88   As for *konton* (Ch. *hun-tan*) in Chinese cosmogony see, N. J. Girardot, 'Behaving Cosmogonically in Early Taoism', in R. W. Lovin and F. E. Reynolds (eds), *Cosmogony and Ethical Order*, pp. 67-97. The first articulated ki cosmogony is found in the *Huai-nan Tzu*, a Taoist work from about 120 BC.

89   This *genki* thought (*genki-ron*) contrasts with the early 'atomic' thought in the West. If the atom was considered the smallest part of a material world in the West, the *genki* comprised the totality of a vitalistic, interdependent world of energy-matter in the East.

90   This passage is based on D. C. Lau, 'Introduction' to his translation of the *Mencius*, p. 24. The quotations are adapted to fit the context. Man's endowment of ki was considered purer than the ki of other things and beings.

91   Ki is 'a difficult term to define and translate, referring as it does to both the

material and the energy that pervade the universe and everything in it' (D. K. Gardner, op. cit., p. 49). There are various attempts at an English translation, for example, 'breath, states or processes of psycho-physical energy, etc.' (Hoyt Cleveland Tillman), 'mutable matter' (Joseph R. Levenson), 'vital gas', 'vapour' (Derk Bodde and Fung Yu-lan), 'fluidum' (Forke) 'connotations of material energy, breath of life, atmosphere', 'ether' (I. McMorran, J. P. Bruce, and others), 'substance' (W. E. Hocking), 'living force' or 'life force' (N. Hiraishi), 'material force', 'vital force', 'matter-energy' (Wing-tsit Chan, Ariane Rump and Joseph Needham), 'energy-matter' (Edward Schafer), 'The Great Ethereal' (Carsun Chang) 'vital breath' (Donald Holzman), 'primordial ether' (Charles O. Hucker), 'material force' (G. Elison), 'psychophysical stuff' (D. K. Gardner) and 'universal energy', 'pure spirit', 'building block of the universe' (A. Wittenborn). Also 'pneuma' (Gk: breath) is found in the literature. The concensus and conclusion is that it is a difficult term to translate. See H. Cleveland Tiliman, 'Consciousness of T'ien in Chu Hsi's Thought', in HJAS, vol. 47: 1, p. 34; Fung Yu-lan, A History of Chinese Philosophy, 2 vols,. Princeton, 1952; The Spirit of Chinese Philosophy, p. 175; and The Philosophy of Chu Hsi; I. McMorran, Fang I-chih and the Neo-Confucian Tradition in The Unfolding of Neo-Confucianism, p.443 et passim; and W. E. Hocking, 'Chu Hsi's Theory of Knowledge', in HJAS, vol. 1, p. 113. Cf., J. P. Bruce, Chu Hsi and His Masters, pp. 100-25, B. I. Schwartz, The World of Thought in Ancient China pp. 179-84, J. R. Levenson, Modern China and its Confucian Past, pp. 3-4, Wang Pi, Commentary on the Lao Tzu, p. 130 and D. K. Gardner, Learning to be a Sage, p. 90ff. The preferred translation here is 'energy-matter', because it connects with modern science. Mostly, however, the term is left in its Japanese (or Chinese) form: Ki (ch'i).

92   J. Farquhar, quoted in R. T. Ames and D. L. HalL op. cit., p. 21. Adapted.

93   'Quotations, slightly adapted, from Y.-s. Yu, '"O Soul, Come Back!" A Study in the Changing Conceptions of the Soul and Afterlife in Pre-Buddhist China', in HJAS, vol. 47: 2, p. 377. Yü bases himself on the Ho-shang Commentary on the Lao Tzu.

94   Ibid., p. 374. Y.-s. Yü reasons that the dual concepts of hun and p'o and yin and yang, like also the dual concept of heaven and earth developed in Chou times and were fully accepted in Han times – when reality was a ki reality.

95   C. O. Hucker China's Imperial Past, p,71.

96   The I Ching, The Lao Tzu and The Chuang Tzu are the three early works which equally proclaim a ki (super)naturalism. As for the Lieh-tzu, see A. C. Graham, The Book of Lieh-tzü, and the Huai-nan Tzu, see B. E. Wallacker, The Huai-nan Tzu and C. Le Blanc, Huai-nan Tzu, Philosophical Synthesis in Early Han Thought.

97   Y.-s. Yü, op. cit., p. 376-7.

98   I. Robinet, Taoism, Growth of a Religion, pp. 15-18.

99   Tao-te-ching, ch.. 42. In 'Commentary on the Lao Tzu by Wang Pi', Ariane Rump (tr.) in collaboration with W.-t. Chan, in Monographs of the Society for Asian and Comparative Philosophy, no. 6, The University Press of Hawaii, 1979, p. 128. Cf., S.-h. Liu and R. E. Allinson, Harmony and Strife, Contemporary Perspectives, East & West, p. 214.

100 See J. Needham, op. cit., pp. 21-3.

101 As for the Kuan tzu, see W. A. Rickett, Kuan tzu, A Repository oF Early Chinese Thought, pp. 1-37.

102 A. C. Graham, *Disputers of the TAO*, p. 101.

103 W. A. Rickett, *op. cit.*, p. 158. Translation modified.

104 *Ibid.*, p. 164. Translation modified.

105 For Chang Tsai and his philosophy see, for example, Fung Yu-lan, *A Short History of Chinese Philosophy*, pp. 278-80 and *The Spirit of Chinese Philosophy*, pp. 175-8. As for a full analysis of his thought see I. E. Kasoff, *The Thought of Chang Tsai (1920-1077) in toto* and W. Eichhorn, *Die Westinschrift des Chang Tsai. Ein Beitrag zur Geistesgeschichte der nördlichen Sung* also *in toto.* And below.

106 *Chung Yung*, Ch. 30, partial translation by Yung-wei Lao in 'On Harmony: The Confucian View', in S.-h. Liu and R. E. Allinson, *op. cit.*, p. 197.

107 It should be noted that we deal with two kinds of science. The term refers mostly to western 'modern science' or 'natural science' in this work. When it refers to 'Chinese science' or 'kyūri' science, it concerns a wider, unwesternized reality that includes metaphysics. 'Proto-science' has been used for pre-modern science in this work.

108 For this whole passage I am much indebted to C. A. Ronan and J. Needham, *op. cit.* pp. 27-158.

109 *Chu Tzu ch'üan-shu*, 49: 1a, quoted in *Sources of Chinese Tradition*, p. 481.

110 *Chu-Tzu yü-lei*, I: 1b. Cf., J. Needham, *op. cit.*, pp. 472-89.

111 See M. Miyake, 'Jukyō ni okeru gōrishisō', in *Nihon shisō-shi kōza 4*, (*Kinsei no shisō, 1*), p. 148, where *Chu Hsi yü-lei* is quoted and J. P. Bruce, *Chu Hsi and His Masters*, p. 121.

112 *Chu-tzu yü-lei* 1:2a, quoted by J. Ching, *op. cit.*, p. 29.

113 *Chu-tzu yü-lei*, 94: 6a. *Mutatis mutandum* one finds Chu Hsi close to especially Aristotle and also other western thinkers, such as Aquinas and Whitehead. Such comparisons are useful even if relative. See J. Ching, *op.cit.*, p. 243 and J. Visarius, *Untersuchungen zur Metaphysik des Chu Hsi*, pp. 86-91.

114 See J. Needham, p.480

115 Quotations from J. Needham, *op. cit.*, pp. 480-1.

116 C.Schirokauer, *A Brief History of Japanese Civilization*, p. 163.

117 J. P. Bruce, *Chu Hsi and his Masters*, p. 126 and *Chu Tzu ch'uan-shu*, 49: 1 a-b.

118 See A. Wittenborn, *op. cit.*, p.22 and J. Ching, *op. cit.*, p. 98.

119 See A. Wittenborn, *op. cit.*, p. 22. Cf., C. A. Ronan and J. Needham, *The Shorter Science & Civilization in China: 1*, pp. 239-40.

120 H. Busch, *The Tung-Lin Academy and Its Political and Philosophical Significance*, in *Monumenta Serica, Journal of Oriental Studies*, vol. XIV (1949-1955), p. 131.

121 As for entelechy and Aristotle, see, for example, W. Durant.

122 It is tempting, however, to assume that Chu Hsi saw the 'germs', 'seeds' or 'beginnings' (ki) of the ri in the Unlimited, stored for the Great Ultimate world – thus close to Plato's ideas. J. Ching notes that ri and ki are passive and active, while Aristotle's form and matter are active and passive, respectively. J. Ching, *op. cit.*, p. 29.

123 Specifically, it is Chu Hsi's comments on the following passage in the *Chung Yung* (I:1): 'What Heaven ordains is called nature; to follow nature is called tao; cultivation of the tao is called instruction.'

124 As expressed by Yamagata Daini, in *Yanagi-shi shinron*, Ch. 3.

125 The *Ta Hsüeh* presented a simple programme in eight points about how to cultivate and discipline oneself, three of the points pertaining to social functions and five to personal cultivation, a simple system for moral order in personal life and in society. *Ta Hsüeh*, 1: 4 and *Sources of Chinese Tradition*, p. 114. See also above, n. 32.

126 Cf., R. L. Taylor, 'Confucianism: Scripture and the Sage', in *The Holy Book in Comparative Perspective*, pp. 194-5. The Five (Six) Classics (*I Ching, Shih Ching, Shu Ching, Ch'un Ch'iu, Li Chi, (Yüeh Chi)*) 'were not simply materials for the history of an age; they were texts for the ages'. J. R. Levenson, *Confucian China and its Modern Fate*, p. 92.

127 Yi T'oe-gye was an orthodox Chu Hsi scholar, representing Korean ri-ki-ism as it developed during the Yi dynasty. He was unknown in China but in Japan was recognized by scholars such as Fujiwara Seika, Hayashi Razan and Yamazaki Ansai. He played an important role in Tokugawa Neo-Confucian thought. 'Yi T'oe-gye's way of approaching the Chu Hsi philosophy was rather metaphysical, Chinese-like and individually-oriented and one based on spiritual cultivation.' Y. Abe, *op. cit.*, pp. 22-6.

128 *Mencius*, II, 1: 6.

129 *Mencius*, VII, 1:21,4.

130 Chu Hsi did not include trustworthiness among the 'beginnings'. See *Kinshiroku* (*Chin-ssu lu*), I: 41, where he explains that trustworthiness 'occupies no fixed position' (W.-t. Chan's translation, *op. cit.*, p. 30) and cannot be a moral beginning.

131 As for the debate that took place among Korean Confucian scholars about Chu Hsi and ri and ki see, for example, J. H. Berthrong, *Transformations of the Confucian Way*, pp. 146-9.

132 *Li Chi*, vol. 4. Desires are encoded in man's nature and their restraint is incumbent upon every man on his way to becoming a sage. Chu Hsi did not condemn the human emotions and desires but he distrusted them. He said: 'For nourishing the mind, there is nothing better than to have few desires.'

133 He has even been called 'the uncrowned emperor of China'.

134 No metaphysical system is presented, but Confucius hints at something when he says, 'Does Heaven say anything? The four seasons run their course and all things are produced. Does Heaven say anything?' Heaven speaks in its own way! *The Lun Yü*, 17:19.

135 *Ta Hsüeh*, 10: 6 and 7.

136 *Chung Yung*, 10:5 and *Lun Yü* 2:4.

137 P. J. Ivanhoe, *Ethics in the Confrucian Tradition*, pp. 9-10.

138 The *Lun Yü*, 2:4.

139 S.-h. Liu, *Understanding Confucian Philosophy*, p. 29.

140 O. Zierer, *Ideen bewegten die Welt*, p. 77.

141 'If scholars want to argue that there is nothing like Western metaphysics or cosmology in Confucianism, the Sung achievement proves otherwise. The Sung Neo-Confucian movement organizes the world in terms of principles and insights taken from its reading of classical Confucianism and modified by its response to the

Buddhist challenge.' J. H. Berthrong, *Transformations of the Confucian Way*, p. 86. See, also, M. Miyake, 'Jukyō ni okeru gōrishisō', in *Nihon shisō-shi kōza 4. (Kinsei no shisō, I*), p. 143.

142 C. O. Hucker, *op. cit.* p. 364.

143 T. H. Fang, *The Chinese View of Life*, p. 67 and C. A. Ronan and J. Needham, *op. cit.*, pp. 127-90.

144 D. J. Wyatt, 'Chu Hsi's Critique of Shao Yung: One instance of the Stand Against Fatalism', in *HJAS*, vol. 45:2, p. 650.

145 J. Needham, *op. cit.*, p. 507.

146 A. D. Birdwhistell, *Transition to Neo-Confucianism. Shao Yung on Knowledge and Symbols of Reality*, p. 58.

147 Chang Tsai quoted in T. Kuwako, *Seikan no tetsugaku*, p. 136. For the *Huai-nan Tzu*, see A. C. Graham, *Disputers of the TAO*, pp. 332-3.

148 Chang Tsai quoted in *Sources of Chinese Tradition*, pp. 466-7.

149 Quotation from Chang Tsai, found in I. E. Kasoff, *The Thought of Chang Tsai (1020-1077)*, p. 49. Much of the passage about Chang Tsai profits from Kasoff's clear presentation.

150 *Ibid.*, p. 72. Translation adapted.

151 I. E. Kasoff, *op. cit.*, pp. 52-3. The quotation is adapted. Ch'eng-Chu: the Ch'eng Brothers and Chu Hsi in abbreviated form.

152 J. H. Berthrong, *op. cit.*, pp. 104-5. See the *Chu Hsi yü lei* which runs like a paraphrase of Chang Tsai when it is said that all cosmos emanates from the One Primal Ki (*ichigenki*), 'Human beings, plants, trees, animals emanate from there. . . . All of them are ki.' For a discussion, see M. Miyake, 'Jukyō ni okeru gōrishisō', in *Nihon shisō-shi kōza 4, (Kinsei no shisō, I*), pp. 141-2.

153 For Chou Tun-i's Diagram, see, for example, J. P. Bruce, *op. cit.*, p. 129.

154 For the Chinese original, see *Kinshiroku* (Chin-ssu lu), I: I, and for a translation, W.-t. Chan, *op.cit.*, pp. 5-7. The present translation is also based on *Sources of Chinese Tradition*, pp. 513-4 and J. Needham, *op. cit*, pp. 460-2. The translation is adapted.

155 The *T'ai-chi t'u-shou* is probably based on an interpretation of the *I Ching*, perhaps in the light of both Taoist and Buddhist concepts. See D. K. Gardner, *Chu Hsi and the Ta Hsüeh*, p. 12. J. P. Bruce likens *t'ai-chi* to the 'roof ridge of a house, the highest point that can be reached . . . and the zenith in the heavens beyond which even thought cannot pass, . . . simply the law of the universe'. In today's parlance it would stretch to where the 'Big Bang' occurred. See J. P. Bruce, *Chu Hsi and His Masters*, pp. 133-7. Chou Tun-i, wisely, says nothing about the *wu chi*, lit. 'without limit', the yonder side of *t'ai-chi*.

156 The term *wu-chi* originates from the *Tao Te Ching*, ch. 28, which bespeaks a return to the Unlimited Infinite (*wu chi*). Early Chinese thought, not only Taoism, was aware of 'a beginning that was before all beginnings, sometimes termed "chaos"'. The *t'ai-chi* comes from the *I Ching*. 'Chu Hsi was preoccupied all his life with the cosmic origins of the universe.' J. Ching, *The Religious Thought of Chu Hsi*, pp. 35-40, passim.

157 *Chu-Tzu Yü-lei* 94: 10a, p. 3773. See also W. W. Lai, 'How Principle Rides on Ether: Chu Hsi's Non-Buddhistic Resolution of Nature and Emotion', in *Journal of*

Chinese Philosophy II (1984), 31-65.

158 For an excellent discussion of the *wu chi* ending up in the 'highest good', see Wm. T. de Bary, 'Neo-Confucian Individualism and Holism', in D. J. Munro (ed), *Individualism and Holism: Studies in Confucian and Taoist Values*, pp. 336-9.

159 Ch'eng Hao is revered for his sagely qualities. Quotation taken from R. L. Taylor, *The Religious Dimensions of Confucianism* p, 69.

160 W.-t. Chan, *A Source Book in Chinese Philosophy*, p. 523.

161 Words by Ch'eng Hao, quoted by R. L. Taylor, *op. cit.*, p. 19.

162 J. Needham, *op. cit.*, p. 458.

163 P. J. Ivanhoe, *Confucian Moral Self Cultivation*, p. 50. Chu Hsi has been described as 'der grosse Systematiker der neo-konfuzianischen Philosophie'. B. Lewin, *Kleines Lexikon der Japanologie. Zur Kulturgeschichte Japans*, p. 51.

164 For Chu Hsi, life and philosophy, see, for example, W.-t. Chan, *A Source Book in Chinese Philosophy*, pp. 588-653.

165 One can divide the history of Confucian thought into four (or five) periods. First, the classical *I Ching* era when things were loosely distinguished on the magic cosmic level; second, the Confucian period when human values adjoined the cosmic world; third, the first Confucian synthesis including all significant elements – Confucian, Taoist, Yin-Yang, Five Elements, Legalist – in one coherent whole in the Han (Han Confucianism); and fourth, the second Confucian synthesis which added a metaphysical ri-ki rationalism to earlier thought. If there is a fifth era today, it is one without a Heaven. For a different division of the Confucian tradition, see C.-y. Cheng, *Tai Chen's Inquiry into Goodness*, pp. 4-17.

166 P. J. Ivanhoe, *ibid.*, p. 49.

167 J. H. Berthrong, *op. cit.*, pp. 110-1.

168 The *Book of Odes*, the *Book of History*, the *Book of Changes*, the *Book of Rites* and the *Spring and Autumn Annals*. Originally there were the Six Classics, including the *Book of Music* that was lost – if it ever existed. The Classics and the Books were referred to as the *Shisho-gogyō* 'Four Books and Five Classics'. They 'comprised the database of customs, institutions and etiquette of ancient China'. S. A. Thornton, 'Ogyū Sorai', in I. P. McCreal, *op. cit.*, p. 373 and *ibid. Chu Hsi's program.*

169 This was in contrast to earlier Confucian studies, in which the earlier Five Classics came first. See D. K. Gardner, *Chu Hsi and the Ta Hsüelt*, pp. 5-6 and *ibid*, 'Chu Hsi' Program of Learning', *HJAS*, vol. 49: 1, pp. 145-50.

170 The early classics and books were further grouped together as the Thirteen Classics under Neo-Confucian influence. The Thirteen Classics consisted of the Five Classics, the Four Books, the *I li*, '*Ceremonies and Rituals*', the *Chou li*, 'Rituals of the Chou Dynasty', the *Kung Yang ch'uan*, 'Kung Yang's Commentary [to the Ch'un-Ch'iu]', the *Ku Liang ch'uan*, 'Ku Liang's Commentary [to the Ch'un-Ch'iu]', the *Chiao Ching*, 'Filial Piety Classic' and the *Er ya*, 'Continued Correctness'.

171 S.-h. Liu, *op. cit.*, pp. 173-4.

172 Reference to H. C. Tillman, *The Idea and the Reality of the 'Thing' during the Sung: Philosophical Attitudes toward WU*, p. 75, and C. Chang, *The Development of Neo-Confucian Though*, pp. 309-31.

173 *Chu-Tzu yü-lei*, 94:10a, and W. H. Lai, 'How Principle rides on Ether: Chu Hsi's Non-Buddhistic Resolution of Nature and Emotion', in *Journal of Chinese*

Philosophy II (1984), pp. 31-65.

174 C. O. Hucker, *China's Imperial Past*, pp. 370-1. For a complete translation of the *Chin-ssu lu* (*Kinshiroku*), see W.-T. Chan *Reflections on Things at Hand*, New York and London, 1967. For a discussion of the *Kinshiroku*, see Wm. T. de Bary, 'Neo-Confucian Cultivation and the Seventeenth-Century', in *The Unfolding of Neo-Confucianism*, pp. 153-60. de Bary translates the *Kinshiroku* as 'The Essentials of Learning'.

175 It must not be forgotten that ri is always 'embedded in ki'. It has been discussed whether Chu Hsi took a negative attitude toward feelings. W.-t. Chan means that 'all he wanted was to have human desires in the proper measure'. W.-t. Chan, *Chu Hsi, Life and Thought*, p. 30 and P. J. Ivanhoe, *Confucian Moral Self Cultivation*, p. 57.

176 W.-t. Chan, *Chu Hsi, Life and Thought*, pp. 139-61. The above paragraphs are much indebted to this passage.

177 Y. Abe, *op. cit.*, pp. 28-9. As an idealist, Chu Hsi belongs in the Mencian fold by upholding that the essential nature of man is good, while, as a realist, he explains human evils by means of the physical nature of man.

178 'He was a follower of Lu Chiu-yüan (Hsiang-shan), whose system he inherited and completed'. J. Ching, *op. cit.*, p. 193.

179 Introspective self-examination and mental tranquility should come first, external activities afterwards. First a Sage within, then a king without. (*nei sheng wai wang*, Jpn. *naisei gaiō*), close to Socrates who emphasized that 'All true insights come from within.'

180 M. Yoshida, 'The Chinese Concept of Nature', in S. Nakayama and N. Sivin, *Chinese Science, Explorations of an Ancient tradition*, p. 84.

181 J. R.Levenson, *Modern China and its Confucian Past*, p.4.

182 Metaphor used by Wang Yang-ming, quoted in P. J. Ivanhoe, *op. cit.*, p. 50.

183 W.-t. Chan, 'How Buddhistic Is Wang-Yang-ming?', in *Philosophy East and West*, 12: 3, pp. 232-3.

184 J. H. Berthrong, *op. cit.*, pp. 124-5.

185 Quotation in J. Ching, *To Acquire Wisdom, The Way of Wang Yang-ming*, p. 83.

186 C. Chang, *Wang Yang-ming*, pp. 18-19.

187 As for 'gradual' and 'sudden', see R. L. Taylor, 'The sudden/gradual Paradigm and Neo-Confucian mind-cultivation', in *Philosophy East and West*, XXXIII, 1 (1983), pp. 17-34.

188 See J. Ching, *To Acquire Wisdom, The Way of Wang Yang*, pp. 57-103 *et passim*, W.-m.Tu, *Neo-Confucian Thought in Action, Wang Yang-ming's Youth (1472-1509)*, pp. 13-54, *passim* and the *Ta Hsüeh*, I: 1.

189 See *Sources of Chinese Tradition*, p. 515.

190 Quotation from Ph. J. Ivanhoe, *op. cit.*, p. 73.

191 Ph. J. Ivanhoe, *ibid.*, p. 74.

192 *Liang chih* is a term from Mencius. See Ph. J. Ivanhoe, *ibid.*, p. 80. The Wang Yang-ming scholars tended eventually both towards pure intuition close to Zen Buddhism and to moral cultivation close to orthodox Chu Hsi thought. *Sources of Chinese Tradition*, pp. 524-6.

193 *T'ien* can refer to (1) the 'natural heaven', the physical blue sky, (2) to a ruler

(*chu-tsai*, Jpn. *shusai*) in the cosmic process and (3) philosophically to a moral heaven. Perhaps, in earliest times, to an anthropomorphic deity. See Y.-S. Kim, *op. cit.*, 135-71 and J. Ching, *op. cit.*, p. 55. (*Chu-tzu yü-lei*, 1: 22,8).

194 For discussions of Heaven, Shang Ti and the concept of a divine law-giver, see J. Needham, *Science and Civilization in China*, vol. II, p. 518 *passim*, and D. Bodde, 'Evidence for "Laws of Nature", in Chinese Thought', in *HJAS*, vol. 20 (1957), pp. 709-27.

195 W.-m. Tu, *Confucian Thought, Selfhood as Creative Transformation*, p. 38, with reference to W.-t. Chan, *A Source Book in Chinese Philosophy*, p. 264.

196 The tao of Lao Tzu was a cosmic tao, inner and unwritten, a tao of Nature, while the tao of Confucius was moral and written. The tao of the Legalists was thereupon a tao of Law.

197 *Kinshiroku*, XIV: 4.

198 J. Ching, *Confucianism & Christianity*, pp. 124-5. It is close to Spinoza's pantheism expressed as *Deus sine natura*.

199 Wang Ch'ung (*Lun heng*), quoted in J. Ching, *ibid.*, p. 125.

200 H. T. Kim, 'Transcendence Without and Within: The Concept of T'ien in Confucianism', in *International Journal for Philosophy and Religion*, III: 3 (1972), p. 160.

201 *Kinshiroku*, IV: 31. Cf., *ibid.*, IV: 37.

202 See P. Nosco, 'Nature, Invention, and National Learning: The *Kokka hachiron* Controversy, 1742-46', in *HJAS*, vol. 41: 1, p. 78.

203 This is in Confucian thought. In Taoism, tao comes first. In the *Chuang-tzu* it is said, 'Before Heaven and earth came into being, tao existed from all eternity. . . . It gave birth to Heaven and Earth' – 'It is the mother of all things under heaven'. The *I Ching* speaks of the three primal powers, the tao of Heaven, the tao of Earth and the tao of man which combine in the hexagrams. *Chuang-tzu*, ch. 6. D. H. Smith, *Chinese Religions*, pp. 75-7 and A. Waley, *The Way and Its Power*, p. 141.

204 J. Ching, *op. cit.*, p. 123.

205 Cf., R. L. Taylor, *The Way of Heaven, An Introduction to the Confucian Religious Life*, p. 24, and *ibid.*, *The Cultivation of Sagehood as a Religious Goal in Neo-Confucianism*, *in toto*.

206 For a comprehensive discussion of *jen*, see W.-t. Chan, 'Chinese and Western Interpretations of *jen* (*Humanity*)', in *Journal of Chinese Philosophy*, 2:2 (1975), pp. 107-29.

207 The Chinese word *jen* (Jpn. *jin*) is, as J. Needham concludes, 'almost impossible to translate'. Legge chooses 'benevolence' or 'virtue' and Waley uses 'goodness', but, he says, 'this does not convey (to my mind) the warmth of the conception. . .'. Wing-tsit Chan uses the term 'humanity' and 'human-heartedness'; and P. Boodberg uses the term 'co-humanity', stressing that *jen* is realized only in interaction with others. N. Needham, *op. cit.*, p. 11 and W.-t. Chan, *op. cit.*, pp. 119-20. In 'The Evolution of the Confucian Concept', in *Philosophy East and West*, 4:1, p. 1, W.-t. Chan lists sixteen different translations of *jen*.

208 W.-t. Chan, *op. cit.*, p. 122.

209 J. Ching, *Confucianism & Christianity*, p. 9.

210 Itō Jinsai said it almost as shortly in his *jinsetsu*, '*Jen* Doctrine: Goodness (*jin no*

toku) can be expressed with a single word "love" (*ai*)' See the *Lun Yü* 12:5, the *Meng Tzu* 6B: 2 and the *Lun Yü* 12:22.
211 The *Lun Yü*, 14:36, 3.
212 The *Chung Yung*, ch. 12.
213 Ch'eng Hao, *op. cit.*, p. 79.
214 Translation by R. L. Taylor, *The Confucian Way of Contemplation*, p. 14. A full version is found in *Sources of Chinese Tradition*, pp. 469-70.
215 Quotation in W.-t. Chan, *op. cit.*, p. 56.
216 In Y. Nakamura. *Kinsei no shisô*, pp. 1-41.
217 See O. G. Lidin, *Ogyū Sorai's Distinguishing the Way, An Annotated English Translation of the* Bendō, p. 38.
218 G. Leinss, *Japanische Anthropologic, Die Nature des Menschen in der konfuzianisache Neoklassik am Anfang des 18. Jahrhunderts, Jinsai und Sorai*, p.3, *passim*.
219 For the views on human nature in China, see C. Leinss, *op. cit.*, pp. 1-12, *passim*, and W.-t. Chan, 'The Concept of Man in Chinese Thought', in *Neo-Confucianism, Etc.: Essays by Wing-tsit Chan*, Harvard University (Oriental Society), pp. 117-85.
220 See, for example, *Kinshiroku*, IV: 30-41. W.-t. Chan, p. 136-40.
221 *Chu-tzu yü-lei*, 12: 7a. Quotation in J. Ching, *op. cit.*, p. 122.
222 *Kinshiroku* (*Chin-ssu lu*) (I: 21). W.-T. Chan's translation in *Reflections on Things at Hand*, p. 20.
223 I find it pedagogically correct to use the term *kokoro* for the mental apparatus that stands for human consciousness, mind and heart and (Gr.) *psychê*. It refers to both feeling and thought and is therefore translated, depending on context, as mind, heart, or 'heart-and-mind'. See R. L. Taylor, *The Centered Self: Religious Autobiography in the Neo-Confucian Tradition*, pp. 272 and 277 and W.-t. Chan, *Neo-Confucian Terms Explained*, pp. 56-61.
224 *Chün-tzu chi-chieh* 17: 206. Translation by Watson, pp. 80-1, and quoted by A. D. Birdwhistell, 'Knowledge heard and seen', in *Journal of Chinese Philosophy*, II (1984), p. 69.
225 *Chu-tzu ch'üan-shu* 14: 2a, and the *Meng Tzu*, 6B: 16.
226 The *Kuan-tzu*, Ch. 49, tr. in W. A. Rickett, *op. cit.*, p. 160.
227 J. Ching, *op. cit.*, p. 96.
228 J. Ching, *ibid.*, p. 137. *Chu-tzu yü-lei* 98: 7b and 5: 9a. Quotation found in J. Ching, *op. cit.*, p. 97.
229 D. K. Gardner, *Chu Hsi's Program of learning*, p. 170.
230 See *Shinkiroku*, IV: 48, 53 and 55.
231 Ph. J. Ivanhoe, *op. cit.*, p. 62.
232 Compare with W.-m. Tu, 'Subjectivity in Liu Tsung-chou', in D. J. Munro (ed.), *Individualism and Holism: Studies in Confucian and Taoist Values*, pp. 215-38.
233 J. Ching, *op. cit.*, p. 59-60. Opposite *t'ien-hsin* we find *jin-hsin* the human mind, which is 'precariously unstable' as it is influenced by human desires and passions. See also H. C. Tillman, *Consciousness of T'ien in Chu Hsi's Thought*, pp. 40-50.
234 Mostly later religious Taoism. See Fung Yu-lan, 'The Rise of Neo-Confucianism

and its Borrowings from Buddhism and Taoism', in *HJAS*, vol. 7, pp. 113-25.

235 *Jōri* is a term that may be followed through the whole Confucian tradition. It can be traced to the *Meng tzu* (V.II: 1-6) with the approximate meaning of 'harmonization'. Other sources give the meanings of 'inscape', 'pattern of ri in nature', 'logic (of nature)', '(blood) veins', 'reason',

236 Wang Pi is quoted in J. Ching, *op. cit.*, p. 153. Wang Pi (AD 226-249) initiated the *t'i* (substance) and *yung* (function) thinking.

237 Cf. *Bible*, 'Exodus', 3: 13.

238 *Kuan-tzu* quoted in R. H. Minear, 'Ogyū Sorai's "Instruction for Students": A Translation and Commentary', in *HJAS*, vol. 36 (1976), p. 44.

239 C. Blacker, *Japanese Enlightenment*, pp. 41-2.

240 The *Lun-yü*, 2: 4. Translation based on A. Waley, *The Analects of Confucius*, p. 88.

241 *Kinshiroku* (*Chin-ssu lu*), II: 59; W.-t. Chan, *op. cit.*, p. 66.

242 The examinations became a means for advancement and success. They were indispensible for official positions.

243 *Kinshiroku* (*Chin-ssu lu*), II: 1, W.-t. Chan, *op. cit.*, p. 35.

244 See Chu Hsi's *Method of Learning*, in D. K. Gardner, *op. cit.*, pp. 102-11.

245 *Kinshiroku*, X: 27. Tr. W.-t- Chan, *op. cit.*, p. 247.

246 R. L. Taylor, *op. cit.*, p.14 and *ibid, The Cultivation of Sagehood as a Religious Goal in Neo-Confucianism*, pp. 77-88 and 195-200. Li T'ung (1093-1163), Chu Hsi's teacher, recommended quiet sitting and looking within oneself for finding the Way.

247 There seems not to have been any single method for quiet sitting. 'Just act in an ordinary fashion and let quietude come forth from silence' was perhaps the general rule. 'It was not formalized like *zazen*, it was just quiet sitting.' R. L. Taylor, *The Cultivation of Sagehood as a Religious Goal in Neo-Confucianism*, p. 199. See also Wm.T. de Bary, *op. cit.*, pp.178-84.

248 *Chung Yung*, 1:4. Translation from R. L. Taylor, *op. cit.*, p. 36.

249 He was accused of being 'Bodhidharma half of the day and a Han scholar half of the day', that is, half a Buddhist and half a Confucian. W.-t. Chan, *op. cit.*, p. 27.

250 See J. P. Bruce, *Chu Hsi and His Masters*, p. 121.

251 See R. L. Taylor, *op. cit.*, p.17. Taylor refers to J. Wach's criteria for a religious experience, expressing that the Neo-Confucian reverence suggests a religious response to what is viewed as an Absolute. J. Wach, *The Comparative Study of religions*, pp. 27-58.

252 W.-t. Chan, *op. cit.*, pp. 84-5 and Y. Abe, *op. cit.*, p. 22.

253 The literati (samurai in Japan), peasants, artisans and merchants.

254 Or as C. Blacker expresses it vividly: 'The passage of the seasons and the movements of the stars, the way a hawk flies and a fish leaps, were manifestations of the same ultimate principles as those which prescribed that man should be filial to their parents and loyal to their lords, that there should be a proper distinction between husband and wife and mutual trust between friends.' C. Blacker, *The Japanese Enlightenment*, p.45.

255 In Chang Tsai's *Western Inscription*. See above ch.11.

256 See, for example, Chu Hsi's *Shinkiroku*, chs VIII-IX, and my translatation of Ogyū Sorai's *Seidan*, ch. II.

257 M. Maruyama, *Studies in the Intellectual History of Tokugawa*, pp. 191-2 *passim*.
258 Chu Hsi says,for example, in the *Kinshiroku*, IX: 3: 'When the principles of people's livelihood come to an end, the system of ancient sage-kings may be changed.' The criterion was, in other words, impoverishment. When poverty struck, even the sagely system could be changed. Translation: W.-t. Chan, *op. cit.*, p. 220.
259 *Kinshiroku*, I: 13, I: 19 and I: 30 (W.-t. Chan, *op. cit.*, p. 13 and pp. 24-5).
260 See M. Maruyama, *op. cit.*, pp. 94-5 *passim*.
261 As for Ch'en Liang, see H. C. Stillman, *Utilitarian Confucianism, Ch'en Liang's Challenge to Chu Hsiu, in toto*. The quotation comes from p. 157.
262 Ricci came to Peking in 1601 and aroused much interest in European science and had translations of books on mathematics, astronomy and other subjects made. C. O. Ronan and J. Needham, *op. cit.*, p. 57.
263 See M. Sugimoto and D. L. Swain, *Science & Culture in Traditional Japan*, p. 261-2.
264 See J. R. Levenson, 'The Abortiveness of Empiricism in Early Ch'ing Thought', in *The Far Eastern Quarterly*, vol. 23, Issue 2 (1954), pp. 155-65. If one defines modern science as 'an organized (that is, sustained and systematic) and empirically oriented effort to explain natural phenomena', 'it is indisputable that modern science emerged in the seventeenth century in Western Europe and nowhere else'. R. Stark, *For the Glory of God*, p. 146. Stark quotes E. Grant, *The Foundations of Modern Science in the Middle Ages*, p. 168. The question remains, asked by Einstein and others: Why did modern science develop in Europe and not in China?
265 See J. Ching, *To Acquire Wisdom, The Way of Wang Yang-ming* and W.-m. Tu, *Neo-Confucian Thought in Action, Wang Yang-ming's* youth.
266 For a presentation of Lo Ch'in-shun and his (ki) thought see I. Bloom, 'On the Abstraction of Ming Thought: Some Concrete Evidence from the Philosophy of Lo Ch'in-shun', in *Principle and Practicality*, pp. 69-125 and *passim*. See also Wm. T. de Bary, *op.cit.*, pp. 200-1.
267 See W. J. Peterson, 'Fang I-chih: Western Learning and the "Investigation of Things"', in *The Unfolding of Neo-Confucianism*, Wm. T. de Bary (ed.), New York and London, 1975.
268 See I. McMorran, 'Wang Fu-chih and the Neo-Confucian Tradition' in *The Unfolding of Neo-Confucianism*, pp. 413-67 and *The Passionale Realist, An Introduction to the Life and Political Thought of Wang Fuzhi (1619-1692)*.
269 W. J. Petersen, 'The Life of Ku Yen-wu (1613-1682)', in *HJAS*, vol. 28: 1 and vol. 29: 2 and J. R. Levenson, *Confucian China and its Modern Fate*, p. 4.
270 J. R. Levenson, *op. cit.*, p. 6.
271 Wm. T. de Bary, *Neo-Confucian Cultivation and the Seventeenth-Century Enlightenment*. It should not be forgotten, however, that Ieyasu was a devout Buddhist. *The Unfolding of Neo-Confucianism*, p. 195.

PART II

272 He was a pragmatist who understood where to find the ideology that suited his Tokugawa state best. It should not be forgotten, however, that Ieyasu was a

devout Buddhist. 'Confucianism was the ideal instrument of moral discipline for the two-sworded class' (J. Murdoch, p. 117).

277 *Sengoku*, 'the country at war' and *gekokujō*, 'the overturning of those on top by those below'.

274 A. Craig divides the Tokugawa Confucian tradition into four periods: (1) The first relative pure Chu Hsi Confucianism, as represented by Fujiwara Seika and Hayashi Razan; (2) The second period when independent thinkers of the *ōyōmei* and *kogaku* gave the tradition new directions; (3) The third period which showed 'great complexity ... with overlapping developments' and eclectic tendencies; (4) The fourth period beginning in 1790 which was equally complex, now acerberated by the 'barbarian' menace but partly under shogunal control. See A. Craig, 'Science and Confucianism' in M. B. Jansen (ed.), *Changing Japanese Attitudes Toward Modernization*, pp. 155-6. It is also possible to divide Confucianism into three periods (1) the unorganized first era, ending with (2) the *Shoheizaka* era from 1691 when it became an established creed, and (3) the era beginning 1790 when it was declared the national orthodoxy.

275 See Y. Abe, 'Development of Neo-Confucianism in Japan. Korea and China: A Comparative Study', in *Acta Asiatica*, Nr. 19, p. 16, *passim*.

276 Buddhism, however, was much alive and the religion among the people. It was the intellectuals, mostly samurai, who stood aloof from Buddha.

277 T. H. Kang, mentions in his work, *The Making of Confucian Societies in Tokugawa Japan and Yi Korea*, p. 146, that Matsudaira Sadanobu included the Japanese gods in his han's Confucian shrine.

278 See *Japanese Religion, A Survey by the Agency for Cultural Affairs*, pp. 21-3.

279 M. Hane mentions in *Japan, A Historical Survey*, p, 93 that Ieyasu frequently invited Seika to lecture on Confucianism from 1593.

280 Text and translations as regards Fujiwara Seika are based on K. Murakami, *Rinrigaku*, pp. 375-8 and W. J. Boot, *The Adoption and Adaption of Neo-Confucianism in Japan: The Role of Fujiwara Seika and Hayashi Razan*, pp. 7-34 and 118-46, *passim*.

281 Y.-I. Fung, *A Short History of Chinese Philosophy*, p. 271.

282 *Suntetsuroku*, a work that discusses among other things sayings by Confucius. This quotation is found on p. 27 in *Nihon shisō taikei*, 28. Translation by H. Ooms, *Tokugawa Ideology*, p. 114. The letter is also quoted and translated by H. Ooms, same page. The term *kyōgen* (Ch. *hsiang-yüan*) is discussed in the Lun-yü, 17: 13 and in the *Mencius*, 7B: 37, 8-13.

283 Matsunaga Sekigo is known for his *Irinshō*, 'Comments about the Eternal Human Relationships', in which he presents the (Neo-) Confucian ethical principles in easy terms for people who might have been confused by Buddhist and Christian beliefs. See M. Rüttermann, 'Die Schreibregularien (*Shorei kuketsu*) des Kaibara Ekiken. Übersetzung und Kommentar. Erster Teil', in *Japonica Humboldtiana*, vol. 2 (1998), pp. 103-63.

284 Utsunomiya Ton'an is mentioned by Ihara Saikaku. See P. Nosco, 'Introduction: Neo-Confucianism amd Tokugawa Discourse', in P. Nosco (ed.), *Confucianism and Tokugawa Culture*, p. 12.

285 Official Confucian scholars were categorized with Buddhist monks in early

Tokugawa times (until 1691).

286 Hayashi Razan is quoted in K. Murakami, *Rinrigaku*, pp. 379-81. The exact source is not given.

287 Quotation in C. Totman, *Early Modern Japan*, p. 171. Totman in turn quotes Lu, *Sources*, 1: 236. Cf., T. Sagara, 'Ninsei jukyō no tokushoku', in *Nihon shisō-shi kōza 4*, *(Kinsei no shisō, 1)* p.69.

288 Quotation in D. J. Lu, *Japan, A Documentary History*, p. 246-7.

289 For Razan's Shinto studies, see H. Ooms, *op. cit.*, pp. 94-105 and Y. Abe, *op. cit.*, 19-21. Yoshida Shinto was founded in late Muromachi times by Yoshida Kanetomo (1435-1511), also called Yuiitsu Shinto. It incorporated much Confucian thought.

290 Quotation in Lu, *ibid.*, p 247. For a presentation of the *ōdō* concept, see D. M. Earl, *Emperor and Nation*, pp. 15-6 and Y. Nakamura, 'Itō Jinsai', in Y. Nakamura *et al.*, *Kinsei no shisō*, pp. 31-2. 'Ōdō is goodness and righteousness *(jingi)*' (Itō Jinsai).

291 *Nihon shisō taikei*, vol. 28. pp. 161-2.

292 For the *Santoku-shō*, see *Nihon shisō taikei*, 28, pp. 152-86. The translated part is found pp.161-5.

293 H. Ooms, *op. cit.*, pp. 82-3.

294 M. Maruyama, *op. cit.*, p.155.

295 I am grateful to William E. Deal for his analysis of Hayashi Razan. See *Great Thinkers of the Eastern World*, 1. P. McGreal (ed.), p. 347.

296 For a translation of the *Hai Yaso*, see G. Elision, *Deus Destroyed, The Image of Christianity in Early Modern Japan*, pp. 149-53 and H. Müller, *Hai Yaso Anti Jesus*, MN 2 (1939), pp. 268, 275.

297 Quotation found in C. Elison, *Ibid*, pp. 171-2. For a discussion of the *Myōtei mondō* and *Ha-deusu*, see *ibid.*, pp. 142-84.

298 T. Maruyama, *Nihon no kokoro, nihonjin no kokoro*, p. 10.

299 M. Anesaki, 'Japanese Criticisms and Refutations of Christianity in the Seventeenth and Eighteenth Centuries', in *TASJ*, 2nd Series, vol. VI (1929), pp. 1-3.

300 Even his original Japanese name is not known.

301 H. Bolitho, *Bereavement and Consolation*, p.21.

302 The Ōyōmei School was later criticized for being close to Zen. One of the critics was Bitō Nishū (1745-1813). T. Okada, 'Neo-Confucian Thinkers in the Nineteenth Century', in P. Nosco (ed.), *Confucianism and Tokugawa Culture*, p. 238.

303 In *Tōju sensei zenshū*, 1, pp. 215-7, as cited in Tsunoda *et al.* (eds), *Sources of Japanese Tradition*, vol. 1, p. 375.

304 M. E. Tucker, 'Nakae Tōju', in *Great Thinkers of the Eastern World*, p. 351.

305 Nakae's thought was intimately connected with a metaphysics of '(filial) piety' *(kō)* which, in an elaborate way, denoted the way of heaven, the origin of divine reason, creation and moral life.

306 On how he became Nakae Tojū's student and his life, see G. M. Fisher, 'Kumazawa Banzan, His Life and Ideas', in *TASJ*, vol. 16, pp. 223-58.

307 In this service Banzan received the unparalleled stipend for a Confucian scholar of 3.000 *koku*.

308 For a translation, see G. M. Fisher, 'Dai Gaku Wakumon, A Discussion of

Public Questions in the Light of Great Learning', in *TASJ*, vol. 16. (1938), pp. 259-356.

309 S. R. Turnbull, *The Samurai, A Military History*, p. 278.

310 M. Maruyama, *Rinrigaku*, p. 393, quotation from *Shūgi washo*, in *Nihon shisō taikei*, vol. 30, p. 141.

311 The *Shūgi washo*, is quoted in K. Murakami, *op. cit.*, pp. 394-5. See also *Nihon shisō taikei*, vol. 30, pp. 13-14.

312 Kumazawa Banzan, *Miwa monogatari*, quoted in K. Wildman Nakai, 'The Naturalization of Confucianism in Tokugawa Japan: The Problem of Sinocentreism', in *HJAS*, vol. 40: 1 (1980), p. 163.

313 Translation (*Shūgi washo*, VI: 234) in M. Maruyama, *Studies in the Intellectual History of Tokugawa Japan*, by M. Hane, p. 203 and in *Nihon shisō taikei*, vol. 30, p. 145.

314 Quotation from Banzan's *Shūgi gaisho*, found in *Edo jidai no shisō, Kindai Nihon no meicho*, vol. 1, p. 284.

315 Quotation from M. Maruyama, *op. cit.*, p. 203.

316 *Shūgi gaisho*, Book III, quoted in M. Maruyama, *op. cit.*, p. 213.

317 The virtue of *kei* was highly valued by orthodox Chu Hsi Confucian (ri) thinkers while the virtue of *sei* (*makoto*) came first among 'progressive' (ki) thinkers like Itō Jinsai and Katayama Kenzan. See T.Sagara, 'Kinsei jukyō no tokushoku', in *Nihon shisō-shi kōza 4*, (*Kinsei no shisō, 1*), pp. 55-66. *Keigi* (also read Moriyoshi) was symbolically his *azana* alias.

318 For a full quotation see R. Rubinger, *Private Academies of Tokugawa Japan*, p. 43.

319 The above quotations from the *Hekii* is found in *Nihon no shisō*, vol. 17, pp. 229-50.

320 S. Taira, 'Shintō shisō', in *Nihon shisō-shi kōza 4*, (*Kinsei no shisō, 1*) pp. 171-6.

321 The three commentaries were *Kinshiroku*, 'Reflections on things at hand', Hakurokudō-shoin, *Regulations for the White Deer Cave, and Shōgaku*, The Lesser Learning.

322 I am indebted to H. Ooms' excellent work, *Tokugawa Ideology, Early Constructs, 1570-1680*, Princeton, 1985, especially pp. 230-86. I have profited much from his vocabulary and phraseology.

323 R. L. Taylor, *op. cit.*, p. 27. Cf., T. Sagara, *op. cit.*, pp. 73-8.

324 Quotation in H. Ooms, *Tokugawa Ideology*, 233.

325 J. V. Koschmann, *The Mito Ideology*, p. 10.

326 Tentative translation 'Testament Offering Peace'.

327 From Tamaki Isai (Masahide) we know that Yamazaki Ansai created a cult of his 'self' late in life. See H. Ooms, *op. cit.*, p. 231.

328 D. M. Earl, *op. cit.* 61-5.

329 T. Najita's succinct description of the work. T. Najita, 'History and Nature in Eighteenth-century Tokugawa Thought', in *The Cambridge History of Japan*, vol. 4, *Early Modern Japan*, 615. Rai San'yō was a renowned littérateur, whose rich production embraced both verse and prose. For a full translation of the *Tokushi yoron*, see J. Ackroyd, *Lessons from History: Arai Hakuseki's Tokushi yoron*, University of Queensland, 1982, and for a pointed review of the same, see H.

Ooms, 'Hakuseki's Reading of History', *MN* 39: 3 (1984), pp. 333-50.
330 T. Najita, *ibid.*, p. 645.
331 D. Keene, 'Characteristic responses to Confuciasnism in Tokugawa Literature', in *Confucianism and Tokugawa Culture* P. Nosco (ed.), Princeton, 1984.
332 M. Bitō, 'Thought and Religion, 1500-1700', in *The Cambridge History of Japan*, vol. 4. *Early Modern Japan*, p. 409.
333 G. Wm. Knox, 'Ki, ri and ten', in *TASJ*, 1st series, XX (1892), p. 157.
334 R. Minamoto, '"Jitsugaku" and Empirical Rationalism', in de Bary and Bloom (eds), *Principle and Practicality*, p. 415. Quotation from *Nippon rinri ihen*, 8: 95.
335 M. Kassel, *op. cit.*, p. 70.
336 T. Okada, 'Practical Learning in the Chu Hsi School: Yamazaki Ansai and Kaibara Ekken', in Wm. T. de Bary and I. Bloom, *Principle and Practicality*, p. 281.
337 R. Minamoto, *op. cit.* p. 413. Quotation from *Nippon rinri ihen*, 8: 95.
338 See M. E. Tucker, *Moral and Spiritual Cultivation in Japanese Neo-Confucianism, The Life and Thought of Kaibara Ekken (1630-1714)*, pp. 73-5, *passim*.
339 R. Minamoto, *op. cit.*, 414. Quotation from *Nippon rinri ihen*, 8: 95.
340 J. Needham, *op. cit.*, p. 506. One is reminded of Spinoza who lived about the same time (1632-77) and also expressed a pantheistic view of the world.
341 In this connection, see Y. Abe, 'Development of Neo-Confucianism, in Japan, Korea, and China: A Comparative Study', in *Acta Asiatica*. Nr. 19 (1970), pp. 31-9. *passim*.
342 M. E. Tucker, *The Life and Thought of Kaibara Ekken*, p. 123, and 'Kaibara Ekken', in I. P. McGreal, *op. cit.*, p. 369.
343 For a translation, see Basil Hall Chamberlain, 'Teaching for the Young', in *TASJ*, vol. IX (1881), pp. 223-72.
344 The *Yamato zokkun* is translated in M. E. Tucker, *op. cit.*, pp. 131-220.
345 Or in James Legge's words, 'The great attribute of heaven and earth is the giving and maintaining of life'. *I Ching*, Hsi-tz'u chuan. *Sacred Books of the East*, vol. 16, p. 381.
346 *Ekken zenshū*, vol.2, pp. 173-5.
347 M. E. Tucker, 'Kaibara Ekken', in I. P. McGreal, *op. cit.*, p. 370.
348 Y. Abe. *op. cit.*, p. 26.
349 For a presentation of Yamaga Sokō, Itō Jinsai and Ogyū Sorai, see *Sources of Japanese Tradition*, vol. I, pp. 384-424.
350 Quotation from Carmen Blacker, *The Japanese Enlightenment, A Study of the Writings of Fukuzawa Yukichi*, p. 43.
351 For a full translation of the *Haisho zanpitsu*, see S. Uenaka, 'Last Testament in Exile', in *MN* 32:2 (1977), pp. 131-50.
352 The *Haisho zanpitsu*, in *Nihon no shisō*, vol. 17, pp. 331-3. Translation by S. Uenaka, *Last Testament in Exile, Yamaga Sokō's Haisho zanpitsu*, in MN, vol. 32, 2, pp. 125-50.
353 In *Yamaga Sokō zenshū*, 12:172, quoted in R. Minamoto, *op. cit.*, p. 432.
354 The three virtues of the accomplished *kunshi* were goodness/benevolence, knowledge/wisdom, and valour.
355 S. R. Turnbull, *op. cit.*, 282.
356 For the cultural tension between Japan and China through the centuries, see

D. Pollack, *The Fracture of Meaning*, in toto.
357 S. A. Thornton, 'Yamaga Sokō', in *Great Thinkers of the Eastern World*, 359.
Cf., Yamaga's *Kōtō yōryuku*, quoted in E. Ozawa, 'Kinsei rekishi shisō', in *Nihon shisō-shi kōza 5 (Kinsei no shisō 2)*, p. 89, which says, 'to honour the court and the emperor and to live up to the great rules and propriety of the military'.
358 C. Tolman, *Early Modern Japan*, pp. 173-4.
359 See T. Najita, 'History and Nature in Eighteenth-Century Tokugawa Thought', in *The Cambridge History of Japan, vol. 4, Early Modern Japan*, J. W. Hall (ed.), pp. 596-659. I have profited from pp. 612-3.
360 See *Edo jidai no shisō. Kindai Nihon no meicho*, vol. I, p. 181, where Yamaga Sokō's *Shidō* chapter from the *Yamaga gorui* is given.
361 See J. J. Spae, *Itō Jinsai, A Philosopher, Educator and Sinologist of the Tokugawa Period*, p. 102 and *passim*. Jinsai likened heaven and earth to one great box with the yin and yang being the ki inside. Spae, p. 102. J. A. Tucker, *Itō Jinsai's Gomō jigi and the Philosophical Definition of Early Modern Japan*, p. 25. The first piece of the translation I owe to J. J. Spae, the second piece to J. A. Tucker.
362 His studies demonstrated that, for example, 'quiet sitting' is not mentioned in either the *Lun Yü* of the *Meng Tzu*.
363 Translation of title by J. A. tucker, *ibid.*, p. 1.
364 *Gomōjigi*, ch. 1: 3. J. A. Tucker, *op. cit.*, p. 74. Since Tucker is using the translation 'generative force' for ki, this rendering of the term is kept in the quotation from his work. After all, 'generative force', 'life force' and 'energy matter' are synonymous terms.
365 Also this translation (slightly adapted) comes from J. A. Tucker, *op. cit.*, p. 73.
366 Quotation found in C. Totman, *op. cit.*, p. 180, based on R. Minamoto, 'Jitsugaku and Empirical Rationalism', found in de Bary and Bloom (eds), *Principle and Practicality*, pp. 149-50. The phrasing is de Bary's.
367 From *Dōjimon*, quoted in Minamoto, *op cit.*, pp. 434, 439; 446-7 and Totman, *op. cit.*, p. 181.
368 S. A. Thornton, 'Itō Jinsai', in I. P. McGreal, *op. cit.*, p. 363.
369 Quotation from de Bary, *Sagehood as a Secular and Spiritual Ideal*, pp. 148, 151.
370 Itō Jinsai, like Ogyū Sorai later, denied that poetry, as contained in the *Shih Ching, Book of Odes*, served as a vehicle for ethical morality as the Chu Hsi orthodoxy had it.
371 Reference to H. Ooms's review in *The Journal of Japanese Studies*, 22: 2 (1996), p. 386. Ooms mentions that the translation of Lo's work was published 'four years before Jinsai took on Sung Confucianism'.
372 J. A. Tucker describes how Itō Jinsai was also influenced by Chen Pei-ch'i Jpn. Chin Hokukeik (1159-1223), whose work *Hsing-li tzu-i, The Meanings of Neo-Confucian Terms*, was known and read in in his time. J. A. Tucker, *op. cit.*, pp. 19-26. It is in the end impossible to know which sources influenced a scholar like Jinsai the most. He read much and might have been influenced from many quarters. A fact is, however, that he was close to Ming thought.
373 S. H. Yamashita indicates that Jinsai 'did not move easily' from the Ch'eng-Chu philosophy and that there was an in between period, from 1662 to 1777, before his

opposition to it was clearly expressed. See S. H. Yamashita, 'The Early Life and
Thought of Itō Jinsai', in *HJAS*, pp. 465-7.
374 Translation found in S. Matsumoto, 'The Idea of Heaven: A Tokugawa
Foundation for Natural Rights', in T. Najita and I. Scheiner, *Japanese Thought in the
Tokugawa Period, Methods and Metaphors*, p.189.
375 R. Minamoto, *op. cit.*, pp. 436-7.
376 Quotation from C. Totman, *Early Modern Japan*, p. 180. Totman is in turn
quoting R. Minamoto, *Jitsugaku and Empirical Rationalism*, p. 436.
377 D. J. Lu, *op. cit.*, p.248.
378 M. Bitō, *op. cit.*, p. 423.
379 P. Nosco, *Remembering Paradise*, p. 36.
380 As he said in the *Benmei* 'Goodness (*jin*) is virtue, it is not human nature (*sei*),
so how could it be *ri*? *Jin naru mono wa toku nari, sei ni arazaru nari, iwanya ni wo
ya.*
381 O.G. Lidin, *The Life of Ogyū Sorai, a Tokugawa Confucian Philosopher*, pp. 99-
100.
382 K. Yoshikawa, *Jinsai, Sorai, Norinaga*, p. 84, *passim.*
383 None of the commentaries were published in Sorai's life-time. See Yoshikawa
Tesshi and Ishida Ichiro, 'Jukyō shisō no tenkai' (Imanaka, Kanshi), in *Nihon shisō-shi
kôza 4. (Kinsei no shisô, 1)*, pp. 91-5.
384 *Benmei*, in *Nippon rinri ihen* 6: 32, quoted in R. Minamoto, *op. cit.*, p. 440.
Translation by R. Minamoto, slightly changed.
385 See M. Maruyama, *op. cit.*, p. 241, *passim.*
386 Opening line in Sorai's *Kenen danyo*, a dubious work according to K.
Yoshikawa, *op. cit.*, p. 252.
387 S. Matsumoto, *op. cit.*, p.190.
388 K. Yoshikawa, *op. cit.*, p. 252 *et passim.*
389 The *Lun Yü* quoted in K. Yoshikawa, *op. cit.*, p. 251.
390 See O. G. Lidin, *Ogyū Sorai's Discourse on Government (Seidan), An Annotated
Translation*, Wiesbaden, 1999.
391 One can conclude that a man's talent(s) were the *ri* for Sorai, The rest was *ki*.
392 Chu Hsi had expressed the same in *Kinshiroku*, IX: 2.
393 Mukai Genshō studied medicine in Nagasaki and afterwards opened a school in
Kyoto. He is known for his antagonism to Aristotelian cosmology.
394 A. Craig, *Science and Confucianism in Tokugawa Japan*, in Marius B. Jansen,
Changing Japanese Attitudes Toward Modernization, pp. 140-1. Adapted quotation.
This is a reference to a classic (the *I Li*, ch., XXIII: 2) which says 'The birds and the
beasts know their mothers, not not their fathers.' See J. Steele, *The I-Li or Book of
Etiquette and Ceremonial*, vol. II, p. 19.
395 Quotation from Arai's *Saishikō* translated in K. Wiidman Nakai, *Shogunal
Politics*, p. 186.
396 The *Seiyō kibun* is found in *Nihon shisō taikei*, vol. 35, pp. 8-82. The first
volume is translated by W. B. Wright, 'The Capture and Captivity of Père Giovanni
Batista Sidotti in Japan from 1709 to 1715', in *TASJ*, vol. IX (1881), pp. 156-72.
397 See Li Su-ping, 'The Phiiosophical Concept of Ii in Chinese and Japanese Neo-
Confucianism: A Comparative Study', in *The Japan Foundation Newsletter* vol. XXIII,

no. 4 (January, 1996), p. 13, *passim*. Further, see *Sources of Japanese Tradition*, pp. 470-2.

398 As for Sidotti, see, for example, J. Murdoch, *A History of Japan*, vol. III, *The Tokugawa Epoch, 1652-1868*, pp. 304-6.

399 *Seiyō kibun*, ch. 3, in *Nihon shisō taikei*, vol. 35, p. 79.

400 S. Katō, (Katō Shūichi), *A History of Japanese Literature, The Years of Isolation*, p. 170. Expression attributed to Miura Baien.

401 K. Kasaya, 'The Identity of *Samurai* in the Tokugawa World', in *Two Faces of the Early Modern World: The Netherlands and Japan in the 17th and 18th Centuries*, pp. 168-9.

402 See M. E. Tucker, *op. cit.*, p. 37.

403 T. S. Smith has presented one of the 'technologists' in an excellent article, 'Ōkura Nagatsune and the Technologists', in A. M. Craig and D. H. Shively (eds), *Personality in Japanese History*, pp. 127-54.

404 M. Maruyama, *Nihon seiji shisō-shi kenkyū*, pp. 145-6.

405 See M. Kinski, *Knochen des Weges, Katayama als Vertreter des eklektischen Konfuzianismus im Japan des 18. Jahrhunderts*, p. 94.

406 T. Najita, 'Method and Analysis in the Conceptual Portrayal of Tokugawa Intellectual History, in T. Najita and I. Scheiner (eds), *Japanese Thought in the Tokugawa Period*, p. 15.

407 T. Okada, *op. cit.*, p. 217.

408 For Tominaga Nakamoto, life, writings and philosophy, see M. Pye, *Emerging from Meditation*, London, 1990.

409 See translation of *Okina no fumi*, in M. Pye, *op. cit.*, p. 53.

410 Printed in 1766. Probably written much earlier (by 1750?). See T. Najita, *Visions of virtue in Tokugawa Japan*, p. 130.

411 For Asada Gōryū and his studies, see M. Sugimoto and D. L. Swain, *op. cit.*, pp. 354-7.

412 For Hoashi Banri and his comprehensive scientific work, see M. Sugimoto and D. L. Swain, *op. cit.*, p. 305.

413 I gratefully admit that I have been influenced by T. Najita, 'History and Nature in Eighteenth-century Tokugawa Thought', in J. W. Hall (ed.), *The Cambridge History of Japan*, vol.4, *Early Modern Japan*, pp. 625-7.

414 See, for example, *Fukuzawa Yukichi on Education, Selected works*, tr. Eiichi Kiyooka, Tokyo, 1985.

415 The passage is much indebted to T. Najita's work about the Kaitokudō, its scholars and scholarship: N. Najita, *Visions of Virtue in Tokugawa Japan*.

416 The Sino-Japanese ri was read *kotowari* by Motoori Norinaga, as proven in this *waka* poem by him: *Kusuwashiki, Kotowari shirazute, Karahito no, Mono no kotowari, Toku ga hakanasa*, 'How wretched, Without understanding our ri (*kotowari*), Of the mysterious, To expound the Chinese, ri (*kotowari*) of things'. D. Pollack, *The Fracture of Meaning*, p. 185. Pollack's translation adapted.

417 This paragraph from P. Nosco who is quoted almost verbatim. See P. Nosco, *Remembering Paradise*, p. 86, *passim*. Quotation from *Nihon shoki jindai no maki satsuki*, in Nosco, *ibid*.

418 The result was the *Kojiki-den*, a translation and commentary of the *Kojiki*.

419 See, for example, M. Conte-Helm, *The Japanese and Europe*, p.8. Hirata acknowledged, however, European skills in astronomy and medicine.

420 The above paragraph is based on, first of all, *Sources of Japanese Tradition*, pp. 592-603.

421 This led, lastly, to the rallying cry 'sonnō-jōi', 'Revere the Emperor and Oust the Barbarians', by the Meiji Restoration.

422 M. Mehl, *Private Academies of Chinese Learning in Meiji Japan*, p. 15.

423 Katō Shūichi, 'Tominaga Nakamoto, 1715-46, A Tokugawa Iconoclast', in *Monumenta Nipponica*, XXII, 1-2, p. 178.

424 S. H. Yamashita, *Master Sorai's Responsals, An Annotated Translation of Sorai sensei tōmonsho*, p. 18.

425 For Andō Shōeki generally, see E. H. Norman, 'Andō Shōeki and the Anatomy of Japanese Feudalism', in *TASJ*, 3rd Series, vol. 2 (Dec. 1949).

426 For Andō Shōeki's ki 'theology', see K. Murakami, *Andō Shōeki no sekai*. pp. 77-116.

427 Both quotations are found in C. Totman, *op. cit.*, p.361. They come from E. Herbert Norman, *op. cit.*, pp. 221-2 and 243.

428 So anonymous in fact that he was 'discovered' as late in 1899. See T. Yasunaga, *Ando Shoeki*, p. 3, *passim*, and E. H. Norman, *Ando Shoeki and the Anatomy of Japanese Feudalisim, in toto.*

429 T. Najita, 'History and Nature in Tokugawa Thought', *op. cit.*, pp. 632-3.

430 J. Joly, p. 365. On Yamagata Daini see T. Najita, 'Restorationism in the Political Thought of Yamagata Daini (1725-1769)' in *The Journal of Asian Studies*, vol. XXXI, no. 1 (1971), pp. 27-31.

431 In a letter to Taga Bokkyō, *op. cit.*, in G. K. Piovesana's translation, *op. cit.*, p. 428.

432 M. Yanagizawa, 'Miura Baien to sono shūhen', in *Nihon shisō-shi kōza 4. (Kinsei no shisō 1)*. pp. 114-115 R. Mercer, *op. cit.*, p. 182. Mercer's translation is adapted.

433 See R. Mercer, *Deep Words, Miura Baien's System of Natural Philosophy*, p. 5, *passim*.

434 The above discussion of Miura Baien is based on R. Mercer's *Deep Words, Miura Baien's System of Natural Philosophy*, pp. 4-5, *passim*. See also G. K. Piovesana, 'Miura Baien, 1723-1789, and His Dialectic & Political Ideas', in *MN* vol. XX, no. 4 (1965), pp. 389-443.

435 It is not fully clear when the heliocentric theory was presented to scholars in Japan and certainly not clear when Miura learned about it. As he mentioned it in his letter to Taga Bokkyō in 1777, it must have reached him before then. See R. Mercer, *op. cit.*, p. 194, where it is mentioned that he had read a work on astronomy, the *Tenkei wakumon*, already at twenty-four years of age. This would mean that he was acquainted with European astronomy, at least the Tychonian (Tycho Brahe) system, before 1750. The former Chinese cosmic view of a round-heaven-square-earth was replaced by a European cosmic view of a round-heaven-round-earth, a fact that must have disturbed Baien's thinking of opposites.

436 Baien did not often leave his abode in Bungo on Northern Kyushu, where he was both a farmer and a doctor. He took a genuine interest in medicine which included dissection of animals. This interest might have influenced his jōri thought.

See M. Yanagizawa, 'Miura Baien to sono shūhen', in *Nihon shisō-shi kōza 4, (Kinsei no shisō, 1)*. pp. 106-13.

437 In letter to Taga Bokkyō, translation by R. Mercer, *op. cit.*, p. 156.

438 The letter to Taga Bokkyō with this recommendation is, dated 1777.

439 G. K. Piovesana, *op. cit.*, p. 401. Miura Baien says himself in the letter to Taga Bokkyō that *jō* originally meant a branch of a tree, and referred to the grain of the wood. In the following paragraph he exemplifies how ki is conveyed along the grains of the wood. The grain determines the pattern in which the ki moves. See translation by R. Mercer, *op. cit.*, p.161.

440 R. Mercer refers to both Itō Shuntarō and Yukawa Hideki who both pointed to Niels Bohr's theory about the 'complementarity of the wave and particle of light' R. Mercer, *op. cit.*, p. 165.

441 There are three letters to Taga Bokkyō in the *Baien zenshū*. This letter is of especial value because it presents Miura Baien's thinking in fairly simple terms. It is found in *Baien zenshū*, vol. II. According to R. Mercer it is an exposition of Miura Baien's philosophical theory as it is found in the final version of the *Gengo*.

442 Letter to Taga Bokkyō translated by G. K. Piovesana, in *MN*, vol. XX, no. 4, pp. 434-5.

443 *Ibid.*, p. 434.

444 Correlations are part of the Chinese thinking since earliest times. For example, earth is the correlate of heaven and yin is the correlate of yang. Miura Baien was thus in the mainstream of Chinese philosophy with his warp and woof thought. How close he is to Chinese thought he shows when he presents a cosmogony that says: 'Heaven and earth are but the names given to the original ki and the concrete things (*mono*). Ki forms heaven whereas the concrete things form earth.'

445 R. Mercer, *op. cit.*, p. 196.

446 'Science of the southern barbarians', the first wave of European, mainly Portuguese, learning in Japan. See, for example, M. Cooper, *The Southern Barbarians, The First Europeans in Japan*, pp. 139-44 and O. G. Lidin, *Tanegashima, The Arrival of Europe in Japan*, pp. 180-4.

447 The title of the work is *Anatomische Tabellen*, in Japan referred to as *Tafel anatomia*, written by Adam Kulmus (1689-1745), a German professor at Danzig; first printed in 1722. It was a Dutch translation, printed in 1734, *Ontleedkundige tafelen*, that reached Japan by 1770. M. Sugimoto and D. L. Swain, *op. cit.*, pp. 317-28.

448 M. Sugimoto and D. L. Swain, *ibid.*, pp. 330-1. For the story of *rangaku* learning in Japan, see, for example, M. Sugimoto and D. L. Swain, *op. cit*, pp. 223-399. It should be noted that the heliocentric thinking was accepted much quicker in the Confucian world than in the Christian world, where the church tried to suppress it.

449 For the story of Sugita Genpaku and the introduction of Western science see Sugita Genpaku's *Rangaku kotohajime*, 'The Introduction of Rangaku' (1815), R. Matsumoto and E. Kiyooka (tr.), Tokyo 1969.

450 K. T. Hosuck, *The Making of Confucian Societies in Tokugawa Japan and Yi Korea: A Comparative Analysis of the Behavior Patterns in Accepting the Foreign Ideology, Neo-Confucianism*, p. 195 and H. Passin, 'Modernization and the Japanese Intellectual: Some Comparative Observations', in *Changing Japanese Attitudes*

Toward Modernization, pp. 447-87.

451 For a thorough review of these developments, see T. Okada, 'Neo-Confucian Thinkers in the Nineteenth Century', in P. Nosco (ed.), *Confucianism and Tokugawa Culture*, pp. 21550.

452 See D. H. Shively, 'Tokugawa Tsunayoshi, the Genroku Shogun', in *Personality in Japanese History*, A. M. Craig and D. H. Shively (eds), pp. 114-5, *passim*.

453 Cf., R. Rubinger, *Private Academies of Tokugawa Japan*, pp. 24-33, *passim*.

454 Quotation from *Jurin hyō*, in M. Kinski, *Knochen des Weges*, p.4.

455 From Matsudaira Sadanobu, *Kagetsu sōshi* (1812), quoted by H. Ooms in *Charismatic Bureaucrat*, p, 132. I am indebted to Professor Ooms for vocabulary and phraseology in the passage, pp. 122-50. It shows the complicated educational situation in the eighteenth century which led to Matsudaira's reform.

456 The Kansei prohibition was the first 'conscious policy to define the relationship of Confucianism to the national government'. See R. L. Backus, 'The Kansei Prohibition of Heterodoxy', *HJAS*, vol. 39: 1 (1979), p.66 *passim*.

457 See H. Ooms, *ibid.*, pp. 40-8.

458 Suzuki's *Shinbu no michi* primarily advocates ki thought. Ki penetrates all existence, 'including man, who inhales it through respiration. Man lives in it, and it lives in him, like a fish in the water.'

459 Tentative translation: 'Four Records of Word and Will'.

460 'Some referred to Issai as Chu [Hsi] on the outside, Lu [Hsiang-shan] on the inside'. T. Okada, *op. cit.*, p. 218.

461 Quotation in W. W. Smith, *Confucianism in Modern Japan*, p. 27.

462 Bitō is quoted in R. L. Backus, *op. cit.*, p. 79. Translation is adapted. Original in *Nihon rinri ihen*, VIII, pp. 409-10.

463 Tentative translation of title: 'Short Scripture about the Elimination of What is Wrong'.

464 Quotations found in *ibid.*, p. 25, in G. Wm Knox, 'Ki, ri and ten', in *TASJ*, 1st series, XX, p. 163 and in M. Maruyama, *op. cit.*, p. 307.

465 See for example, the *Nihon shisei taikei*, N. Mizuta and Arikata (eds), vol. 43, pp. 142-616.

466 S. Kato, *A History of Japanese Literature, The Years of Isolation*, p. 174.

467 Quotation from R. E. Kristensen, 'Western Science and Japanese Neo-Confucianism: A History of Their Interaction and Trapnsformation', in *Japanese Religions*, vol. 21: 2, p. 266.

468 *Yume no shiro*, Ch. 1: 30. Translation by T. Najita, in *Visions of Virtue in Tokugawa Japan*, p. 256.

469 S. Kato, *op. cit.*, p. 175.

470 K. T. Hosuck, *The Making of Confucian Societies in Tokugawa Japan and Yi Korea: A Comparative Analysis of the Behavior Patterns in Accepting the Foreign Ideology, Neo-Confucianism*, p. 195 and H. Passin, 'Modernization and the Japanese Inlellectual: Some Comparative Observations', in *Changing Japanese Attitudes Toward Modernization*, pp. 447-87.

471 *Yume no shiro*, II: 16, *Nihon shisō taikei*, 43, p. 253.

472 S. Kato, *op. cit.*, 175-6.

473 *Yume no shiro*, II: 15. *Nihon shisō taikei*, 43, pp. 254-9.

474 Translation (adapted) in S. Kato, *op. cit.*, p. 180.

475 Totally without a credo he seems not to have been. In ch. 1: 31 he finds everything in the universe unfathomable (*fusoku*) but ends up making the 'sun and heart' (taiyō-shin) the source of things. *Nihon shisō taikei*, 43.

476 As for Yamagata Bantō, see T. Najita, *op. cit.*, pp. 222-84.

477 T. Najila, *ibid.*, p. 253.

478 Two sections of the *Keiko-dan* are translated by M. Kinski in *Japonica Humboldtiana*, vol 1, pp. 143-95 and vol. 4, pp. 65-127.

479 For Kusama Naokata who is mostly forgotten in literature, see T. Najita, *Visions of Virtue in Tokugawa Japan*, pp. 227-48.

480 H. Bolitho, *Bereavement and Consolation*, p. 107. For the Kangien school, see also M. Mehl, *Private Academies of Chinese Learning in Meiji Japan*, Mehl mentions that the curriculum at Kangien included mathematics, medicine, military studies, astronomy, geography, National Learning, Dutch learning and etiquette, an indication of the wider education offered in the private schools in the 1800s.

481 See R. P. Toby, 'Both a Borrower and a Lender Be', in *MN*, vol. 46, no. 4 (1991), pp. 483-512.

482 Towards the end of the Tokugawa age we have the 'rational'-'irrational' dichotomy, *kaikoku*, 'open the country', on the one side and *jōi*, 'expel the barbarians' on the other. *Kaikoku* was the new rational thought asking for the opening of the country for foreign intercourse while *jōi* was the 'irrational' thought, opposing foreigners and foreign things.

483 Quotation in W. W. Smith, *Confucianism in Modern Japan*, p. 27.

484 For a study of the Neo-Confucian scholars in the nineteenth century, see T. Okada, *Neo-Confucian Thinkers in the Nineteenth-Century Japan*.

485 W. W. Smith, *op. cit.*, pp. 87-8.

486 See B. T. Wakabayashi, 'Katō Hiroyuki and Confucian Natural Rights, 1861-1870', in *HJAS*, vol. 44: no. 2. pp. 469-92. I have profited from this article.

487 Nishi Amane took an interest in the ri which he divided into *shinri*, 'mental ri' and *butsuri*, 'physical ri'. The word *tetsugaku* came from the day of its introduction to have the connotation of western positivistic philosophy. See T. R. H. Havens, *Nishi Amane and Modern Japanese Thought*, pp. 131-40 *passim*.

488 For Inoue Tetsujirō and his production, see G. K. Piovesana, *Recent Japanese Philosophical Thought 1862-1996*, pp. 37-44.

489 Among recent Confucian scholars in China, although in the shadow of the prevailing materialism and Mammonism, are Fung Yu-lan (1895-1990) and Mou Tsung-san (1909-95). For Okada Takehiko, see R. L. Taylor, *The Confucian Way of Contemplation, Okada Takehiko and the Tradition of Quiet-Sitting, in toto*. For today's Neo-Confucianism among Chinese, see S.-h. Liu, *op. cit.*, pp. 260-3.

PART III

490 Cf., R. Stark, *For the Glory of God*, p. 146.

491 See R. Mercer, *Deep Words*, p. 4. Kaibara Ekken and Miura Baien represent these scholars.

492 Joseph R. Levenson means that the Chinese empiricists never advanced

beyond pre-scientific nominalism, as represented by Peter Abelard (1079-1142) in Europe. They observed things, but they never came to observe things 'with a method and a purpose'. 'They stopped short on the scientist's long way to a universality, now, of laws, which govern the mutual relations of particular things.' J. R. Levenson, *op. cit.*, pp. 158-60.

493 Quotation from the *Hsün Tzu*, in J. Needham, *op. cit.*, p. 28.

494 Numata, Jirō, *Western Learning*, tr. of Matsudaira Sadanobu, *Uge no hitogoto*, p. 177.

495 Quotation from W. E. Hocking, *Chu Hsi's Theory of Knowledge*, p. 116, adapted.

496 W.-t. Chan, 'The Concept of Man in Chinese Thought', p. 176. Tr. of Chu Hsi's commentary on the *Ta Hsüeh*, ch. 5.

497 Or as D. K. Gardner puts it in *Learning to be a Sage* (pp. x-xi): 'Study was thus the road to self-awakening, the process of returning to one's true self; *for Chu Hsi its aim was never the acquisition of knowledge for its own sake*' (emphasis added).

498 Or as D. K. Gardner puts it in *Learning to be a Sage* (pp. x-xi): 'Study was thus the road to self-awakening, the process of returning to one's true self; *for Chu Hsi its aim was never the acquisition of knowledge for its own sake* (emphasis added).' See also P. Nosco, (ed.) *Confucianism and Tokugawa Culture*, Introduction, p. 6.

499 One need only stand in front of a Ming vase or a samurai sword to understand what Chinese and Japanese practical science could achieve.

500 J. Needham, *op. cit.*, pp. 152-4 and pp. 474-510.

501 W. Heisenberg, *Physics and Philosophy*, p. 167, and *Across the Frontiers*, p. 127. However, 'The separation of God and science of magic was not achieved until the seventeenth century; in traditional China it was never fully achieved.' C. A. Ronan and J. Needham, *op. cit.*, p. 86.

502 Enmity and tension existed, however, in the West between philosophy and reason. Bitter fights took place between the church and the new science and it was not until after the Reformation that the Scientific Revolution was fully free to move forward in earnest. This engendered the vision of a future of transformation and progress.

503 R. Stark, *For the Glory of God*, pp. 158-76, *passim*.

504 W. Heisenberg, *Physics and Philosophy, The Revolution in Modern Science*, p. 139, *passim*.

505 Cf., I. McMorran, *Wang Fu-chih and Neo-Confucian Tradition*, p. 439.

506 See Karl R. Popper, *The Open Society and its Enemies*, vol. 2, p. 221 and *passim*.

507 A. Craig, 'Science and Confucianism in Tokugawa Japan', in Marius H. Jansen, *Changing Japanese Attitudes Towards Modernization*, pp. 140-1. Adapted quotation. This is in turn reference to a classic (the *I Li*) which says 'To know the mother and not the father is to be a bird or a beast' (*kinjū haha shirite chichi shirazu*).

508 The beginnings of democracy can of course be discussed. In one sense Switzerland was first and incipient democratic rule can be watched in other countries. We are not far from the truth when we see England and the United States as the first one person one vote democracies.

509 'We have almost entirely overlooked the long succession of technical

discoveries coming from the Chinese during the first thirteen centuries of our era.'
C. A. Ronan and J. Needham, *op. cit.*, p. 4.
510 D. L. Hall and R. T. Ames, *Thinking Through Confucius*, p. 328.
511 Cf., R. E. Carter, *op. cit.*, p. 194.
512   R. E. Carter, *ibid.*
513 The *Chuang tzu*, *Great Knowledge*, quoted in T. Merton, *The Way of Chuang Tzu*, p. 40.

Glossary

NOTE: The Chinese characters for all entries in this Glossary are available from the Author by writing to the Publishers.

A

ai (awaremi)	sorrow
ai	love
ai jen	to love people
aku (nikumi)	hatred

B

banbutsu	all things
bu	warfare
bun	scholarship
bushidō	way of the warrior
butsu	things or affairs
butsuri	modern physics
butsuri-gaku	natural science

C

chang chih (jōchi)	ordinary knowledge
chen chih (shinchi)	real knowledge
cheng	fairness
ch'eng (sei)	inner sincerity
ch'eng (makoto, sei)	sincerity
ch'eng-i (seii)	sincere intention or will
ch'i ch'ing (shichijō)	seven emotions
chidō	Way of Earth
chih (chi)	arrive at or to reach
chih (chi)	wisdom
chih-hsing ho-i (chikō gōitsu)	unity of knowledge and action
chih-san (shizen)	highest good
ching (kei)	outer sincerity
ching (sei)	stillness
ching-tso (seiza)	quiet sitting
chiri	earthly dust
chiri-gaku	geography

ch'iung-li	the pursuit or inquiry of ri
chū	loyalty
chung (chū)	equilibrium
ch'ün tzu (kunshi)	the superior man
chu-tsai (shusai)	lord

D

Dai-Nihon	Great Japan
denki	electricity
do	earth
dōgaku	Learning of the Way
dōitsu shinbutsu	oneness of spirit and material matter
dokuritsu	independent
dōri	truth

F

fūfu	husband and wife
fukoku	rich country
fukoku kyōhei	a rich country and a strong army

G

genki	the primal ki
giri	duty or ethical performance
gogyū	Five Elements
gojō	Five Constant Virtues
gorin	the five relations
gōsō	will
gu	receptacle

H

hakugaku	wide learning
hankan-gōitsu	oneness of opposite aspects or synthesis of contraries
hao-jan chih ch'i (kōzen no ki)	flood-like ki
hen no ri	changing ri
ho (wa)	harmony
honmatsu	root and branches
hsin (shin)	trustworthiness
hsing (sei)	human nature

hsing-erh-hsia (keijika)	impure ki world below forms
hsing-erh-shang (keijijō)	pure ri world above forms
hsing-p'o (keihaku)	form soul
hsin-hseh (shingaku)	learning of the mind
Hsüan (Gen)	Primal Origin
hun (kon)	soul at macrocosmic level
hun-tun (konton)	pre-existing undifferentiated chaos
hun ch'i (konki)	spiritual soul

I

i (gi)	righteousness
ichi-genki	One Primordial Energy
I Ching (Ekikyō)	The Book of Changes
i-fa (ihatsu)	manifest activity
iki	respiration
ikiru	to live
ikki	one ki
ikki-konten	one-ki chaos
ikki no shintai	advance and retreat of the one ki

J

jashū	evil creed
jen (jin)	goodness or benevolence
jen-ho (jinwa)	essential harmony among men
jiki	magnetism
jinsei	good government
jinshinron	godliness in man
jinyoku	selfish desires
jitsugaku	useful learning
jōge bunken	distinctions between high and low
jōki	steam
jōri	lines and veins
jubutsu itchi	Confucian-Buddhist syncretism
juka-shintō	Confucian-Shinto syncretism

K

ka	fire
kaikoku	open the country
kakubutsu-kyūri	the study of and pursuit of things in ri
kami	spirit

kanbun	Chinese composition
kanri	administration
katachi	physical form
katsubutsu	living thing
kei	reverence
keiten-aijin	love of people
kenkyō	forced interpretations
ki	energy-matter
ki (yorokobi)	pleasure
kiatsu	atmospheric pressure
kin	metal
kisetsu	bravery, loyalty and integrity
kishin	ghosts and spirits
kishitsu	character or disposition
kishitsu no sei	earthly nature
kisho	weather conditions
ko (kaku)	arrive at
kō	filial piety
k'o (kyaku)	guests
kochū	ancient commentaries
kōkiatsu	high air pressure
kokoro	mind-and-heart
kokutai	national essence
koshiraegoto	selfish fabrications
kōshō	philological or evidential research
kotowari	truth
ko-wu-chih-chih (kakubutsu-chichi)	to investigate things and attain wisdom
ku	fear
kuei (ki or oni)	spiritual
kusare jusha	rotten Confucians
kyōgen	frauds and cheats
kyōhei	strong army
kyokei	abiding in reverence
kyomu	empty nothingness
kyūri	investigation of li (ri)

L

lei (rui)	class or category
li (rei)	rites or ritual or propriety
li (ri)	principle

liang chih (ryōchi)	innate good knowledge
li-yüeh-hsing-cheng (rei-gaku- *kei-sei)*	rites, music, penal law and government

M

makato no michi	Way of truth
meitoku	bright (illustrious) or heavenly virtue
mizunomi	water-drinking, poor
moku	wood
mushi-mushū	without beginning, without end
mushin-mubutsu	without gods, without buddhas
myōgō	wondrous amalgam

N

nichigaku	a Three-Creeds-in-One School
niki	two ki
ninjō	human feelings
nu (ikari)	anger

P

p'o (haku)	soul at microcosmic level
p'o ch i (hakki)	sentient soul

R

rei	rites
reigi-hatto	law and order
reihō	inborn jewel
ri	principle
ri	profit
ri-ka	science
rō	narrow and vulgar

S

sakui	invention or creation
san-chiao (sankyō)	three teachings
san-kang (sankō)	Three Bonds
sei	nature
seido	established system

seiri	principle of life
sei-sei	growth of life
seiza	quiet sitting
sei zen nari	nature is good
shen (shin or kami)	divine
sheng-sheng (sei-sei)	generation and regeneration
shih-wu (shibutsu)	external objects and affairs
shiji	dead words
shinjubutsu-itchi	Shinto-Confucian-Buddhist eclectic syncretism
shinki ki	advances or holy ki
shinri-gaku	psychology
shizen	nature
shori	management
shōtenchi	microcosm of Heaven and Earth
shugyō-roku	religious record
shujin	Lord
shūri	repair
sodoku	heart
ssu tuan (shitan)	Four Beginnings of virtue
sui	water
suijōki	vapour

T

tai	body
t'ai-chi (tai-kyoku)	Great Ultimate
T'ai-chi-tu (Taikyoku-zu)	Diagram of the Great Ultimate
taigi	great duty
t'ai ho (taiwa)	great harmony
t'ai hsü (takyo)	Great Vacuity
t'ai-i (taiitsu)	the Great One
taiki	ki retreats
taikyoku	the Great One or the Great Ultimate
taiwatai	question and answer style
tao (dō)	way
tao-hsin (dōshin)	moral mind
tao-li (dōri)	the Way-Principle
Tao Te Ching (Dōtokukyō)	The Book of the Way
tatami	straw mat
teikiatsu	low air pressure
tencho no dōri	Way of Heaven and Earth

tendō	Way of Heaven
tenjin-gōitsu	union of Heaven and man
tenka no ri	ri of the world
ten no chōri	grace of Heaven
tenshu	heavenly lord
t'ien (ten)	Heaven
t'ien ch'i (tenki)	heavenly ki
t'ien chih hsing (ten no sei)	Heaven's nature
tien-ming (tenmei)	Mandate of Heaven
t'ien-tao-ch'i (ten-dō-ki)	vital energy matter
t'ien ti (tentei)	Celestial Lord
ting ti (teitai)	fixed specificity
toki-tokoro-kurai	time, place and circumstance
tōyō dōtoku, seyō gijutsu	Eastern morality, Western technology
tsune no ri	constant ri
tuan (tan)	the mass of seeds
tung (dō)	movement

W

wan wu (banbutsu)	myriad things
wei-fa (mihatsu)	unmanifest stillness
wu	nothingness
wu-chi (mukyoku)	Unlimited or Limitless
wu-wei (mui)	nonbeing

Y

yōgaku	Western studies
yoku	desire

Z

tso-ch an (zazen)	sitting meditation

Index